P9-DFV-899

Francis A. Drexel
LIBRARY

Harvard Business School

Core Collection

1998

SAINT JOSEPH'S UNIVERSITY

Up the Loyalty Ladder

ALSO BY MURRAY RAPHEL

Tough Selling for Tough Times (with Neil Raphel)
Mind Your Own Business
The Great Brain Robbery (with Ray Considine)
The Do-It-Yourself Direct Mail Handbook (with Ken Erdman)

Up the Loyalty Ladder

Turning Sometime Customers

into Full-Time Advocates

of Your Business

MURRAY RAPHEL AND
NEIL RAPHEL

HF
5415.5
R36
1995

ST. JOSEPH'S UNIVERSITY

3 9353 00308 6186

HarperBusiness
A Division of HarperCollins*Publishers*

UP THE LOYALTY LADDER. Copyright © 1995 by Neil Raphel and Murray Raphel. All rights reserved. Printed in the United States of America. No part of this book may be used or reproduced in any manner whatsoever without written permission except in the case of brief quotations embodied in critical articles and reviews. For information address HarperCollins Publishers, Inc., 10 East 53rd Street, New York, NY 10022.

HarperCollins books may be purchased for educational, business, or sales promotional use. For information please write: Special Markets Department, HarperCollins Publishers, Inc., 10 East 53rd Street, New York, NY 10022.

FIRST EDITION

Designed by Jessica Shatan

Library of Congress Cataloging-in-Publication Data
Raphel, Murray, 1928–
     Up the loyalty ladder : turning sometime customers into full-time advocates of your business / Murray Raphel and Neil Raphel. — 1st ed.
          p. cm.
     Includes index.
     ISBN 0-88730-725-6
     1. Customer relations. 2. Advertising. 3. Consumer satisfaction. 4. Word-of-mouth advertising. 5. Success in business—United States. 6. Businessmen—United States—Interviews. I. Raphel, Neil. II. Title.
     HF5415.5.R36 1995   94-43548
     658.8'12—dc20

95 96 97 98 99 ❖/RRD 10 9 8 7 6 5 4 3 2 1

Contents

PART 5: THE ADVOCATE

Foreword

It is an icy winter morning in a big city in America. One hundred and fifty merchants invited by American Express from the metropolitan area shrug off the chill, check in at a reception desk, and chat over a continental breakfast. At precisely 9:00 A.M., an enthusiastic fellow merchant bounces onto the stage and proceeds to entertain and enlighten the merchants.

Soon the icy morning is forgotten. A warm feeling envelops the room. One of the best business speakers has captured his audience. He is showing them by example, by encouragement, by explanation why satisfied customers are the key to a successful business.

The enthusiastic merchant's name is Murray Raphel. His mission: to show big and small businesses how the key to their survival is bringing customers to the top of their "loyalty ladder."

One of my assignments for American Express is to help our merchants do more business. The better American Express merchants do, the better American Express does.

We have been running seminars on direct marketing, business ideas, and customer loyalty for American Express merchants for the last several years. Murray Raphel has been one of our most successful seminar leaders. I think his success with business audiences can be attributed to several factors:

- He and his family ran a successful retail clothing business and shopping center for over forty years.
- Murray and Neil Raphel are active in producing direct mail and marketing campaigns for varied kinds of businesses.
- Murray and Neil write columns and books and produce audiotapes and videotapes, which helps them keep up with the new trends and ideas in marketing and advertising.

Because of their backgrounds, Murray and Neil are able to have empathy with the business owner's plight: There is just so much the businessperson has to do to keep his business operating. Where is the time to think creatively about marketing and customer satisfaction?

In this book, Murray and Neil produce clear and concise answers to that problem. They give techniques to help businesspeople move their customers up every rung of the loyalty ladder. They provide a media guide for every step of the loyalty ladder, with clear rules on how to use newspapers, radio, television, direct mail, and other media most effectively.

Above all, when you read this book you will catch Murray and Neil's enthusiasm for business. Their passion for helping businesspeople succeed comes through on every page. Their easy-to-read writing style makes you want to keep turning page after page to learn more.

By the time you finish this book, you'll be Murray and Neil Raphel Advocates.

Like me.

KAREN QUINN
Vice President, Marketing Education
Epsilon
a subsidiary of the
American Express Corporation

Acknowledgments

A friend once warned us to "never say 'thank you' to anyone in the room when you're speaking or in a book you write because you will always wind up forgetting someone."

He was right.

But while realizing we will unfortunately not mention many of the people who helped us through the years, we must thank our partner, wife, and mother, Ruth, who brings everything together while the two of us go off in a hundred different directions. Shirley Gordon, our retailing partner of four decades, is an invaluable part of our marketing team. We also want to thank our secretary, Mary Liguori, who typed up all the interviews and cheerfully proofread our copy.

Through the years, our worlds of retailing, speaking, and consulting put us in contact with hundreds of other people who kept on pushing us to the top of THEIR Loyalty Ladder. Among them are:

- Ray Considine, who taught us how to speak and gave us ideas for the Loyalty Ladder, which, in turn, he received from Ray Cusato.
- John Groman, Executive Vice President, Epsilon, a division of American Express, with whom we first spoke in Montreux, Switzerland.
- Speaking of American Express, we appreciate the help and assistance of Karen Quinn, Vice President, Marketing Education,

Epsilon, a division of American Express, who helped us spread the word of the Loyalty Ladder in seminars throughout the United States.

• Bob Aders, former president and CEO of the Food Marketing Institute, who helped us become "experts" in food marketing.

• Tom Haggai, CEO of IGA supermarkets, who is a mentor and close friend.

• Walter Schmid, who started us on our international speaking tours throughout Europe.

• Eddy Boas, who has helped us become speakers in Australia and the Far East.

• Ken Erdman, our pal, friend, and co-author of our direct marketing book for small retailers.

• Dave Usher from Greenwich Workshop, who first heard us speak ten years ago and said, "How can we take your ideas and have them help our retailers?"

• And we can't forget Adrian Zackheim from HarperBusiness, who invited us to his office, listened to the outline for this book, and in five minutes (or less) said, "I like it. Let's do it!"

Did we mention Neil's wife Janis and our daughters (and sisters) Paula Crowley and Caren Franzini, the greatest Advocates we could ever have?

And . . . (*ooops, we've run out of room. If you're not here, we'll include you in the next book . . .*)

MURRAY & NEIL RAPHEL

How to Use This Book

Here's how to make your business grow: Start with your current customers. Figure out who they are, how you can attract new ones, and how you can increase the loyalty of every person who does business with you. Think about the Loyalty Ladder and how you can move people to the highest rung.

This book is divided into five sections that correspond to the five rungs of the Loyalty Ladder:

- **Prospects**—people who may be interested in buying from you;
- **Shoppers**—people who visit your business at least once;
- **Customers**—people who purchase one or more products or services from your business;
- **Clients**—people who regularly purchase your products or services; and
- **Advocates**—people who tell anyone who will listen how great your business is.

Each section contains an introduction, interviews with successful businesspeople, a guide on how to use specific types of advertising, stories, and case histories.

You can read this book straight through or pick your spots, browsing through the individual sections. You can use the media guides as references. You can pass out the rules for success to your employees.

Any way you use this book, remember to have a smile on your face and enthusiasm in your heart. Because to move consumers up *your* Loyalty Ladder, you must first motivate yourself and your employees.

And may all your Customers become Advocates.

Introduction

———■———

YOU ARE ALWAYS A PROSPECT

You wake up in the morning, open the newspaper, and are confronted by a blizzard of ads. Turn on the TV, and in between the weather and the news there is one sale after another. The radio, the billboards, the buses on your way to work all have a special offer for you. The phone often brings an unsolicited query with special pricing, today only. The mail brings you catalogs, offers, deals, and steals. Wherever you turn, somebody is trying to sell you something.

Prospects are great. Prospects are necessary for a business to succeed. But many businesses have the misguided notion that to be successful all they have to do is to attract more and more Prospects. They forget Raphel's Number One Rule for Businesses: "It is far, far easier to sell more to the Customer you already have than to sell to new Customers."

It costs five times as much to sell to a new Customer as to sell to a customer you already have. A new Customer doesn't know you, doesn't know your products, is suspicious of your business's quality. Existing Customers know your product or service. They have already spent money with you. They have already been Prospects and have climbed several steps up the Loyalty Ladder. You should court new Prospects, but put most of the emphasis on the Customers you already have.

YOU ARE FREQUENTLY A SHOPPER

You need a new suit. Your toaster oven is on the blink. You promised the kids you'd take them to Disneyland. There are birthdays. Holidays. Anniversaries. Something won't work. You need more. You need better. You need a computer. An answering machine. A new watch. A pencil. Food. There are catalogs to browse through, stores to visit, malls to traverse.

Once a person has made it from the Prospect to the Shopper rung of your Loyalty Ladder, you are in business. The Shopper has made an effort to get to know you and your business. But you only have a brief few seconds to impress Shoppers that they should give you their business.

A national survey of one million Customers says Customers make up their minds whether they will buy or not in the first eight seconds they are in your store. It's an amazing statistic, but it makes sense when you think about it. In the first few seconds, you take in the atmosphere, the attitudes, the merchandise. If your employees are courteous, if your selling space is nicely laid out and clean, if your prices are competitive and clearly displayed, you have a good chance of taking a Shopper up the next step of the Loyalty Ladder.

YOU ARE OFTEN A CUSTOMER

You like to eat in the Alley Deli because the roast beef is fresh and so are the waitresses. You shop at Wal-Mart because the prices are right even though they don't always have everything you want. You like to go to the Towne 16 movie theater because they have the best foreign films. You buy your computer supplies from MacZone because of the good pricing, fast service, and next-day delivery.

You have a Customer once someone buys something from you. Now is the time you have to redouble your efforts to get that person to buy something else from you. Here's why.

A recent survey of bank customers showed:

If your customer has . . .	The odds of keeping him or her are . . .
A checking account	1 to 1
A savings account	2 to 1
Checking and savings accounts	10 to 1
Checking, savings, and a loan	20 to 1
Checking, savings, a loan, and a safe-deposit box	100 to 1

The odds are similar in other businesses. If you have a life insurance policy from an insurer, you may switch policies if a better salesperson approaches you. But if you have a life insurance policy, pension program, and car insurance from the same agent, your loyalty to that agent has skyrocketed.

You Are Sometimes a Client

You buy your kids' clothing from Hanna Andersson because the clothes are beautiful and they hold up for years. You eat breakfast every day at Joe's Place because where else can you can get delicious eggs, bacon, toast, and an endless cup of coffee for $2.50?

Once businesses discover their frequent buyers, they cannot afford to ignore them. Saks Fifth Avenue discovered that the top 10 percent of their customers accounted for more than 50 percent of their business. They started a Saks First Club for these best customers.

Saks is not alone. JCPenney sent Privilege credit cards to one million customers who charged at least $800 in each of the past two years and paid on schedule. Cardholders receive rewards such as advance notice of sales, an exclusive shopping hour, discounts on merchandise, extended warranty and buyer protection on certain merchandise, free JCPenney catalogs ($5 each to noncardholders), free gift-wrap certificates, and a quarterly newsletter.

Sears and Neiman-Marcus and Dayton-Hudson and Montgomery Ward all have similar programs. It's becoming rare to find a large retailer that does not go out of its way to track its best Customers and entice them to buy more.

But rewarding loyal Customers is even more crucial for a small business owner. If a large retail corporation with $1 billion in annual sales loses ten Customers who spend $1,000 each, it has lost .01 percent of its business, a number that will barely impact sales. But if a company doing $200,000 a year in sales loses ten Customers who spend $1,000 each, it has lost 5 percent of its business. And that 5 percent may account for 25 percent of its net profits. A small business must cultivate and seek to enlarge its best customer base. That business's very survival is at stake.

YOU ARE RARELY AN ADVOCATE

You spend a whole day telling people what great service you received from Avery labels after you bought a bad batch. They sent you a new shipment that arrived the next day at no charge. They offered to repair the printer. They were nice and considerate on the phone. You will never buy any other label than an Avery label.

Advocates can spur the growth of your business. Here's how:

If you need a lawyer, you could scan the yellow pages of your local phone book and have hundreds of choices. Or you can ask your next-door neighbor how she liked the lawyer she went to recently. If she replies:

> Dan Smith is the best lawyer in town. He handled my personal injury case and got a far better settlement than I thought was possible. He was always cheery and friendly, he also returned phone calls, and he worked hard on my behalf. In fact, he even prepared a will for my husband and myself for free!

Your next phone call will probably be to Dan Smith.

In fact, your next-door neighbor probably did not wait until you asked her advice on a lawyer. She probably knocked on your door one day and told you the whole story.

Unsolicited testimonials are probably the strongest form of advertising. Your neighbor does not have a financial stake in Dan Smith's success. Yet she goes out of her way to tell everyone she meets how happy she was with Dan. With a few Advocates like that, Dan Smith will soon

have to work long hours to take care of all the new business he will
receive.

John Groman, vice president of Epsilon, a division of American
Express and one of the largest database companies in the United
States, says there are only three ways to have more business. ("People
might give you a list of a dozen or fifty or more. But there are only
three.") Here they are:

1. Have more Customers. New Customers and Shoppers will
increase the volume of business by exposing more people to the
goods or services you sell.

2. Have your Customers shop more often. The more times a Customer contacts your business, the more you are going to sell him
or her. Make the law of averages work for you by giving your Customers many reasons to come shop with you again.

3. Have your Customers buy more when they come in. This happens when you turn your Customers into Clients and Advocates.
By giving your best Customers better service and especially by
giving them rewards, you can dramatically increase your business from the Customers you already have.

In your everyday life, you are at one time or another at every rung
on the Loyalty Ladder. The businesses that succeed in pleasing you
the most will receive the most transactions from you.

This book will show you how to make people climb your Loyalty
Ladder and become Advocates for your business. It will show you the
ways to tailor your message to Prospects, Shoppers, Customers,
Clients, and Advocates. The more people that can be induced to climb
yet one more rung up your Loyalty Ladder, the more successful your
business will be.

Part 1

THE PROSPECT

Introduction to Prospects

———————————————— ∎ ————————————————

Pros-pect /pras-pekt *n. Someone interested in buying
something from you.*

Prospects are people who may know about you but have never spent
money with you. How do you bring them to your business?

It's not easy. And the failure to attract Prospects and turn them into
Shoppers is why many small businesses cannot get out of the starting
gate.

For many years, businesses have thought that the way to compete
was by having more selection and lower prices than their competitors.
**Ironically, too much selection and too low prices are two of
the main reasons businesses fail!** The reasons:

1. Too much selection can lead to too much inventory and
declining profitability. Think about your niche in the marketplace and what you are really trying to sell.

2. Too low prices can be a death knell for many small and even
many large businesses. If you don't have the operating efficiency
of a Wal-Mart, you can't compete with Wal-Mart on price. Stress
your positives: specialization, customer service, knowledgeable

salespeople, guarantees, home deliveries, repair service, gift wrapping, etc. . . . Stress your differences with the Wal-Marts of the world if you can't compete with Wal-Mart on price.

Let's talk about selection in detail.

The average person is faced with hundreds of commercials every day from TV, newspapers, radio, billboards, inside taxis, and, in Sydney, Australia, on the back of bathroom stalls.

More than 15,000 new products appear in the marketplace every year and more than 90 percent fail!

Think of this:

- Owners of an IBM PC or clone can choose from more than 30,000 software programs.
- Car buyers can choose from 572 makes and models.
- If you have a credit card, you receive more than 300 catalogs from September to Christmas.
- Toothpaste comes in 138 different varieties (that's *not* brands, that's varieties: tubes, dispensers, decorator colors, for smokers, nonsmokers, for folks with sensitive teeth, for coffee and tea drinkers, for yellow-stained teeth . . .).

David Pittle in *Consumer Reports* writes, "We hear over and over again people have trouble making choices about buying decisions."

For some businesses, the Big Selection *does* work. Charles Lazarus, founder of Toys "Я" Us, says, "When parents have no clear idea of what to buy, they go to the store with the biggest selection." Great for Toys "Я" Us, but difficult for the small toy shop on the corner. It isn't there anymore. It went the way of the small stationery and office supply shop that fell to the huge selection from Staples.

So what's going to make the Prospect come to you?

A huge selection is rarely the answer for the small businessperson. The reason: the cost of the inventory.

Let's look at the second surprising reason many businesses fail: They try to compete with the big boys on price.

Huge discounters will win on price. They have the buying power and low overhead relative to sales to achieve business success on very low markups. They have gobbled up billions of dollars from the American consumer, saying, "Nobody beats our prices" or similar slogans. In 1993 discounters sold more apparel than department stores for the first time. Budweiser beer cut beer prices for the first time in its 116-year history. Philip Morris slashed Marlboro prices 40 percent to protect its share of the cigarette market.

Does this work? It can . . . for the big boys. But even for huge players like Philip Morris the results can be mixed. The short-run effect can be an increase in sales but a decline in profits. The day Marlboro made its price-cutting announcement, its stock price fell. Investors didn't think Marlboro's increased Prospects would translate into a better bottom line. More than a year later, the financial analysts are still sorting out the fallout from what is now termed "Marlboro Friday." Marlboro's market share did climb, but competitors are fighting back by reducing the prices of their premier brands. In the end, the smoking public is benefiting from lower prices, but the cigarette industry may be less profitable.

Let's look at American Airlines. American was scoring the highest ratings from air travelers year after year as the airline they liked most. Then American decided to increase business by offering lower prices for air travel. Seemed like a good idea at the time. After all, airlines had different "special" prices at different times of the year (sometimes different times of the day). Why not take the confusing which-price-do-I-pay-today rules and make a few simple easy-to-understand price rules? The problem was that all the other airlines followed American's lead. The small airlines such as Southwest Airlines and Alaska Airlines were successful because they did not have the union problems and overhead costs of American. American soon switched back to what made them successful in the first place.

Today's consumers know who does what. They place your business in a slot in their where-to-buy decision ladder. Bestselling authors Jack Trout and Al Reis call it "Positioning"—how consumers position your product in their minds.

Says futurist Laurel Cutler, "The consumer of the nineties is the smartest consumer ever. We are training people to be very smart."

The problem with being lower in price is it can lead to price wars. You can soon find yourself in the position of the Kroger supermarkets in Cincinnati, which fought the new food discounters (or as the food industry euphemistically likes to call them, "alternative format stores") to the point where pig farmers came in to buy milk at 5 cents a quart because it was cheaper than the usual pig feed.

So "price" and "selection" may not be the best ways you can bring the Prospect up the Loyalty Ladder.

WHAT CAN YOU DO?

The rest of this chapter will give you some examples of specific techniques that can be used to attract Prospects into your business. But to give you an idea of what can be done, let us tell you a story about our first foray into business. We competed with price and selection, but limited that competition to a specific category of items in our store.

When we started in business, our annual volume for our tiny children's shop was $25,000 a year. What would make the potential Prospect come to see us, passing up the giant department store and the large specialty shops? My father-in-law came up with an idea: "Have an inexpensive category of items with the biggest selection in town."

It was the fall, and we wondered, "What did customers want for winter that was not expensive?"

How about something to keep children warm like gloves or mittens or scarves? Fitted the description: Inexpensive, and we would offer the biggest selection in town.

We hand-lettered signs for the windows: THE BIGGEST SELECTION OF CHILDREN'S GLOVES, MITTENS AND SCARVES IN THE CITY!

Soon people would come to see our large selection of mittens and gloves. And, while they were there, we offered a snowsuit (probably the smallest selection in town). But the sale of one snowsuit equaled three dozen pairs of gloves.

We did sell an occasional snowsuit. Or little boy's suit. Or little girl's dress.

All because we had something the customer wanted—in the biggest selection.

So although we did not supply the biggest selection in *everything*, we did have the biggest selection in *something* our customers wanted.

What were we doing? Converting Prospects into Shoppers.

You must make the Shopper's first impression of your business a strong, warm, caring-about-you experience. If you do this, you attract future Customers. If you ignore—or worse, insult—these Shoppers, you lose them forever. And, even worse, they tell the story to a dozen (or more) of their friends.

We had a recent experience in a supermarket that resulted in that store's losing our business . . . perhaps forever. And since we buy as a family over $100 a week in groceries or over $5,000 a year or over $100,000 in the next twenty years, the loss could be significant for the store involved.

We went to buy some cold cuts from the deli counter. The clerk looked up at us and said, "Take a number!"

"What?" we said.

"Take a number," repeated the clerk, motioning to a machine with paper tear-off numbers. "That way I'll know who's next."

"But, uh," we said, "there's no one else here except us!"

"If you want to get taken care of, you have to have a number. That's the rule!" the clerk repeated, now annoyed.

We walked over to the machine and tore off the next number, 61.

The clerk looked at the numbers on a wall indicator and yelled out, "Sixty-one is next!"

"That's us!" we said, and we were taken care of.

What's happening here? The people taking care of you, trying to convey an impression of professionalism and authority, have forgotten the human element. They remember only that everything has to be "by the numbers." Robots act that way. People don't. Shouldn't. Can't . . . if they want someone to climb up to the next rung of the Ladder . . . and become a **Shopper.**

"What's Your Yield per Acre?"

—————————■—————————

Stan Golomb runs marketing programs for dry cleaners, restaurants, dentists, health spas, pizza parlors, and assorted other businesses. When he takes on new clients, he invariably asks them to focus on one key business question:

"What's your yield per acre?"

"Farmers use yield per acre to measure their productivity," says Stan. "They look at how many bushels of corn or beans they harvest per acre. If the average is 100 bushels per acre, the farmer getting 60 bushels per acre knows he's doing something wrong."

So why can't a businessperson compare his crop to determine his or her "yield per acre"? The yield is measured in business done within an existing market area. The "acreage" would be the amount of potential business available within an area that could be serviced by one location. Want to know how well you're doing? Focus on your "yield per acre."

Start by defining your market. Your primary market is where 80 percent of your Prospects presently live. Find the addresses of 300 of your present customers. From that sampling, you can project where most of your customers live. If you're like most small businesses, more than 80 percent of your customers will come from a three- to five-mile radius from your business.

Next: Find out how many family units there are in your market area. Visit your post office. The postmaster knows how many carriers cover the area and how many homes each carrier serves. Say there are 5,000 homes in the area. You do business with 1,000 customers. That's a 20 percent yield. You have 20 percent of your available market.

Your task: Find out how you can improve your yield per acre!

There are two ways to increase your yield:

1. Increase the percentage of households that do business with you.
2. Have the households that do business with you spend more with you.

When you know your percentage of the market, you can go about systematically increasing your share. Even if you had every customer in your market, you could still dramatically increase your sales by motivating your regular customers to spend as much as 50 percent more with the right kind of inducements.

Your sales will depend on a number of factors:

1. The geographical boundaries of your market
2. The density of the market
3. The income level of the market
4. The type of work the people in the market perform
5. The social lifestyle of the market
6. The ethnic characteristics of the market
7. The median age level of the market
8. The weather of the market
9. The amount of competition in the market
10. The nature of the competition
11. The nature of your own competitive activities

The combination of these factors determines why one business does $5,000 a week in sales and another similar business in the same town struggles to do $2,000. Whatever factors you have to contend with, you can always improve your business yield.

Think of what farmers do to improve their yield per acre. They add water, they use fertilizer, they use chemicals to eliminate insect problems. They hybridize their seeds. They plant, they cultivate, and they work at the job of getting as much of a profitable crop out of each acre as they can. What can you do in *your* business?

You have to live with some unchangeable elements. Consider them as givens. You can't change the economy of your area, or the density, or the geographical boundaries. You can't do much about your location, or how your competitor promotes or charges for his products or services.

But you can do a lot about making your own business more successful. And it's only you and your actions that can change things. Do nothing and you can bank on it—nothing will change, except the external factors that influence any business.

Take a dry-cleaning business, for example. The range of annual sales can run from a low of $50,000 to a high of $1,000,000, the potential amount of annual over-the-counter business for one location.

But this business can increase its yield, whatever it is, by 20 percent, 50 percent, or even more. It can only be done by understanding its market and taking action.

For example: There's an expressway to the north. No sales come into a business from the other side of that barrier. There are railroad tracks to the south. Very little comes from south of the tracks. There's a golf course to the west. Nothing much west of that point, and to the east there seems to be a boundary at Fairview Avenue. If this was your business, located on Ogden Avenue right in the center of all the X marks, you'd limit your promoting to within those boundaries. Direct mail, phone, and circulars are the only way to go. And concentrate on your store's appearance—the windows, outdoor signs, and internal promotions using customers as the media to spread your word. A recent survey by American Research Associates said four out of ten prospects decide whether or not to enter your business by what it looks like from the outside.

Once you have the hang of viewing your market the way a farmer views a crop, you'll begin to figure out how to work the field to increase your yield—and profits.

INTERVIEW
Sid Friedman

■

"If it ain't broke, break it!"

Forbes magazine ran a cover story listing America's top salespeople, including Arnold Schwarzenegger, Michael Jordan, Ralph Lauren, and Sid Friedman.

Sid . . . who?

Sid is one of the world's top insurance salesmen. When we want to find out how to find prospects, we call Sid. He supervises thirty insurance salespeople but still works dawn to dusk every day selling insurance himself. One of the most repeated phrases in his writings and seminars is this one: "If it ain't broke, break it."

What's Sid saying?

This: It is not enough simply to do what everyone else is doing. And, more important, it is not enough simply to repeat that which worked before. Peter Drucker writes that "every business has to be prepared to change . . . everything!"

Simply because an idea, concept, theory in business worked for years, that does not mean it will continue to work for years. In fact, it probably will not. It's part of the "the only thing permanent is change" philosophy.

Sid Friedman's willingness to upset the applecart extends to prospecting for new business. We interviewed Sid to gain insight into how he became one of the country's top salespeople.

Q. How do you identify the universe of people who may need your services in the first place?

A. I do target marketing. I find people who have something in common with each other. It is impossible for me to say that the universe is my market. It is not. I live near Philadelphia, but Philadelphia is not my market. Neither is New York or Atlantic City.

My market is people who have something in common with each other. So if I were prospecting funeral directors, I would go where funeral directors go. I would go to their meetings, I'd be a speaker at their meetings, I'd want to write articles for their magazine. When I get to know them and they get to know me, we develop a relationship with each other.

Once I have one funeral director as a customer, I can go to other funeral directors. I would bring a copy of the list of funeral directors to my one client and say, "Joe, do you know anybody on this list that I could talk to and show them what kind of work I do?" I would go to people who have an affinity to each other and I would work those connections.

I want to be very specific about whom I'm trying to sell. Not just doctors, but neurosurgeons.

The universe is not your market. You can slip through and be successful but you'd be one sperm cell against the billion that make a baby. I don't want to do that. It's no value. I'd rather know which one works and use that one cell.

Q. How about people who have used your services once? Do you do anything special to encourage them to use other services or come back to you?

A. Yes. We cross-sell. Once you buy something from me, I'm not a stranger and you become very valuable to me. Now I have to keep on keeping you. That's number one. How do I keep on keeping you? Through birthday cards, by a letter, by "I saw this newspaper article and thought it would be of interest to you." Things I see every day that would be of special interest to you.

Once you've bought product A and I think product B or C or D would be good for you, I will try to see you about it. For example, if you bought group insurance from me, I might talk to you about a private pension, annuities, terminal funding for your pension plan, let you know I do that. And I wouldn't expect you to buy every time I call you, but I'll put you in a mood that when you do decide to buy, you might consider me.

Q. Do you have to eliminate potential business to reach those people who really need your services?

A. It begins with the planning process, doesn't it? What am I going to pull the trigger for until I know what I'm shooting at? It isn't ready, fire, aim. If I know what I want to target, I've got to find out can they afford me, do they make enough money, is the business profitable? If they are profitable, are they the type of people who generally care? If I went to them, would they buy from me? For all the money in the world, I won't work with engineers because I can't deal with them.

The personalities, the demographics, the location, the geographics, all those things go into picking the market that I want to work in.

Q. Most people are shy about giving details of their financial life. How do you break down that barrier to evaluate whether these people can use your services?

A. I don't think they have to rely on their shyness or their brazenness to give me the information. It's kind of public. I know dry-cleaning people all over America, all over the world, make a lot of money. Some of it is green and some of it is checks, but they make money. Owners of more than one dry cleaner make even more money. If I wanted these prospects as customers, I would target the dry-cleaning industry. I would find out where they have their meetings, see if I can join those meetings as an associate member, infiltrate that group in some way. I'd tell them I'd like to contribute. I want to find out what they like and dislike. I want to write for their magazine. I want to speak to their organization for free. I want to become a resource for them so they can become a resource for me.

I have a battle plan. I don't know how anybody can go to war without a plan. While this is not a war it *is* strategic planning that is required before you can get to the actual planning.

Q. How do you deal with complaints or people who have a problem getting hold of you?

A. Nobody has a problem, I give out my private number. It's part of the obligation of the president of a company. He is the chief complaint department. Two things should get to the president. One is great things where someone in your company did a fabulous thing and they want to tell you about it. The second is the customer who has a big problem and the president is the only person that can do something about it.

Q. Do your employees do the same sort of relationship marketing that you do?

A. Not all of them. I wish they did because it would make their life easier and they would make a lot more money. I think you make a lot more money by service than you do by sales. There are more cars sold in the service department than in the showroom.

Q. What special efforts will you take to make a sale?

A. One client said he couldn't see me because he was going to Chicago. I said, "What time do you leave tomorrow morning?" The client replied, "I'm on the 7:00 plane, flight 1260 from Philadelphia to Chicago." I said, "Are you flying first class or coach?"

I asked if I could join him and he said, "Absolutely. Come on." I called the airline, got a ticket, and I sat in the seat next to that person. We had a two-hour presentation. I walked out with the sale and a thank you from the client for having the courage to make time when he was available. I took the next plane home.

I've done it many times. As far as L.A. I have the client to myself for two hours to Chicago and for six hours to L.A. It's my client. I own him. He's got nowhere to go, can't leave me, can't get off. He can't do anything but sit in a chair next to me.

Here are fifteen secrets from Sid Friedman on how to increase customer loyalty.

1. **Promise a lot and deliver more.** Otherwise, this is what happens:

The average customer buys five policies in a lifetime . . . from four different agents. Here's why:

3 percent relocated.

5 percent developed other relationships.

9 percent left because someone else had a better price.

14 percent were dissatisfied with the product they bought.

68 percent left because of an attitude of indifference to the customer.

2. Always give 100 percent. If we had to live with 99.9 percent, we'd have one hour of unsafe drinking water every month, two unsafe plane landings at Chicago's O'Hare every day, 16,000 pieces of mail lost every hour, and 500 incorrect surgical performances every week.

3. **Always be a pro.**

• A pro is good at what he does and knows how to do it again.

• A pro keeps on getting better.

• A pro critiques his performance every single time.

4. Keep a personal idea book. If you hear or read something you like, write down the note or phrase.

5. View your life as a journey. Keep charge of your growth. Be the person you want to be. First: Set a destination. What is your goal? Second: Do you know your strengths and weaknesses? Third: Plan your trip.

6. **Have the courage to dream big dreams.** Dream in color.

Have an image of what you want. See it. Draw it. Ordinary people can do extraordinary things.

7. Be a first-rate "you." You don't want to be me. You'll only be a second-rate "me." You're an original. Take tips from people you admire. Keep on playing tapes in your mind. But erase the tapes that are not positive.

It only takes a .300 batting average to be a baseball Hall of Famer. That means you don't make a hit 70 percent of the time. The difference between a champion and an average player is a small fraction.

8. Manage your time and you'll manage your life. Here's how:

On a piece of paper, draw three columns. At the top of column 1 write URGENT. At the top of column 2 write IMPORTANT. At the top of column 3 write EVERYTHING ELSE. Carry this list wherever you go.

9. Remember the four Ds of time management. Put everything on your desk in one pile. Take up the first piece. You can't put it down until you:

Do it or

Delay it (but put a date on when you'll Do it) or

Delegate it or

Destroy it.

10. Discover what the rest of the world is doing and don't do it. Stop competing. Start creating.

11. Make your personality such that it brings out the best in people around you. Develop a personality so that other people are drawn to you. Work to eliminate your negative behavior.

12. Recognize the destructive behavior of a loser. Here are some telltale characteristics of losers:

• They are preoccupied with themselves and don't have time for anyone else.

• They can't handle responsibility.

• They are inflexible.

• They can't see the big picture. They won't venture into new territory.

- They resent authority. They would rather fail than take instruction and win.
- They are lazy. They won't devote their time or talent without asking for more money.
- They are critical and blaming. They find excuses. They say problems are unsolvable.

13. In contrast, here are the characteristics of winners:
- They have a sense of humor.
- They won't give up until the job gets done.
- They are disciplined to do what it takes to achieve success.
- They have a good balance in their lives. There is more to life than work.
- They are goal-oriented.
- They understand exactly how *you* feel. They give you undivided attention and honesty.
- They have a healthy self-image and a good mental attitude.

14. Don't take yourself too seriously, but take what you do very seriously.

15. If it is to be, it is up to me. Ten words. Each only has two letters. But they provide a guidepost for your life.

MEDIA TIPS
Newspapers

—————■—————

Prospecting Through Newspaper Ads

In this book, we will give you tips on how to use different media to entice your customers to climb the Loyalty Ladder. We start with newspapers because they are an easy way to reach a broad range of prospects for your business.

FACT: Newspapers reach more than 113 million adults in the United States every day. About six out of ten say they read every page. Nine out of ten read the general news. And if your business is looking for a specific gender, remember nine out of ten men read the sports pages and eight out of ten women read the entertainment pages.

Most newspaper readers are subscribers (seven out of ten), which means it's a guaranteed delivery into the home of your customers, unlike radio or TV, which deliver to the home only when the viewer or listener decides to view or listen.

It's a very important medium to consider for your business, since more ad dollars are spent in newspapers than any other medium— nearly $34 billion a year.

Because so many people read newspapers every day, newspaper advertising can be a great way of introducing prospects to your product or service.

Newspapers eat up 25 percent of the ad dollars spent nationwide—

but for local advertising, they use half the available ad dollars. (Next: TV and yellow pages with about 13 percent each.)

Here are some guidelines on headlines, copy, and illustrations we learned through the years to attract prospects to your business through newspaper advertising.

THE HEADLINE

Readers look at a newspaper page an average of four seconds before turning the page. In those four seconds they look at the news headlines first. You better say something that makes them want to stop and read the headline of your ad. Something that makes them want to keep on reading.

The average woman reads only four ads in an average newspaper, so put *news* into the headline. Something that is new, just-arrived, first-time, unique—those are key words that make the prospect read your ad.

1. **Promise a benefit or provoke curiosity.** Remember there are only two things that people buy: solutions to problems and good feelings. Think of those two criteria next time you sit down to write a headline for one of your products or services. Stress the benefit of your product, not the product itself. If the shoes you sell have crepe soles (feature), say they are "shock absorbing" (benefit). If the suits you sell are a blend of Dacron and wool (feature), say they can be worn "year-round" (benefit). Advertisements with headlines that promise a benefit are read by four times more people than headlines that don't have benefits. Charles Mills, vice-president of O.M. Scott, the largest grower of lawn seed in the world, said, "People are interested in their lawns. Not in our seeds."

2. **Put the name of the product in the headline if possible.** Not the name of your business. Put your name someplace else in the ad. Not in the headline, unless it has a special meaning: "ONLY AT (name of your business) WILL YOU FIND (name of item)."

Most people like to see the name of their business at the top of the ad. Most customers couldn't care less. The bottom of the ad is fine. . . . And don't forget to add your address, phone number, and someone's name to request more information.

3. Long headlines pull as well (and often better) than short headlines. Headlines with more than ten words have much better readership than shorter headlines.

4. Don't be clever for the sake of being clever. A recent ad for automobiles promoted new cars with catalytic converters with this headline: ARE YOU ALLERGIC TO CATS? A reader that was stopped reading after the first sentence, but the ad had nothing to do with cats.

5. Have a "big idea." Advertising guru David Ogilvy said, "Unless your campaign is built around a big idea, it will pass like a ship in the night." You have to find out what's unique about the product you are advertising. The more yours-alone facts you put in your copy, the easier it is to sell your merchandise.

6. Sell one idea at a time. Otherwise you confuse the reader.

7. Make it "news" worthy. A "new" product. A "new" solution. Ads with news in the headlines pull about 20 percent better.

8. Use certain words in headlines because . . . they work. They include (but are not limited to) *new, free, how to, amazing, introducing, guarantee, you, now.* If your ad is directed to a certain audience, put them in the headline (asthmatics, people with rheumatism). One headline that worked: SIXTY DAYS AGO THEY CALLED ME BALDY. You can be sure bald men read THAT ad.

9. Include a local reference if possible. Supermarkets that promote products grown in their state report a dramatic increase in sales. People want to be identified with indigenous merchandise. There's a pride in buying that which is theirs. Which is one reason Mondale won Minnesota and Dukakis won Massachusetts when almost every other state turned them down.

10. Don't be clever. Double entendres, puns, headlines written to grab your attention but have no follow-through simply don't work. A cable TV network ran a series of ads with prominent people making statements like, "Murphy Brown moves to *60 Minutes.*" They began each of these ads with copy that said,

"Well, that isn't true, but if it *were* true . . ." And most people stopped reading. We once wrote an ad for snowsuits we bought in Finland as follows: WE WENT TO HEL-SINKI AND BACK TO BRING YOU THESE SNOWSUITS. Funny. But didn't sell snowsuits.

The following week we ran the same ad but changed the headline to: IN OUR THIRTY YEARS IN BUSINESS, WE NEVER SOLD SO MUCH OF ONE ITEM IN SO SHORT A TIME. That headline sold sixty-three jackets. People read the headline and said, "That jacket must be terrific."

11. **Put the headline under an illustration.** Why? Because that's how people read. Look at your newspaper or the layout of news magazines. If your ad looks more like an editorial page, your readership will increase.

12. **Don't write your headline in capital letters.** Setting your ad lowercase INSTEAD OF SETTING IT LIKE THIS will increase readership. Here's why: We learn to read in lowercase letters like this sentence. Yes, the headline will be set in a larger typeface, but still set it in lowercase.

13. **Make the headline easy to understand.** John Caples, an expert in headline writing and former VP of the advertising agency BBD&O, said, "People are thinking of other things when they see your ad." Don't make them think. Make them act.

14. **Make it believable.** I'll read HOW TO LOSE TEN POUNDS IN TWO WEEKS. I won't read HOW TO LOSE TEN POUNDS IN 24 HOURS. One is believable. One isn't.

15. **Make it for your audience.** You use a different headline if your audience is a young mother or a sixty-year-old grandmother.

16. **Tell a story.** People like to read stories, and your headline will keep them reading into the body copy if the story is interesting. Here's a headline we used for men's terry robes: WE FIRST SAW THESE IN THE CRILLON HOTEL ON THE PLACE DE LA CONCORDE IN PARIS. We actually did. First time we saw thick, terry robes hanging in a hotel room's closet. We came home and ordered them for our store, and this headline sold the robes!

17. **Solve a problem.** We found we could monogram a child's name on an inside tag or the front of a special brand of children's raincoats. Most children's raincoats are yellow, and you can't tell one from another in the cloakroom. Your child often comes home with someone else's coat. Our headline read: CAN'T LOSE THIS RAINCOAT 'CAUSE IT HAS THEIR NAME ON IT. We sold out in three days!

18. Fulfill a dream. John Caples wrote this classic: THEY LAUGHED WHEN I SAT DOWN AT THE PIANO. It sold courses on learning to play the piano through mail instruction.

19. Offer excellent value. After forty years of writing headlines, we have found that there are less than a dozen that work every time. Here's our favorite. It will work for your business by simply substituting the prices and the items: WOULD YOU BUY A $30.00 SHIRT ON SALE FOR $14.99? It tells the original price, sale price, and makes you want to read more to find out why. This headline is easy to adapt for your business.

20. Last, but not least, don't forget to use a headline. If you think that sounds unbelievable, look at the automobile and food ads in your local newspaper. They either have no headline (just the name of the business up there at the top) or innocuous phrases like MIDWINTER CLEARANCE, which means . . . nothing.

A final word: Try different headlines for the same product. John Caples said he tried different headlines for the exact same product and one would pull as much as twenty times more business than the others.

Doubleday books ran this headline successfully for years: BUY THESE FOUR BOOKS FOR 99¢

Until someone came up with the same offer—but a different headline that worked much better: BUY THREE BOOKS FOR 99¢—GET ONE FREE.

THE COPY

The body copy of your ad is read by only one out of ten readers. The trick is to catch them with the headline and keep them reading with the first few paragraphs. If you can get readers to read the first 50 words of what you write, they will probably read the next 250 words. It is impossible to underestimate the power of words. Or even a word. Some examples:

• One word doubled the business of a shampoo. The instructions read, "Wet hair. Apply lather. Rinse thoroughly." And then a bright copywriter added one word that doubled the business: "Repeat."

• World-famous salesman Elmer Wheeler was known for using a phrase for added business. A drugstore chain wanted to increase its sales of milk shakes. At that time, some customers requested an egg in their milk shake, which added to the cost (and profit). Wheeler's suggestion tripled sales: When the customer asked for a milk shake, the counter person would say, "One egg or two?" Almost everyone said "one" (the others said "two").

•Helena Rubinstein cosmetics couldn't understand why department stores were turning down the free giveaway Rubinstein offered. We analyzed their presentation and came back with the answer:

"You are using two wrong phrases. The first one is when your headline says, A GIFT FROM HELENA RUBINSTEIN." Wrong. It should be a gift from the store.

Second: If you are an upscale store, do not offer the customer a "free coupon." It should be a "gift certificate." "Supermarkets give coupons. You give gift certificates. Same product. Different word." By making these two simple changes, nearly every department store participated in the Helena Rubinstein promotion.

• When you visit Disneyland or Walt Disney World, you are not a customer. You are a "guest." This simple word change is reflected in courtesy shown. We are nicer to "guests" than we are to "customers."

• I like the way our British cousins call life insurance companies life *assurance* companies. I guess that means I'm paying money to "assure" I keep on living. U.S. companies tell me I win only if I die.

And so, when writing the copy for your ad, remember the importance of words.

And . . . Here Are Twenty Ways To Keep Them Reading:

1. **Get to your main point . . . fast!** Most teachers of copywriting will show how you can cut out the first three paragraphs and probably make the copy more salable. Your beginning copy should expand on the benefit promised in the headline.

2. **Make sentences short.** Only twelve to fifteen words. Make paragraphs short. Two or three sentences. This gives you lots of "white space" around your copy. Makes it easier to read. Remember, readers "scan" rather than "read."

3. **Don't set copy wider than three inches.** Here's why: The eye drops down to the next line after three to four inches. Especially at normal newspaper 8-point type size. (This is 11.5 point.)

4. **Don't exaggerate.** Make sure "the story isn't better than the store." Promise a lot and deliver more.

5. **Be specific.** The Five *Ws* still work. To quote Kipling:

I keep six honest serving men

(They taught me all I knew);

Their names are What and Why and When

And How and Where and Who.

6. **Write as though you were talking to someone in your living room.** Chatty, comfortable, easy to read and understand.

7. **Set your copy in serif type. Not sans serif.** Here's why: Sans serif is difficult to read. This copy is set in serif type. It has little "hooks" on the end of each letter, which makes it easier for the eye to follow along. This copy is set in sans serif. You can see it is more difficult to read than the previous sentence.

8. **Long copy sells as much as short copy.** As long as it's interesting to read.

9. **Write in the present tense.** Positively, absolutely avoid the past tense. The "has been" or "were done." Writing in the present tense means something is happening now. Writing in the past tense means it's over with, long gone, in the past . . . who cares?

10. Use words or references people understand. I once wrote copy on a new song that I said "was the best music I've heard since Glenn Miller went down in the English Channel." I showed the copy around the office and everyone younger than thirty asked me, "Who's Glenn Miller?"

11. Use testimonials. Of people who actually bought from you or used your product. Your local customers are much less expensive to use than celebrities and can be just as effective. ("Hey, here's a picture of Mary Simpson. I know Mary. . . .")

12. Include the price. We once ran an ad for a little girl's sheepskin coat. The price was very high, and our buyer advised us against telling the price in the ad. We persuaded her by saying, "Why did you buy it if you didn't think you could sell it?" Nine out of ten newspaper readers said pricing influences their product selection and desire to buy. If you don't tell them, you haven't influenced them.

13. If it's on sale, tell me how much I'm saving. Food ads are most guilty of this. They yell "sale" at the top of their ads but don't tell me how-much-was-it. If it's on sale, great. But tell me two things: (1) the original price and (2) how much I'm saving.

14. Read the award-winning ads and copy them. Why not? Go to the art museum and see the artists copying the masters. Most popular singers tell you they started by copying the style of someone they admired. That's how you start. Eventually your own style will develop.

15. Does your ad include all the pertinent information? Take a look at the copy in mail order catalogs. In a very small space they tell you what you want to know. Is it washable? What sizes does it come in? What colors? The more you tell, the more you sell.

16. The word "FREE" is still the most powerful word in the English language. "Buy one for $10, get one *free*" pulls 40 percent better than "Half Price" or "50 percent off."

17. Put a coupon/gift certificate in the ad and increase response. At least 10 percent more people will remember seeing your ad if you include a coupon. When Danielle Barr took over as head of advertising at National Westminster Bank in London, she came from a background of direct marketing. She called in the agencies responsible for the bank's advertising and told them she wanted a coupon in all future advertising. The agencies squirmed, were uncomfortable, mentioned "disturbing design layout" and "not the image of the bank" and "what's the reason." Danielle carefully explained that in the million-plus readership in the London newspapers, someone, somewhere, somehow would respond to the coupons. And they were excellent prospects for area managers to follow up with because they now had the customer's name and address. (Yes, it worked.)

18. **Put the coupon/gift certificate in the lower outside corner.** Here's why: It's easier to tear out.

19. **Anticipate questions.** What would you ask yourself about the offer you are making? That's what most folks are asking themselves while they're reading. Sooooo, answer their questions. That's one reason Question and Answer copy is so effective. Gives you a chance to anticipate the objections . . . and answer them.

20. **Remember the rule of three.** Say what you're going to say. Say it. Say what you said. Follow that outline, and you're way ahead of most copywriters.

THE ILLUSTRATION

A headline and copy capture your attention and explain what you have to sell. If, however, you can add an illustration to your ad, you will increase readership. Here are twenty rules to follow to make sure they keep on reading after they see the illustration.

1. **Show the product in use.** Photos of people using your product enhance credibility.

2. **Put the illustration at the top of the ad with a caption underneath.** And then the headline. And then the body copy. That's how people read.

3. Use photographs instead of illustrations. They attract greater readership and sell more merchandise. Exception: Many newspapers have older presses and cannot reproduce good-quality photographs. That was true with our local paper, and so we used illustrations. Also, certain fashion ads use illustrations to convey a certain "look." Good example: Lord & Taylor's ads in the *New York Times.*

4. Does the finished ad "look" like *your* business? Or *any* business? The reader should recognize the ad as your ad and not someone else's. In an advertising class we taught, we would place in the front of the room ads from five local supermarkets with the store names taken off. We gave the class a paper with the names of the supermarkets and told them to match the names on their papers with the ads displayed. No one ever did it correctly.

5. Does the picture alone tell the story? This rule also works in television. Here's how: Turn off the sound. Just look at the pictures. Do you know what is being advertised? If you don't, it's not a good ad. Same for illustrations in a magazine. If I covered up the copy and your name, would I know what you're trying to sell?

6. Make the illustration ask, "What does this mean?" If the picture is provocative, the reader will continue reading to find out what it's all about.

7. Make the picture show what happens when your product is used. The clothes come out whiter in the washing machine if they buy your cleaner. The children win prizes in the Easter parade when they wear your clothing. We once did an ad for the service department of an automobile agency with a photograph showing used parts in a plastic bag in the trunk of the car. The point: The firm REALLY did the work and really did put in new parts. And here are the old parts to prove it. Since so many people do not have confidence in auto repairs, this made them feel more "comfortable." And the service department's business increased because of this one illustration.

8. Use photographs of real people. Testimonials are very important. Good example: contests. Does anybody really win?

Publishers Clearing House shows their truck pulling up to winners' houses in their TV ads and videotapes the reactions when people are told they just won a million dollars. That's effective!

9. Keep illustrations simple. One person in the ad. One product in the ad. Keep it uncluttered.

10. If possible: Use a baby or an animal or a good-looking person. These are proven attention grabbers.

12. Use color. More and more newspapers are offering good color reproduction. In the past few offered it, and those that did often had poor registration (the color didn't fall where it should and a hat became part the flesh color of the face and part the color of the hat). Today, modern presses have much better quality control. Your cost is about 50 percent more than it is for black and white. But the ad can pull as much as 100 percent more readership. Good value. Besides, who wants to look at black-and-white meat or black-and-white produce from the supermarket?

12. Be wary of type on color backgrounds. Using black type on a dark blue background might be interesting, but you can't read the copy! If readers can't read the copy, you can't sell the merchandise!

13. Use captions under your illustrations. Twice as many people read them than read the copy in your ad. So make them selling sentences!

14. Vertical ads pull better than horizontal ads. About 25 percent more. One reason: People fold the newspaper, and since most of the editorial appears on the top part, they read that section and then . . . turn the page.

15. The bigger the ad, the greater the response. But not as much as you think. Using a factor of 100 percent reading a full page ad, here are the percentages if the ad is reduced:

> Half-page ad: 74 percent
>
> One-third-page ad: 62 percent
>
> One-quarter-page ad: 68 percent

Carefully think whether the extra exposure is worth the dramatic extra cost.

16. **Running an ad in reverse type (white on black) will not attract readers.** Just the opposite. It turns them off. Too difficult to read, so let's turn the page. The most astonishing example was a recent ad from a motor club that advertised membership with a coupon printed in reverse (white on black). Unless you had a pen with white ink, it was impossible to fill out.

17. **Sell the merchandise, not the design.** Many graphic artists are concerned with winning awards for their great designs, but you're concerned with filling the register. Remind them your goal is what pays their salary.

18. **Make the ads look like they could be news stories.** You see more and more advertising done this way because . . . it attracts about 50 percent MORE readers.

19. **Recheck the basics.** Do you have the name of your business in the ad? Do you have the address? Do you have a phone number for me to call? Do you have the name of someone I can talk to when I call? If you have free parking, have you told me where it is? Do you accept credit cards? Look at the ads in this morning's newspaper. Few, if any, remember to put in all the items we just mentioned.

20. **The Bottom Line:** If an ad works, repeat it.

Newspaper Advertising Pluses
• Believability
• Mass exposure
• Lots of room to write descriptions
• You can go back and read it again
• You can rip it out and save it
• Targeted sections (sports, social)
• Can use coupons
• Can pick days to advertise

Newspaper Advertising Minuses
• Fewer people reading
• Rates climbing faster than circulation
• Your ad is one of many ads

- Average reader spends four *seconds* on a page
- Audiences it does NOT reach well: eighteen- to thirty-four-year-olds, out-of-towners
- Coupon redemption declining
- Can't determine placement of your ad

CASE HISTORY
AMC Kabuki

———————— ■ ————————

We want to show you in detail how some businesses move their customers up the Loyalty Ladder. Every chapter has a case history—a story about a business that succeeds in making its customers come back again . . . and again . . . and again. Here is our first example.

Business: AMC Kabuki 8 Theatres.
Owner: American Multi-Cinema, Inc.
Manager (San Francisco): Larry D. Whittenberger.

Background: Whittenberger, who joined AMC in 1981, has considerable autonomy in shaping the success of the Kabuki 8 complex, which sits in the heart of Japantown. He cut his marketing teeth doing advance work for Ringling Brothers, and the experience has paid off well: The Kabuki is the highest-grossing theater in a town that is among America's most important film markets. It is also among the most innovative. Since the theater opened in 1986, annual ticket sales have doubled, to about a million. It is the only theater that markets to the full spectrum of moviegoers: children, ethnic groups, hard-core enthusiasts, gays and lesbians, occasional moviegoers, and others.

The Kabuki 8 was the first theater complex built by AMC in an effort to upgrade its image as an operator of shopping-mall multi-plexes. The high-impact, urban complex was a risky one. Site acquisition and construction came to $18.5 million, making it one of the most expensive movie-theater houses ever built. The complex employs a staff of eighty-five, including seven managers. Prior to the theater's opening, a jobs committee consisting of representatives from various community-based organizations was formed to recruit and screen applicants, a function it still occasionally performs. The Kabuki donates passes to 103 different organizations to support fund-raising efforts by nonprofit groups.

Besides newspaper advertising, the Kabuki uses the following methods to create satisfied customers and repeat business:

• Advance ticket sales. The Kabuki was the first movie house in town to offer this service. Tickets may be purchased from an ATM machine inside the lobby or over the phone by way of key-pad instructions. Future plans: Use the customer data generated by such transactions to contact specific people who enjoy specific movies.

Advance ticket sales have been particularly useful in conjunction with the screening of movies that attract large crowds. Customers who use the advance can be sure of getting seats. In addition, Whittenberger can count his chickens before showtime, since on numerous occasions he has sold 75 percent of the available seats before the box office even opened. Whittenberger sees advance sales as a particularly good way of attracting those movie-goers who see relatively few movies and who don't want any hassles (e.g., SOLD OUT) when they're out on a busy Saturday night.

• Validated parking. At 50 cents for three hours on weeknights and weekends, it's the cheapest deal in town. Parking is in a garage directly underneath the complex.

•Free popcorn Wednesday nights, free refills of large buckets anytime, and snack bars that offer the best of local specialties: Just Desserts cakes and pastries, biscotti. Other upscale items include China Mist ice tea, trail mix, and Odwalla juices, along with more gourmet desserts from the local Sweet Inspirations.

•All the amenities, plus. The Kabuki is known for showing perfect, scratchless prints with bright images, crisp corners, and perfect sound. "We always screen each print before the public sees it. If there's a problem, we get a new print, or reel if that's what's required, in a hurry."

The Kabuki is also one of the cleanest and most well-maintained of San Francisco's movie houses. The floors are never sticky, the seats are plush and comfortable, and the rest rooms are always in good shape. Burned-out light bulbs get replaced promptly.

One other unusual touch is a staff of ushers and snack-bar personnel that Whittenberger has trained to be "proactive." "We teach them to pay close attention to our customers—they will not wait for you to approach them if they spot a problem."

All of the above make people want to return to the Kabuki 8. But the heart of the theater's Loyalty Ladder—the method used to make theatergoers want to return more often—emphasizes two marketing ideas:

1. Cater to the film buffs, the ones who will return to the Kabuki as many as 200 times a year (some actually do!). In this area, Kabuki is one of the most successful marketers in the country. Build a theater and they will come, but show the right mix of movies, and they will come much more often. To find his best potential customers, Whittenberger has struck up alliances with just about every group of film buffs in town.

The San Francisco International Film Festival (run by the San Francisco Film Society) is the oldest film festival in America, and among the most successful. Attendance has virtually doubled since the Kabuki began hosting it. Prior to that, the festival screened its scores of offerings at venues scattered throughout the town.

Whittenberger convinced the initially skeptical festival organizers to screen films at the Kabuki, and now they won't have it any other way. They love the place, particularly because the hard-core attendees can easily see four movies in one day without having to leave the theater.

Says Whittenberger: "People from all over the world attend the festival, and you can imagine what great publicity we get, not to mention the goodwill with people who really like their movies.

"We [AMC] aren't really an art film specialist—our expertise is in showing films from the major distributors. But San Francisco is a special market, one which particularly enjoys art films. We try to fill that need by catering to various film organizations here. We'll rent them a screen, or several screens, for a day or a week, and that brings many new faces into our theaters. When they see how well we do everything, they tend to return. We get huge goodwill and publicity, and it costs us nothing."

Now, multiply that effect by factoring in these organizations, all of which have come to use the Kabuki for special events:

- The American Film Festival
- National Asian-Americans in Telecommunications Association
- Jewish Film Festival
- Women in Film
- Jazz in the City Film Festival
- Frameline (gay and lesbian film festival)
- Irish Film Festival
- Latinos in Communication
- Cherry Blossom Film Series
- Black Filmmakers
- Friends of the Academy
- Circa Cine Film Society
- Film Arts Foundation

Whittenberger says that the Kabuki has become the unofficial film art center of San Francisco, with the result that a relatively large number of customers are the kind of buffs who spread the word. "I know one woman who saw 200 films last year at the Kabuki. She is a marketing vehicle for us."

2. Kabuki's MovieWatcher frequent moviegoing program provides awards such as free popcorn, soft drinks, and movies at various levels of attendance. Here is how it works:

Detach your MovieWatcher qualification card from a brochure distributed in the lobby. Present the card to the cashier, who stamps it. When you have four stamps, you receive a plastic card with a magnetic stripe to record future data. Each subsequent ticket purchase earns two points. The first ten earn free popcorn. The next ten, a free movie ticket, and so on.

About every two months Whittenberger mails to MovieWatchers to inform them of upcoming screenings and special releases. Members are also entitled to a discount on the purchase of *Premiere* magazine.

"Taken together," says Whittenberger, "our freebies can amount to a pretty good deal. If you come here on a Wednesday night, for instance, you could park for 50 cents, get a free movie ticket on your MovieWatcher card, and all the popcorn you can eat, again for free. That's a pretty hard deal to beat." Indeed, in San Francisco, it's a deal that no one in the movie business has beaten.

Ten Ways to Convert a Prospect to a Shopper

———————————————■———————————————

1. **Create a major reason for a prospect to shop you for the first time.** Offer a wanted item at your cost. Or below. Write it off as "advertising" because . . . that's what it is. Your objective: to have them come to your place of business the FIRST time.

2. **Ask present customers for names of prospects.** Insurance companies have taught this technique for generations. The best source of new customers is existing customers. Call it Networking. Call it Testimonials. Call it Recommendations. Whatever. It is a basic psychological fact that individuals like to persuade others to share their decisions. Think about the movies recommended by friends as a "must see." Restaurants as a "must enjoyment." And your business as a "must go to."

3. **Involve an organization they belong to.** Many supermarkets give 1 percent of a customer's purchase to their designated charity. What this means: The charity, religious organization, community group now become spokespeople for your business and encourage their members to shop with you.

4. **Test direct mail.** Most of your prospective shoppers come from a specific geographic area. If you are a supermarket, they live within two miles of your store. If you're a dry cleaner, they live within a few blocks of your business. If you're a bank, they live as close as your nearest branch office to their home. Whatever. Pick and choose a specific area where your present customers live. The odds are your prospects have not only common geographics but also common demographics. Mail them an offer they can't refuse. If it works, make the next mailing circle wider. . . .

5. Get involved. Most small business owners succeed because they are involved in their community. People know them from Little League, school, civic clubs, business organizations. It is too easy to hide behind the syndrome of "Everybody knows what I do. Everybody knows where I am." False. This means you are suffering from the Curse of Assumption. You assume everyone knows. Most do not. And since 20 percent of the people in your community change their address every year, it makes sense for you to be involved in your community to tell everyone who you are and what you do.

(Always carry a stack of calling cards with you. You never know when you might meet a prospect.)

6. Know your product. People like to buy from people with authority—those who know about the product and can anticipate questions before you ask them. Here's a phrase to remember: Selling is knowledge of stock. Great insurance agents soak up your personal information while the computer inside their head automatically accepts or rejects the different options available within the industry to fit your particular needs. The more you tell, the more you sell. Source of information: your supplier. When new merchandise arrived in our clothing store, we made sure everyone read the tags attached. Very few people do this, but there is a wealth of selling information included in that tiny type.

7. Training and learning. Have weekly meetings with your staff to review what's new and different or about to happen. Go around the room and ask each to contribute their thoughts and ideas. Most people simply do not become involved because they are never asked. There is no limit to where ideas come from. Often from the ones most quiet in the back of the room who rarely have something to say. *But when they do . . .*

8. Do busmen's holidays. Whenever you travel, shop a comparable business. What are they doing that you can copy? Feargal Quinn, owner of Superquinn, Ireland's premier supermarket, runs a twinning program. He takes a person from one of his supermarkets and has him or her switch jobs with someone else in a comparable position at another Superquinn. The employee learns what that store is doing successfully and brings it back to his own store. The program was so successful that he sent his best employees to U.S. supermarkets to do the same thing.

9. Attend trade association meetings. Program organizers look for the different, unusual (and yes, successful) ideas to present at their programs. If you attend a three-day seminar for your industry. If you listen to thirty speakers. If you return with one new idea for your business. *Terrific!* You're ahead of the rest of the competition in converting prospects into shoppers.

10. Read. Watch. Listen. Have cassettes on your business— or just on selling—in your car. You're a captive audience to learn how successful practitioners ply their craft. Watch instructional videos. Read trade journals. Whenever we want to interview the "best" in a particular industry, the first person we call is the editor of that trade association journal. Everyone knows the winners. Every business group is really a small, tight circle where most people might know one another or definitely know the leaders. They are the ones on the audiotapes and videos and written up in books that you want to read. Watch. Listen.

Part 2

THE SHOPPER

Introduction to Shoppers

———————————————— ■ ————————————————

Shop-per / shap-er/ *n. Someone who visits your business at least once.*

Shoppers are one step up the Loyalty Ladder from Prospects. Shoppers are Prospects who have been convinced to visit your place of business.

But Shoppers are skeptics. They know something about your business. But they still haven't made the buying decision. If your products and services are good, if your employees are helpful, if your pricing is fair, many of your Shoppers will climb the Loyalty Ladder and become your Customers. But suppose your business fails to satisfy your Shoppers' needs . . .

We recently visited a local supermarket and were looking for jars of honey. Here's what happened.

We stopped the first person passing who wore an apron with the supermarket's logo and her name printed in large letters: "Pardon me, Janet, can you tell me where the honey is?"

Answer: "Hey, I'm just part-time. I don't know where *anything* is."

We went to the woman working the deli counter and asked the same question.

Answer: "All I know is what is behind my counter."

We went to a man in the meat department.

Answer: Pointing to the blood on his apron, he said, "I'm not in the 'honey' department."

No, he wasn't.

I left the basket half-filled with groceries and walked out, never to return . . .

Sometime, at your next party, if the conversation slows, simply ask the question, "What was the most terrible thing that happened to you when you were shopping recently?"

The conversation will explode with one person interrupting another, each eager to play "Can You Top This" with enough horror stories to fill a Stephen King anthology.

What's happening here?

This: The opportunity to take the occasional Shopper up the Ladder to the more loyal Customer is ignored by many businesspeople.

Like the time when . . .

A new restaurant opened. We went, enjoyed it, returned with friends. One of the dishes was not appetizing. We told the owner on the way out. Her answer: "Well, at least you'll know what not to order the next time."

But "the next time" never happened. . . .

Not that it's easy converting a Shopper to a Customer. It's not. Shoppers, in the vernacular of the supermarket industry, "cherry pick." They go store to store with the newspaper ads clipped out to seek out the lowest price. They shop you only for price. You have to give them a reason to come back. One way: persevere.

Does the cashier see the name of the Shopper on a check and say "Thank you (and their name)" because they see it printed on the check?

Do you ask Shoppers, as they leave, if they were satisfied?

A recent *New Yorker* cartoon showed a wife answering her phone in her home. She turns to her husband and says, "It's the waiter we had at the restaurant this evening. He wants to know if everything was all right."

Do you give them a coupon, a certificate, a "something" that encourages them to come back at least one more time?

If you can have a Shopper come back to your business four times in a row, you have a "steady" Customer. But how do you have them come back four times in a row?

One word: persistence.

You keep on plugging away each time you see the Shopper at your place of business. You make them feel confident, comfortable, and convinced you are their business of choice.

A McGraw-Hill survey said it takes four consecutive calls on a Shopper before you make the sale. So do not become discouraged after the first or second or third try. If you do, the salesperson following you will come in and make the sale you should have made if you had just persevered one more time.

One of the most famous quotes on this topic comes from Calvin Coolidge when he was president. "Silent Cal" was not noted for long conversations or speeches. They tell the story of the woman who met him at a White House party and said, "President Coolidge, I just made a bet with my husband that I could persuade you to say three words."

Coolidge looked at her and said, "You lose."

His quote on persistence is worth repeating:

Nothing in the world can take the place of persistence.
Talent will not; nothing is more common than unsuccessful men
  with talent.
Genius will not; the world is full of educated derelicts.
Persistence and determination alone are omnipotent.

Remember that Shoppers still may not have bought anything from you. They are probably aware of you: through a friend, an advertisement, a direct mail piece, some marketing tool that caught their eye and made them think, "Hmmm, maybe, someday. . . ."

One way to have them buy: Give them their first purchase free.

Many people reading that last sentence might want to stop and reread and say, "Are they kidding?"

No. Not really. What you're looking for is the "lifetime value" of the Customer. How much will that person spend with you over the course of the next few years? If you can have someone come in the first time, if only as a Shopper, you have a chance. If the Shopper doesn't come, you can't sell him or her anything.

One year, Eastman Kodak gave 35mm cameras to every baby born in Rochester, New York, their headquarters' hometown. They also provided photographic material to high school photography clubs. And they realized there were also elementary school photography clubs. Why not give them what they need free as well? Their reasoning: Habits die hard. Once budding photographers use one product—and are satisfied with how it works—they will continue using the same product. And the amateur child photographer of today is the professional photographer of tomorrow.

What are you giving away "free" to your Shoppers to make them want to return to your business as Customers?

Wow!

————————■————————

One of the first things Shoppers notice about your place of business is the ambiance. Are employees happy and are they spreading their enthusiasm to Customers? Is the business fun and cheery or dreary and drab? Shoppers want to come back if employees seem friendly and eager to help. What you need your employees to have is a little bit of "Wow!"—enthusiasm about your business that will be instantly transmitted to your Shoppers.

ENTHUSIASM IS CONTAGIOUS

One person comes in to work every day, greets everyone with a smile and a compliment. People smile back and like that person.

Another person comes into work every day, doesn't greet anyone, looks at the floor as he walks around, never smiles, doesn't make eye contact with other people. This lack of enthusiasm is also contagious. Deadly. People do not smile back and do not like that person.

A friend recently told of an experience he had with a doctor's receptionist who was curt, cold, and gave him a difficult time.

"Well, then," I said, "the doctor is also curt, cold, and will give you a difficult time."

It's true. We tend to imitate what we think is expected of us. Businessman Ross Perot says people don't need to be managed. They need to be led. How you act, react, perform is closely watched by the people all around. They imitate.

ENTHUSIASM IS ALSO HABIT FORMING

People who feel better act better. Stimulate positive feelings within yourself, and those feelings start bouncing back from the people who work with you every day.

Enthusiasm can help counteract tough times. When your customers and employees see the joy and vigor with which you greet the world, they will want to be around you and do business with you.

An enthusiastic example is speaker Charlie "Tremendous" Jones. (When people ask Charlie how he feels, he roars back, "Tremendous!") Charlie greets everyone with a giant bear hug and a cheery "I want you to remember how glad I am to see you!"

Now that's the right way to start every day.

WOW! QUOTES

"Enthusiasm can't be taught. It must be caught."

—DALE CARNEGIE

"A man can succeed at almost anything for which he has unlimited enthusiasm."

—CHARLES SCHWAB

FROM OUR AUSTRALIAN FRIEND TONY INGLETON

"About eight or nine months ago, I had a lot of pressure, financial pressure, in terms of meeting bills, working out the cash flow, etc. . . . And it really started to get me down.

"Then I realized that I had a role as leader of my business. That role didn't mean simply that you made the payroll each week. It also meant that you are in charge of the enthusiasm of the company. And if the head person is giving out very bad vibes, that isn't going to do anyone any good.

"So, even if I am literally bleeding inside, when I pick up the phone I sound happy, positive, as if I didn't have a problem in the world. And, immediately, I start to feel better. If I have a happy look on my face, I find that a positive attitude comes through in my voice."

WHAT PEOPLE WORRY ABOUT

People generally tend to worry too much about everything. Many people invent something to worry about so they can get through the day with a problem that gives them an excuse for not doing the job, making the sale, creating a happy environment.

This is not only self-defeating, it is self-destructive. Doctors have proven that worry cuts down your life span as well as your success span.

Try this one: More Americans commit suicide (the result of stress, anxiety, and yes, worry) than die from the five most common communicable diseases.

Worry causes heart trouble, high blood pressure, asthma, rheumatism, colds, arthritis, migraine headaches, and a host of stomach disorders.

So why are you worried?

A recent survey on "Things People Worry About" broke down as follows:

Things that never happen: 40 percent
Things that can't change: 30 percent
Needless worry about health: 12 percent
Petty and miscellaneous worry: 10 percent
Real problems: 8 percent

Conclusion: 92 percent of the things people worry about, they can't do anything about!

SELLING TICKETS

Sometimes problems seem so huge as to be unmanageable. The solution: Break the problem down to small solvable pieces.

We once did a seminar for the World Hockey Association. One team owner came up to me after the program and said, "I've been listening to you all day and you haven't answered my basic question: How do you sell 10,000 tickets?" We looked at him and quietly said, "One at a time."

It's difficult to focus on 10,000 tickets.

It's easy to focus on *one* ticket.

SPELL YOUR WAY TO SUCCESS

There is a program we do for seminars called "Winners and Losers." We tell the audience it is very easy to tell the difference between one and the other because the first letter of each word spells out the characteristics of both **WINNERS** and **LOSERS.** Since one of the key words is Enthusiasm, this is a good place to tell you how it works:

WINNERS

W **stands for Work Hard.** We don't know any better way for people to succeed than by simply working hard. They cannot do this unless they enjoy what they are doing. Then the work is no longer "work" in the commonly accepted sense. It is simply something people love to do! The artist Pablo Picasso said, "When I work, I relax. Doing nothing or entertaining visitors makes me tired."

I **stands for Ideas.** Never tell Winners there's only one way to do something. "Really?" they'll say and quickly snap off three (or more) ideas you can use to accomplish the same tasks.

N **stands for Now.** Winners do things *now!* They don't wait for tomorrow, next week, or "some other time." They know the desk that is full of work to be done today is twice as full tomorrow if nothing is done. You can always interrupt Winners during the day and ask for advice and direction and they will *never* say, "See me later." They *will* say, "Try this. If that doesn't work, try this. And if *that* doesn't work, come back again. . . ."

N **stands for Natural.** Watch Winners work. People around them shake their heads and say, "How did they do that?" It is much like watching an outfielder catch the difficult fly ball, the tennis player returning the smashing serve. It looks so easy, so natural, that you feel you could do it as well.

E **stands for Enthusiasm.** Which is the subject of this chapter.

R **stands for Repeat.** Winners repeat. If something works, they do it again. Why not? They *will* try to add something new or different to make it work even better. But they will not give up on a winning presentation, idea, or direction until something better comes along.

S **stands for Sell.** Because that's what Winners do best. And all the time.

LOSERS

L **stands for Later.** Losers do *not* do things now. They do them "later."

O **stands for Overworked.** "Wait a minute. I was hired to be a salesperson. You mean I also have to fill out reports. And make action plans. And come up with selling ideas. Hey, I'm overworked!"

S **stands for Sorry.** "I knew I was supposed to handle that sale and I forgot. I'm sorry." "I'm sorry I didn't have the report ready when you wanted."

E **stands for Excuses.** "Let me give you the reasons why I wasn't able to get done what you wanted."

R **stands for Reject.** Every time you come up with a new idea, Losers give you a reason it can't be done.

S **stands for . . . nothing.** Because Losers Never Finish.

Don't be a Loser. Be a Winner. Everybody loves a Winner. Especially one with . . . Enthusiasm.

AN ENTHUSIASTIC THOUGHT

General Douglas MacArthur had a plaque on the wall of his headquarters when he commanded the Allied Forces in the South Pacific in World War II. (Dale Carnegie had the same quote in his office.) It is from Samuel Ullman, a nineteenth-century rabbi and scholar.

You are as young as your faith,
As old as your doubts;
As young as your self-confidence,

As old as your fears;
As young as your hope;
As old as your despair.
Years may wrinkle the skin,
But to give up enthusiasm
Wrinkles the soul.

Start Building Customer Loyalty with a Simple "Thank-You" Letter

———■———

Within the past few months we bought a $5,000 air conditioner, a $600 TV set, a $28,000 car, a $100 pair of shoes, and a $300,000 life insurance policy.

Following these sales, we heard from none of the businesses—except our shoe salesman. He thanked us for coming in to buy and hoped we would "receive much comfort" and would remember him the next time we wanted another pair of shoes.

There's something wrong here.

We called the businesses (except the shoe salesman) and asked if they ever thought of writing thank-you letters after the sale. These are the actual answers:

The Air Conditioner Dealer: "I don't think we ever did that. Well, once in a while our financing company writes a letter to all the people they carry on their books." (What for? He wasn't sure.) "Listen, we know it's a good idea and we know you're going to ask why we don't do it, and the answer is, we guess we just never got around to it. There's so much to do in this business. . . ."

The Television Dealer: "Sending a thank-you letter is the best thing we ever did. Absolutely. We stopped about eight or nine months ago. We're so backed up with all the paperwork in warranties and finance deals that we just don't have the time anymore. But we'll tell you something—from the customer's point of view it was terrific. We used to get a big response. We have to get back to that sometime. . . ."

The Automobile Dealer: "Are you kidding? Why, that's the first thing we do. The day the car is delivered, the salesman sits down and writes a thank-you letter right away. Positively . . . "

Really? Months passed. No letter yet.

The Life Insurance Agent: "We don't send thank-you notes. But we do send birthday cards with our firm's name stamped on them."

What's happening?

All these businesses are ignoring a marvelous opportunity for turning Shoppers into customers.

It is a generally ignored fact of business that it is far, far easier to sell more to the Customer you have than to sell a new Customer.

How do you do that? By taking your customers up the Loyalty Ladder one step at a time.

The businessperson, complaining he is so busy doing other things he "just doesn't have the time," falls into the trap of worrying so much about his store that he forgets about his Customer. It is the old make-work syndrome. Work expands in relationship to the time allotted. If you have a one-hour job but you also have three hours to finish the job, the job becomes a three-hour job.

"But we don't have the time . . . " is really an excuse for "we haven't figured out how to do that in our daily schedule."

Why is it that we never have enough time to do a job—but always enough time to do it over?

You can convert your Shoppers into Customers. It begins with capturing their names for a mailing list. Here are the 1-2-3 easy steps to follow:

1. **Write the customer's name, address, and zip code on sales slips.** If you are an automobile dealer, you have this information. If you are an appliance dealer, you have the name on the sales/delivery slip. If you are a ready-to-wear retailer, take the name when the sale is made.

2. **Hire someone to type these addresses on envelopes . . .**

daily! This saves the salesperson's time. It can be a high school student after school. It can be someone in the office you can spare for a daily hour or two—that's all it takes. This must be done daily. Otherwise the lists pile up. Give the typed envelopes to the people who made the sales for them to send thank-you notes.

To follow up, have an employee type the names and addresses into a computer. Or, save the names and once a month send the names to a mailing house. Voilà! You have an instant mailing list of your customers!

3. The salesperson writes a thank-you note. Daily. In his or her handwriting. On memo paper you supply. Two or three simple sentences: "Thanks for coming in to see us. Hope you enjoy using your (name of product or service). If you have any questions or need more information on (name of product or service) please call me." And includes his or her calling card.

Maintaining this contact will surprise and flatter most customers. They will show your letter to others and say, "How about that!" Because it is unusual in today's competitive retailing world to remember the reason you are in business: to pay attention to your customer.

Making a Customer starts with these simple thank-you notes. You are, of course, also building lists for future sales. If your store sells appliances, you might consider writing the Customer who just bought an air conditioner or TV about a special promotion of refrigerators or toaster ovens or radio clocks or popular-price small appliances for Christmas.

Sandy Bloomberg of Tweeter Etc., a dealer in electronics, automatically sends an offer-to-buy something that ties in with the original purchase. The new offer is sent thirty days after the original purchase. Did the Customer buy a compact disc player for the house? Great. How about one for the car? Did the customer buy a TV? Great. How about speakers for a "surround sound" experience? What is Sandy doing? More business!

How about doing something special for Father's Day or Mother's Day? Most people wait until the last minute before they buy for special occasions. A memo from you will remind them and offer gift-giving solutions.

One local florist recently celebrated his 100th year in business. One person is responsible for sending out reminders on who-sent-what-to-whom last year at this time and the florist will be glad to repeat the order if you simply call. . . .

No wonder the florist is still doing business after 100 years. The Customer contact that made them successful through the years still works.

Although we have received hundreds of business loans through the years, we have never received a thank-you note from one of our bankers. Shouldn't bankers really think of themselves as retailers selling money?

We spoke with Pete Hoke, publisher of *Direct Marketing* magazine, about direct marketing and the small businessman.

"They still haven't learned, have they?" said the publisher. "What will it take to show businesspeople the vast, unexplored, and potentially profitable route available to them by simply taking their Customers up the Loyalty Ladder?"

"Oh," we said confidently, "they're learning. They're catching on. After all, everyone wants to do more business. . . ."

Except, of course, the air conditioner dealer, the television dealer, the insurance salesman, and the automobile dealer in my hometown.

Confidence

—————————■—————————

A recent nationwide survey of buyers across the United States asked the question, "Why do you buy where you buy?"

No, folks, the number one answer was NOT price. (Price was number five.) The number one reason people buy where they buy is **confidence.** Confidence in the business. In the people. In the product. In the service.

(The other reasons in order were: Quality. Selection. Service. And THEN Price.)

People want to shop where they feel they will be taken care of. Where the quality of the product is consistent. Where what you promise is what you deliver.

Having confidence in a product is a reason why all mail order companies have guarantees in their catalogs. That's all MAIL ORDER companies. But most retailers who also do mail order do NOT offer a guarantee.

We called a few of these retailers and asked, "Why don't you have a guarantee in your catalog?" A few hung up on us. Most answered, "Our customers know us. They know we guarantee everything."

We call this the Curse of Assumption. Many businesspeople "assume" their customers know who they are and what they do and why. Not true.

I recently received a catalog of store supplies. One page, in full color, was headlined: POLICY SIGNS PROTECT YOUR STORE.

They had illustrations of policy signs. They read as follows:

NO REFUND. EXCHANGE ONLY.

NO REFUND OR EXCHANGE ON SALE MERCHANDISE.

NO REFUND OR EXCHANGE.

NO REFUND AFTER 7 DAYS ON REGULAR PRICED MERCHANDISE.

Every sign began with the word *NO*.

What an exciting, marvelous, constructive way to inspire confidence in your store. Wherever customers look, they see big gold-and-black signs saying *NO!*

If you have a positive attitude, it affects everyone around you. If you have a negative attitude, it affects everyone around you. Why have signs that say *NO!?*

I want signs that say *YES!*

YES, WE WILL REFUND AND EXCHANGE ANYTHING ANYTIME.

YES, WE WILL MAKE YOU HAPPY.

YES, WE WILL MAKE YOU SATISFIED.

A hot name today in retailing is Nordstrom. Nordstrom came out of the north from Oregon to overstored Los Angeles, where everyone said, "They're successful in Oregon but they'll fail in L.A. Just too many stores here." And in a few short months, they took a major share of the retail market away from the competition.

The oracles gave the same prophecy when Nordstrom moved into Washington, D.C. "They never heard of them here. It'll take years to capture a share of the market." It took a few *months*. Here's why: Nordstrom customers are proselytizers who go forth into the community to spread their word and increase their sales. The stories of service to the customer are legion, and by now may even be apocryphal— but they're so good they're worth repeating:

A man called Nordstrom because his wife had died. He wanted to settle his outstanding bill. He was told it was $1,000 and was asked why he wanted to know.

He told them. A few days later he received a letter from the store saying his wife had been an excellent customer and he was to consider the account paid in full. (Wait, there's more!) The day of the funeral, the store sent flowers.

Another man went to Nordstrom to exchange some shirts. They were bought at another store but put in a Nordstrom box. "That's OK," said the menswear buyer, "we'll take them back for you and you can pick whatever else you want."

The sewing of new buttons, finding of lost buttons, the dozens of extra small services show that Nordstrom knows the result of a recent consumer survey. ("If you make someone happy, they'll tell three other people. If you make someone unhappy, they'll tell eleven other people.") Nordstrom keeps the odds on THEIR side. **Confidence.**

Did you hear about the time Stew Leonard's in Norwalk, Connecticut, America's best-known supermarket, had a complaint from a woman who had found a small piece of wood in her yogurt? The store delivered a fresh CASE of yogurt to her home! (Yes, with a written letter of apology.) **Confidence.**

No wonder the store's in the *Guinness Book of World Records* for doing more business per square foot than any store of any kind in the world.

What are we saying?

This: The techniques that contribute to the growth and success of the small business—honesty, empathy, **confidence**—must be carried out on the selling floor as well. Otherwise you are TWO stores working at cross-purposes.

STOP telling me what I can't do with your merchandise.

START telling me what YOU will do for me. Over and over again, because you believe I am the most important person in the world: your customer.

And if you don't believe that, ask me.

Radio and Television

———■———

"And now, a few words from our sponsor . . . "

Radio and television both have the ability to attract Prospects and Shoppers to your business. When you want to let a broad band of people know who you are, where you are located, and what special deals you can offer, radio and television can deliver the message quickly and effectively. We will first give you some tips on how to use radio.

The customer was someone we had not seen before in our store. She bought several items. As they were being wrapped, we asked the question we always addressed to new arrivals: "Where did you hear about our store?"

"Oh," she said, "I heard your radio commercial just the other day."

"Really," we said, and thanked her for shopping with us.

As she left we realized that the greatest strength of radio is that the commercials never die. In fact, they hardly fade away.

Because . . . *we had not advertised on radio for three months!* Yet she heard our commercial "just the other day."

Yes, it was part of a long-running campaign. But the fact remained we had been off the air all that time . . . and the ad was still remembered.

Radio is a valuable marketing tool for your business. It informs, educates, is flexible, targetable, and intrusive. It reminds Shoppers about your business and encourages them to come back.

Radio's unique strength is that it triggers the imagination. It is far, far more powerful to "think" of an image you hear being described than to see the actual image. Comedian Stan Freberg wrote the following copy for a radio commercial. Imagine you are listening to the radio and you hear . . .

"Okay people, now, when I give the cue, I want the 700-foot mountain of whipped cream to roll into Lake Michigan which has been drained and filled with hot chocolate. Then the Royal Canadian Air Force will fly overhead towing a ten-ton maraschino cherry which will be dropped into the whipped cream to the cheering of 25,000 extras. . . ."

The mental imagery of those words is far more powerful than seeing it happen on a TV screen.

There were those who predicted radio's decline and fall when TV arrived. What really happened: TV became the mass messenger and radio became the niche marketer. Your customers pick, choose, and listen to the type of radio format they like. Formats are many and varied but the most listened to are (in this order) adult contemporary, country, religious, oldies, top 40, news/talk, standards, Spanish, soft rock, urban/black, easy listening, classic rock, jazz, and classical. The top two make up over one-third of all radio stations (country: 16.6 percent, adult contemporary, 19.2 percent.)

What you're doing when *you* choose the station where you advertise: *customizing* your message for your Shoppers.

We found through the years that radio worked very effectively in our retail business when used in one of two ways:

Institutional advertising. Who we are, what we do, and why you should come and shop with us. And the ad runs for weeks and months.

Saturation advertising. When you "own" a radio station with a flurry of radio commercials just before the big sale in your store. You buy a month's worth of commercials and use them up in one to three days. They run every hour of the day because somewhere, sometime, someone is listening to radio.

It figures. Nearly every single person in the United States has at least one radio (99 percent by the last census). And if the radio is not turned on at home, it can turn you on at work (where six out of ten people listen) or in the car (where nine out of ten listen).

With more than 11,000 commercial radio stations on the air (almost evenly divided between AM and FM) and 600 million radios in use—somebody's listening, somewhere, sometime.

The average American listens to radio more than three hours every day! Your goal is to figure out who's listening where. And when.

More and more businesses are spending more and more money on radio. Revenues are over $9 billion and increasing yearly. All businesses—from autos to computers to banks to supermarkets to furniture to drug products—are spending more and more money every year on radio. The more you know about what works and what doesn't, the more successful your ad will be.

Here's the cutting edge of present radio advertising: integrated marketing. Many radio stations are building a database of their listeners from contests and call-ins. They can then approach you with this offer: "When you buy advertising from us, we will send a direct mail piece from your business with a special offer for our listeners only."

Radio represents a small percentage of total advertising in the United States—only about 7 percent of all ad dollars. But it can be very effective if you know the answers to the most-asked questions. So let's play the Twenty Questions Game.

This time . . . about radio.

THE TWENTY RULES FOR RADIO ADVERTISING

1. Hasn't radio reached its saturation point? Is anybody still buying a radio?

A: They're buying and buying and buying and . . . Nearly 600 million radios are in use in the United States. That's up from 456 million in 1980.

2. What radio station should I use?

A: The one your Customers listen to. That's not difficult to find out. Ask. We sent questionnaires to our customers every year asking about different services the store offered, what media they read, listened to, or watched. In our area there are twelve radio stations. We did most of our advertising on the station we liked. After all, if we liked it, our Customers would like it, right? Wrong. When the surveys came back, we discovered that 67 percent of our Customers were listening to one station. *But it wasn't the station we were listening to!*

We switched our advertising dollars to this one station. Because . . . it is a proven fact that your Customer of tomorrow is listening to the same station as your Customer of today. They have the same demographics (age, income, number of children), geographics (live in the same area), and psychographics (have cars, hobbies, participate in similar sports).

3. When should I advertise?

A: Most people tend to listen to the news. We always tried to buy "adjacencies" to the news broadcasts. Yes, it costs more, but if more people are listening, it's worth more.

4. How many commercials does a radio station have an hour?

A: If it seems like there's more commercials than programming, that's not the case it all. It just seems that way. On the AM stations, which have MORE commercials than FM, there are an average of 11.6 commercial minutes an hour.

5. How loyal are radio listeners?

A: More loyal than TV. "This listener loyalty factor is a big plus for radio. It represents a major difference between TV and radio today," says James Garrity, director of advertising, IBM. Echoes Marcos Rada, public affairs manager of American Express Travel Related Services, "We choose radio because it is more flexible and more targeted to pinpoint the specific customers we want by using certain stations. Radio is more effective than TV or newspaper."

6. What products are advertised most on radio?

A: In terms of national advertising, food products are number one, then cars, then financial services, then travel, then beer, ale, wine, then retail stores. Those categories provide nearly 60 percent of radio's advertising dollars.

So if you're in there somewhere, you should consider radio because those folks have figured out it works for them. (Businesses that use radio least: sporting goods, toys, jewelry, photo shops.)

7. What time of the year do people listen most to the radio?

A: Seems constant. In the top twenty-five markets, the difference between the highest listenership (winter) and lowest (summer) is only a few percentage points.

8. Is there one big, terrific advantage over other media?

A: Yes. Speed. If pushed (and you have a cooperative radio station) you can put a message on radio in a few hours. Or less. It simply takes much longer to prepare a newspaper ad. Much, much longer to prepare a direct mail piece. And much, much, much longer to put together a TV commercial.

9. Is it expensive?

A: Yes, but . . . there always seems to be a "deal" in radio. Buy *X* number of spots in the best time spot and they will often throw in "extras" in the wee hours of the morning. You can often barter more easily with radio than with any other advertising medium. ("If you give us ten $25 gift certificates from your business, we'll give you $250 worth of radio advertising if you also buy *X* amount of regular advertising.")

10. Every station that comes into my business tells me they're number one in the ratings and show me their Nielsen or Arbitron charts to prove it. How can they *all* be number one?

A. Believe it or not, they can be—but in different time sequences and different age brackets. One station might be number one in listenership in early-morning drive time. They have a well-known announcer who turns everybody on (or whom everybody turns on). Another station is number one for the adult population ages thirty-four to fifty. Another station is number one for late-night programming. Another station . . . well, you get the idea. The rating services rate different age groups, different time slots. It's difficult for a station NOT to be number one . . . somewhere, sometime. Your job: Select the number one for the audience you want to reach for your business. Ask to see the actual ratings and find out how the station's ratings fit into your potential audience.

AND THEN: Ask who else is advertising on the station. Then call them and ask if they are satisfied. Noncompeting businesses will share this information with you.

11. Is there a technique for writing a radio script that works most of the time?

A: David Ogilvy offers one simple technique in his book *Ogilvy on Advertising.* We've tested it many times and it works for us. Here it is:

1. Identify your brand (the name of your business) early in the commercial.

2. Identify it often (mention your firm's name again and again and again and . . .)

3. Promise the listener a benefit early in the commercial.

4. Repeat the benefit (again and again and again and again and again and . . .)

If you memorize those four points, you are way ahead of most radio commercials, whose writers ignore those four very basic principles.

12. How often should I change my commercial?

A: Not as often as you think. There is an old advertising story about the owner of a major corporation who asked his agency how many people were working on his account.

"Fifty-one," said the head of the agency. "Fifty-one?" said the surprised owner. "What do they all do?"

The agency owner replied, "Well, one of them is working on some new ideas and the other fifty are out there convincing your people NOT to change the ad that's working so well now."

You will become tired, bored, and anxious with your present radio ad much more quickly than the listeners, many of whom will hear it the first time the next time it runs.

One reason why it pays to repeat: Many people will simply not hear the commercial because they are working or preoccupied with some other activity.

13. If you could give me one way to make my commercial more listened to, what would it be?

A: A sound. Something that's "different" and will make people listen. A travel agency did a memorable ad by starting their commercial with the sound of a cruise ship's foghorn. Or an expression. ("We make money the old-fashioned way. We earn it.")

One sound to seriously consider is . . . silence. A very, very powerful tool on radio. But it's so powerful that if used incorrectly it can backfire. An example of the power of silence is a supermarket that wanted to prove to listeners that its store's prices were lower than anyone else's. Here was the commercial:

Good morning, ladies and gentlemen. At this time, Fred's Foodland would like to list for you the names of all the other stores in the area that are presently selling food for less than Fred's Foodland. So grab a pencil and paper and we'll list them for you in alphabetical order. Ready? Here they are. . . .

Which was followed by twenty seconds of silence and then the concluding message: *"The previous message was brought to you as a public service by Fred's Foodland."*

Great commercial if they had timed the silence to last three seconds. But twenty seconds of silence is too long for radio. Listeners called the station to find out why it had gone off the air.

The station promptly canceled the commercial.

14. How much product can I sell in one ad?

A: One. You've probably heard the one from the furniture store listing fifteen items with the original price and the sale price in a one-minute commercial. The audience will remember . . . nothing! Sell a storewide sale. Sell a newly arrived product. Sell a specific brand. That's it.

15. How about music in my radio commercial.

A: Good. If it works. Bad if it doesn't. Be wary of jingles. The good ones are very expensive. Local amateur jingles sound . . . amateur. Another problem with jingles (including the professional ones) is you can't understand many of the words. People don't concentrate on listening to the radio—they just listen to the radio. I like David Ogilvy's line on singing commercials: Would you go into a store and expect the salesperson to start singing to you?

16. Should I use well-known radio personalities?

A: Sure. You might have to pay an extra "talent fee," but the cost is worthwhile because the audience identifies with the individual. We gave well-known radio personalities a very sketchy outline of what we wanted to sell. Often just the product and the price and told them to say whatever they wanted to say. The commercials were far, far better because the audience knew they were off-the-cuff, extemporaneous, and sounded more "believable."

17. Who writes the script?

A: The radio station has full-time people who do just that—they write scripts for what you want to sell. And yes, in smaller stations it can be the salesperson who sold you the time. Insist that the salesperson bring the finished script for you to review and the finished cassette of the ad BEFORE it goes on the air.

Bring in some other folks in your business to listen to the finished advertisement. (You might be caught up in the euphoria of hearing the name of your business and therefore believe that WHATEVER is said must be great because it's *you*.) Your salesmen will make any corrections for you.

18. Should I alternate the times when my ad runs?

A: Yes. Running your ad at different times on different days makes customers feel they hear the ad many more times than it actually runs. There are exceptions. If a certain time slot works for you (like the news adjacencies we talked about), then keep on using it. Another good example is if a special time ties in with a special characteristic of your business. One advertiser became well known because his ad was broadcast every day at the same time because . . . well, let's listen:

"Good morning. It's 9:13. And today's news is brought to you by the Boardwalk National Bank at 913 Atlantic Avenue. . . ."

That worked.

19. Should I use my own voice?

A: Only if it's very distinctive or if your voice has a professional sound. That should eliminate most people reading this sentence. But a distinctive voice can have great appeal because it has a certain "sound." Some good examples: The owner of Carvel Ice Cream, whose obviously nonprofessional, deep-throated gravelly voice gave the product instant identification. And remember the twang of Titus Moody for Pepperidge Farm?

20. All this sounds great to me. Can I get away with just radio advertising?

A: No way. Radio is strictly complementary to your other advertising. It reinforces, reemphasizes, repeats the message you tell in other media. It is the cumulative effect of all your advertising—all carrying the same message at the same time—that makes your advertising work for you.

YOUR TEN-POINT CHECKLIST WHEN BUYING RADIO

We asked several radio salespeople, what are the most asked questions from advertisers when they are thinking about buying time on radio? Here are some of the most asked. If your fellow businesspeople want to know the answers before they commit the dollars, so should you.

1. What kind of music do you play?

2. How far does your signal reach?

3. How large is your audience?

4. Where is your station located on the dial? Is it AM or FM?

5. Do I have to pay anything to have a commercial made?

6. Are you rated in your market? By whom? Can I see the ratings?

7. What does "satellite" mean?

8. What does "drive time" mean?

9. How important are the jocks (radio personalities) in their time frame and will they do my commercial for me at no cost?

10. Will radio really work for my business?

WHAT MAKES A GOOD RADIO COMMERCIAL?

One that makes the customer buy. But first they have to listen. For some reason, humor plays better in radio. Perhaps because the imagination is put to work (like the Stan Freberg commercial mentioned at the beginning of this chapter).

Every year the Clio awards are given to the best commercials. We chose one winner from radio to show you how humor can and does work. (This award winner is from the Campbell-Mithun-Esty agency in Chicago.)

KROGER DOUBLE-PRINT RADIO COMMERCIAL

Nun: You wanted to see me, Father?

Priest: Yes, Sister, I got back the pictures from the parish picnic.

Nun: Oh, so fast!

Priest: Well, I took them to Kroger.

Nun: Ah, Kroger.

Priest: You know, Kroger gives you an extra set of prints free.

Nun: Do they, now?

Priest: And the folks at Kroger say to mail the second print to someone special.

Nun: Ohh.

Priest: So, here's a shot of Mother Superior smashing a spike at the volleyball tournament.

Nun: Ooh, the colors are so vivid!

Priest: Kroger uses Kodak paper and the Kodak Colorwatch System.

Nun: You know, we should send that extra print to the mother's brother, Father.

Priest: Her brother, Sister?

Nun: Or her mother, Father.

Priest: Fine. Here's the deacon sliding into home in the softball game.

Nun: This free print should go to the brother's mother, Father.

Priest: His mother, Sister?

Nun: Or his brother, Father.

Priest: The brother's brother? I thought he had a sister, Sister.

Nun: No, a brother, mother, and a father, Father.

Priest: Oh, and here's the finish of the three-legged race.

Nun: Ooh, Sister Ann and Brother Andrew.

Priest: Who gets the extra free print?

Nun: Well, is a brother's sister more special than a sister's brother?

Priest: But what about the father of the brother and the mother of the sister?

Nun: Aren't you being partial to the father, Father?

Priest: Well, you're pulling for the sister, Sister!

Nun: Oh, Kroger has set a task for us, sure enough.

Priest: Aye.

Nun: Figuring out who to mail that extra free print to could try the patience of a saint.

Priest: Shall we try again?

Nun: Aye, Father.

Priest: Fine. We send the picture of the brother . . .

Both: . . . to the mother of the sister . . .

Voice-over: Double prints . . . at Kroger.

TV or Not TV?

———————■———————

There was a time, not so very long ago, when the person with a small business watched but never thought of advertising on TV. The reason was simple: It cost too much.

This was the time when your TV set broadcast primarily three networks. Yes, you could buy commercials from the local network affiliate station that would broadcast only to the local audience, but the cost was still prohibitive—especially if you were near big-city audiences.

And then, along came cable. Now available in 60 percent of American homes.

Now, instead of choosing one of three channels to watch, the audience can choose from literally dozens!

Now, you can use TV to pinpoint the channel you feel most of your Customers (or potential customers) will watch.

Now you can *customize* what you have to sell to what a specific Customer watching a specific channel wants to buy.

And best of all, now *you can afford it!*

Twenty years ago only 13 percent of local advertising dollars were spent on TV. Most of the rest went to newspapers. Today, that percentage is over 20 percent and could account for nearly 30 percent by the year 2000.

Today, your local TV station will come to your place of business and make you part of the commercial as well as showing what your business looks like. Most times this is included in the rates you pay—especially if you agree to run a certain number of commercials in a certain amount of time.

TV's strong advantage is that it reaches so many homes so quickly on a one-on-one basis. That's you—up there on the screen—in the flesh talking to people in their living rooms all over your selling area. Sometime during the day nine out of ten of your potential customers are watching something on TV (including the annual 30,000-plus commercials). Comparison: Fewer than eight out of ten adults read the newspaper.

In our brief forays into TV, we did our own announcing of new products, sales, and special events. These appearances were invariably followed by people stopping us on the street and saying, "Saw you on TV last night."

TV connotes a glamorous image. Yes, yes, there are those Crazy Charlie auto and appliance ads with screaming salespeople or owners parading around with animals—but, generally, TV exposure creates an aura of interest from the consumer not discernible with radio, newspaper, or direct mail.

TV, more than any other medium, gives you instant identification. That's why most politicians spend most of their money on TV ads. It gives them an identity of who they are and what they say they will do far quicker than any other medium. Many politicians today use TV as their ONLY advertising medium!

TV combines sight, sound, motion, and emotion for powerful selling.

TV is rated by most people as exciting, authoritative, and exerting more influence on their buying decisions.

TV's viewing audience is growing every year—and is now at about five to seven hours per day more than all other media combined!

TV today is more and more competitive as more and more channels open. We have compiled twenty suggestions to consider, think about, and finally do when putting together your first—or next—advertisement on TV.

The Twenty Rules for TV Advertising

1. **The picture must tell the story.** Remember Ogilvy's theory: "Can you turn off the sound and still know what's being sold?" If you can't . . . try again.

2. **Show the product.** Car commercials showing trees, grass, and rivers don't sell cars, as Infinti learned. Blue jeans commercials showing young people in amorous positions attract attention, but do they sell jeans? They may sell an image—but is it YOUR image and, more important, your product? When a local baby furniture store owner wanted the community to know who she was and what she sold, the local cable station did a commercial showing different parts of the store with cribs, beds, strollers. The store received almost instant identification!

3. **Demonstrate how your product or service works.** You see this on the fast-growing infomercial craze. How the cloth with the special ingredient removes scratches on your car. How throwing all your vegetables and fruit into a high-geared mixer makes a delicious drink. If your chairs are made of unbreakable steel, throw them around the studio. (Remember the commercials of the gorilla throwing the Samsonite luggage around his cage?) Visual effects are so effective because TV is . . . visual!

4. **Don't worry about the audience "zapping" your commercial.** Much is written about the fast draw of the TV pad in switching channels when an ad appears. The Television Bureau of Advertising did in-depth research on this perception. Result: It's a minor problem. Nearly 83 percent of the audience say they NEVER switch channels during a commercial break.

5. **Use testimonials.** Yes, we've said this also works in every other medium, but they *really* appear real on TV. Suggestion: Do NOT write a script for customers who agree to say nice things about you. Let them say anything they want. You can edit out the "ummms" and "ahhhs" and extraneous phrases. And if the people you choose do NOT look like models or professionals . . . terrific! That means they look more "real." Paying the extra money for a well-known personality means the viewer will remember the personality—not necessarily your product.

6. Don't mention the competition. This is a growing phenomenon in many of today's TV ads. "Our product is better than (name of competitive product)." The problem is that many of the viewers remember only your competitor's name!

7. Tight close-ups of the face are dramatic. No extraneous arms, legs, props to get in the way of your face (or the announcer you choose) talking directly to the consumer. Very effective. Just like selling face-to-face.

8. Mention the name of your company or product up front. Then repeat it again and again and again and most especially at the end.

9. TV is the most emotional of all media. I watch the *Hallmark Hall of Fame* productions mainly for the commercials. Each is a thirty- or sixty-second piece of art. The morning after the show, it often seems that as many people talk about the commercials as the show.

10. Be wary of TV salespeople who try to sell you on "recall." Many will show you statistics saying how many people remembered a specific TV commercial. Your follow-up question: "I don't care how many *remembered* the commercial. I care how many *bought from* the commercial."

11. Grab the viewer's attention quickly. No different from the headline on the print ad. The same four or five seconds is all the time viewers will give you before they decide whether to watch the rest of the commercial (read the rest of the copy).

12. Have a beginning, middle, and end. Think of each commercial as a ministry. Viewers should be able to follow along and see the problem you present and how you solve it. They must not only see the offer you make but also the benefit they receive.

13. Avoid expensive props and settings. Watch TV commercials on national networks and you will see very effective copy-only commercials. Aetna insurance ads used only words on a screen and voices in the background. It worked.

14. **Use clever film techniques sparingly.** Otherwise you call attention to the editing and not the product.

15. **Certain products sell very well on TV.** That's why you see a lot of soap, beer, and car commercials. A study by Bruskin Associates Market Research asked TV viewers questions about buying their next car. The overwhelming majority knew the car they wanted, but six out of ten did NOT know where they would go to buy. Nearly 80 percent said TV is the medium that tells them about automobiles. So if you're selling cars . . .

16. **Be careful what you say. Somebody's listening.** Every word counts. Your audience is often listening when they're not watching. Your viewer may leave the room during the commercial but can still hear the words.

17. **Don't plan on revisions.** They take time. And money. Your salesperson will review what you want to say ahead of time. Most will give you "storyboards" to look at that show you a sketch of the picture and the words to be spoken. Look at everything very carefully. Ask yourself if your story is being told in a persuasive manner with lots of benefits to the reader. When you see the finished commercial and ask to do certain parts over, you are asking to spend much more money and much more time than changing words in a radio spot or copy in a newspaper ad. It's expensive.

18. **Schedule your ads any season other than summer.** Here's why: TV viewing decreases about 17 percent in summer, but you pay the same for your ad! The exceptions, of course, are if you are advertising summer-only products: patio furniture, bathing suits, suntan lotion. But if your product is year-round, place most of your ad dollars when most people are watching.

19. **Be wary of humor.** Yes, funny commercials make people laugh, but the big question is, do they make people buy? People buy for dozens of reasons that include but are not limited to saving time, saving money, making money, protecting their family, or for achieving comfort, health, and praise. But people don't buy because you made them laugh. It was Claude Hopkins, the father of modern advertising, who proclaimed, "People don't buy from clowns." Yes, humor attracts attention, makes people feel good (which is just a half-step from buying that which makes them feel good), but you have to be very, very careful, since what makes one person laugh makes another person feel uncomfortable, uneasy, and unhappy with what you're trying to sell.

20. **Make it newsworthy.** A tactic we emphasize in every form of advertising because it works in every form of advertising. Is there a way you can tie your product/business into a local event? Special Olympics? Scholastic athletics? Community fund drives? That association gives your business an added luster and creates a positive image.

CASE STUDY
Hanna Andersson

—————————■—————————

How Swede It Is . . .

How do you have someone climb the Loyalty Ladder and become a Customer?

Gun Denhart, owner of the Hanna Andersson catalog, began with a very simple idea. ("Mothers want soft clothes for their children.")

She offered her clothes to friends who were Prospects.

They wanted more. They became Shoppers and Customers. And they told their friends, who also became Shoppers and Customers.

Next she decided to expand her business. She started with a small ad in *Parents* magazine telling her story to Prospects in Parentland. And in a short decade, she built a $50 million business.

To find out how she did it, how she converted Prospects to Shoppers and then to Customers, we went to Portland, Oregon, to interview her.

When thirteen-year-old Gun (rhymes with "tune") Brime accompanied her father on a business trip to the United States in 1959 from her home in Lund, Sweden, she was excited. But if anyone had told her she would return sixteen years later with her husband, move to the West Coast, start a mail order children's clothing catalog, and do nearly $50 mil-lion volume after just ten years in business, she might have smiled wist-fully and said "Hej, hej da" ("Hello, good-bye") and wondered who *this person was predicting these magical fairy tales.*

When Gun Denhart's son Christian was born in Connecticut in 1980, she visited the local children's shops and department stores looking for the soft, all-cotton children's clothing available in comparable shops in Sweden.

"Everything was polyester. They were not soft to the hand. They only lasted a few washings," she said. "Why can't I find the clothing that children wear in Sweden?"

On her next trip back to Sweden to visit her parents, she bought enough cotton clothing for her son's future wardrobe and thought, "Why don't I make this clothing available in the United States?"

She went back to the stores, purchased a large assortment of different styles, came back home, and gave the clothing away to friends and strangers. She said, "We're thinking of selling these clothes here in the U.S. Take them home with you. Use them. Wash them. We'll call you in a few weeks to see what you think of them"

While waiting for her first "test-marketing" results, she reflected on her past and what brought her to what would be her future.

She had left Sweden for Paris in 1973 with her young son, Philip, after separating from her husband. Her sister gave her the name of an American friend in Paris to contact, Tom Denhart, a producer of TV commercials.

The couple met and, after two years in Paris, they moved to Greenwich, Connecticut, and were married. Tom worked as a producer for Ogilvy & Mather; Gun, with her Swedish MBA background, was financial manager of the U.S. branch of a foreign-language-school chain.

By now the test results were back. The friends and strangers not only raved about the clothing but asked, "How do we find more clothes like this?" A difficult question to answer, since there were no more clothes "like this"—unless you took a trip to Sweden.

And then the idea—first thought, then planned, then waiting to be acted upon—became a reality when the I-95 bridge collapsed in 1983 and Gun's daily travels to her job became as long as her husband's.

"We wanted a simpler life," they decided, so they sold their home and moved to Oregon. There they found a larger home for less money. They had $250,000 left over from the sale of their Greenwich home, and they said, "Remember that idea about bringing Swedish baby clothing to the United States? Let's try it."

Fortunately there were no advisers around to tell them of the difficulties. Of the high catalog failure rate. Of all the Reasons It Won't Work.

"If I had known all those reasons, I probably never would have started," says Gun.

But start they did on the proverbial kitchen table. Tom to handle the creative, Gun, the financials—each using their individual experience and talent.

First question: What to call this catalog? Many companies use the name of the entrepreneur who started it all. But the name "Gun" was not pleasing. And then she remembered her grandmother, Hanna Andersson.

It was not only pleasant (and Swedish) sounding, but her grandmother's philosophy would become the theme and direction of the catalog itself.

"My grandmother believed strongly in the Swedish philosophy that equates waste with sin. She would approve of this clothing, which is used over and over and over again."

Gun and Tom returned to Sweden to choose the merchandise and produce the first catalog. She visited several Swedish factories and chose one. She still uses it today—as well as others—and is also a partner in the factory. The models were children of friends. The setting was her parents' house. The shooting was supervised by Tom. Time required to produce the catalog: fourteen days.

Now they had two key ingredients for the success of any catalog: creative and offer. Needed: the List. To whom does she send the catalog?

She found a list broker in New Hampshire who understood her needs. They decided on an initial mailing of 75,000. (And yes, she uses the same list broker today.)

She looked at the finished catalog and there was ... something missing. Yes, Gun's philosophy of the clothing being fun and child friendly was there. Yes, the copy was warm, first person with tucked-in personal messages. The colors were bright, the styling the most wanted from turtlenecks to jumpsuits. But the most important part of all was the "feel." How could customers "imagine" the softness of the fabric?

Conclusion: They couldn't. So, for this first catalog, they cut one-inch squares of the fabric, and rounded up a group of schoolchildren from the Portland area to glue the swatches into the catalogs.

She mailed this first catalog in February 1984. Her first small space ad appeared about the same time in *Parents* magazine.

The headline: WHY ARE SWEDISH BABIES SO HAPPY? The answer: because of the soft cotton clothing they wear. Response rate: 2,500.

They totaled up their results after the first six months: About 1,000 customers and $53,000 in sales. ("Today we do that in a few hours.")

As important as the sales were the letters from customers complimenting Gun on the styling, the coloring, the workmanship, and most of all, the "softness."

She had discovered a niche waiting to be filled. On to the next catalog. . . .

As you browse through her catalogs you see, read, and understand the benefits of Hanna Andersson clothing: The soft combed cotton gives each product the unique Hanna "feel" as well as giving each garment greater strength. Stripes and plaids are yarn-dyed, so colors are not just on the surface to fade with washing. Stripes in fabrics are cut by hand so they match on the seams—time-consuming (read "costs more") but consistent with the quality Hanna "look." Seams are flat-locked to make them more sturdy. Prints are exclusively theirs. Each item has allowance for shrinkage. There's enough room built into the patterns for a proper fit AFTER shrinkage. Unlike many other manufacturers, most of Hanna's expense is in the fabric itself—nearly half the finished cost (sewing is 35 percent and overhead, 20 percent).

Today, a typical catalog has more than 300 styles, and the warehouse holds more than 3,500 stock-keeping units each season.

For the first two years, they ran Hanna Andersson from their home. Says son Philip, now twenty-one, "I didn't have any everyday clothes in my closet. But I had eighty snowsuits."

The rapid expansion forced them to different locations, which finally resulted in their present location: a comfortable five-story 80,000-square-foot warehouse in downtown Portland with loft space, large windows, skylights, and, here and there, Swedish antiques.

There was room on the ground floor for . . . something. So they opened their first retail store.

The clothing is designed in Portland, made in Sweden, Denmark, and the United States, sent to Portland, and then mailed to customers.

In a short ten-year period, the company has grown to $46 million in sales, mailing out catalogs four times a year—a total of ten million.

Each first-time buyer receives a $10 gift certificate "for your next purchase." To ensure accuracy on their mailings, they offer a $5 credit if you receive duplicate mailings and tell them.

From the beginning there was some question of the higher price of the clothing. But the customer soon finds, once bought, once committed. Merchandise ranges from $4 to $90 with an average price of $22. A toddler's T-shirt is $18. A nylon jacket, $48. Gun recalls another of her grandmother's sayings when some critics say the clothing is high-priced: "'Cheap is too expensive,'" said my grandmother. "'You'll soon be buying again.'"

Explaining what makes them quality is one thing. Being aware of new and lower-priced competition is another. Gun feels she solved that problem with her new "Hanna's Worth" logo shown on certain basic items throughout the catalog. They are the best-sellers, so she can charge less and pass the quantity savings on to the consumer.

This philosophy comes to life when the Customer discovers that the clothing seems nearly indestructible as it is handed down from one child to another. Soon other customers came to the same conclusion. Read one of the many testimonials scattered throughout their catalog: "Many of my Hannas are on their third hand-me-down child with the same softness, bright designs and quality—M. E., Madison, Wisconsin."

This hand-me-down knowledge came early in their career and prompted the beginning of "Hannadowns," their most remarked-about program, written up in national magazines from *Fortune* to *Lear's* to *Family Circle* and explained on NBC's *Today* show and CBS's *This Morning.*

"We first mentioned it in our second catalog. We simply said, 'Our clothes are so good, we'll buy them back from you.'" And they do.

When your children outgrow their Hannas, send them back and receive a credit of 20 percent of the purchase price toward future merchandise bought within the year. The company, in turn, donates the returned clothing to charities.

Each catalog explains the program. And, if you are placed on hold when you call in an order, instead of Muzak you hear a description of how Hannadowns works.

Gun remembers a story, oft-told within the company, of the first Customer to bring merchandise back for the 20 percent credit.

She gave the clothing back and, while the credit was being written, suddenly grabbed the clothing back and said, "I can't part with it!" and left.

But many do "part with it." They have given more than $700,000 in Hannadown credit (retail value: more than $3.6 million)—or nearly 150,000 pieces of clothing.

In the beginning, they just put all the clothes in a box. When they filled a few cartons they took them to local charities. Today they receive an average of 3,000 items a month (some months as many as 8,000). Today the charities include local Portland and Oregon agencies and total more than 125 across the United States. UPS sends the clothing for them at no charge. The company also contributes to sudden emergencies like Hurricane Hugo in 1989, when they shipped boxes of clothing through the Salvation Army. Other recipients include the Lutheran Family Service's Russian Refugee program and Romanian orphans.

The "taking care of others" philosophy is a throwback to Gun's Swedish heritage. This accounts for a generous employee program that has the company consistently listed in *Working Mother* magazine as one of the best companies for working parents. Eight out of ten of their 300 employees are women. Most of the staff taking phone orders are working mothers. Among their benefits:

- One-half the cost of child care up to $3,000 a year. Says Gun, "If you go to work worried, 'Is everything all right back home?' you can't do a good job."
- Profit sharing
- Full medical insurance
- Employee fitness classes

- Flexible work schedules: from twenty to forty hours. Whatever works best for the employee and the company.

"We operate on the team approach using ideas developed by Swedish companies like Volvo and Saab," says Gun. "Taking care of your employees is good for everybody."

In the phone room, every article in the current catalog is tacked on large boards. If a customer asks a very specific question about a product, the operator walks over, examines the product, and comes back with the answer.

"Our return rates are lower than average," said a company spokesperson. "I believe it's because we give our customer service reps so much information to share with the customer."

They receive nearly 4,000 calls a day. "We really listen to our Customers. Comments are entered into the computer. Our 800 telephone number is on the label of our garments, so Customers can call easily if they have a question or a complaint." What about complaints? Answer: "If a customer calls and is unhappy with what they received, we send a new one immediately BEFORE we receive back the damaged one."

Also listed on the walls are dozens of small notices headlined YOU DONE GOOD! of current complimentary customer comments about employees for everyone to read.

Also posted: Hanna's Ten Commandments, which begin with (1) Be kind and intelligent with others. . . . and end with (10) Laughter sees us through the day. Have fun.

Starting this year, the firm gives everyone the opportunity to spend eight volunteer hours per year for their favorite charity—and still receive their regular salary.

The firm is the first to set an example of helping others—giving 5 percent of all pretax profits to assist victims of domestic violence.

"Children are our next generation," Gun says. "If they don't get a good start the whole country is in trouble."

All this philosophy resulted in the company receiving the "Business Enterprise Award" from a national nonprofit organization that "honors exemplary acts of courage, integrity and social vision in business."

What about the future?

"We don't want to be the biggest," says Gun, "we want to be the best in what we're doing." Average yearly growth is 15 percent, and they hope to hit $80 million in sales by the year 2000.

To make mailings arrive more quickly, they are adding a new distribution center in Kentucky, closer to their East Coast Customers.

Their newest venture is an Apple multimedia CD-ROM disc program called En Passant that interacts with the user with text, sound, and images. The Customer can specify personal preferences, and the disc gives a range of products and gift suggestions.

Another possible future venture: a Customer Reward Program.

Another: Infomercials. "Maybe. My husband made TV commercials for twenty years. Maybe the circle is coming around.

"We have to explore new ways to reach our customers," says Gun. "We just can't keep mailing more and more catalogs. Customers are upset with receiving too many. I know from my own personal experience."

And it's true. Since 1983, the U.S. population has grown 14 percent, but the number of Americans who shop by mail or phone increased 72 percent, according to DMA figures. In 1980 5.8 billion catalogs were mailed in the United States. In 1990, 13.6 billion.

And most new catalogs fail.

One exception: Hanna Andersson in Portland, Oregon. "The only successful catalogs are those with a distinct personality," says Kate Muldoon of Muldoon Direct. "Hanna Andersson is very warm. You identify with a real person behind the catalog."

True. The clothing has taken on a life of its own. The proof is in the fact that the word *Hannas* has become part of the American idiom, much as "Kleenex," "Scotch tape," and "refrigerator." Consider one of Gun's favorite stories:

"One of Tom's friends was walking in Manhattan and, in front of him, a child was having a tantrum. The mother quietly said, 'If you behave, we'll go home and you can put on your Hannas.'

"The child immediately calmed down, and they walked peacefully away. . . ."

Ten Ways to Convert a Shopper to a Customer

———————————— ■ ————————————

1. **Shoppers decide in the first eight seconds they're in your place of business whether they are comfortable.** That's from a survey of more than *one million* Shoppers. Does someone greet them quickly? Are the frontline people talking on the phone, chewing gum, or (worse) ignoring potential Customers? Wal-Mart has "greeters" as you enter the store, often retired folks who are the most dependable workers and ingrained with old-fashioned service and hospitality. Sainsbury's stores in England have someone up front offering you a shopping cart or a shopping basket. Which do you prefer?

Here's another note: Eight out of ten first-time Shoppers are affected by a dirty parking lot and/or front entrance.

2. **Three out of four Shoppers go to stores because of "sales."** That's a 10 percent jump in just one year. And though this may be a good way to have them come in the first time, remember to practice Feargal Quinn's "Boomerang Theory." It's not difficult to bring someone to your business the first time (like with a "sale"). The question is: How do you have them come back . . . *again?*

3. **Four out of ten first-time Customers judge how much**

you know by how professional you look. And so we go to a local car dealer to lease a car. And the salesman approaches us in a sweatshirt drinking a soda out of a can and asks, "Hey—can I help you?"

Uh . . . no.

4. **Capture their names.** That's where it all begins. You have to know who your Shoppers are before you can treat them like Customers. It begins with capturing their names at the point of sale. They have bought something . . . sometime. Have 3" × 5" cards to write down their name/address/city/state/zip/telephone number, and some penciled notations about what they bought. What they like. Anything that lets you set them apart as individuals.

5. Do Shopper surveys. Ask them what they want. Furr's Markets in Albuquerque remodeled one of the stores. They wrote a letter to 8,000 residents three months before they opened and asked, "What do you want to see in our new store?" More than 2,000 wrote back and said they wanted a scratch bakery up front, a deli near the entrance, and a bigger seafood section. Furr's did it all and *doubled their volume!*

Would they have increased their business anyway? Sure. Would they have *doubled* their business? *No way.*

6. Which brings us to your "suggestion box." Up front where it can be seen by your Shoppers. With plenty of pencils and forms. BIG LETTERS so they can see where it is and are "invited" to say whatever they want to say. Each suggestion is answered each day! A personal letter, and include a coupon and/or gift certificate for them to use next time they come to your business as a "thank you" for giving you the idea.

7. Have an up-front "Mission Statement" or "Guarantee." I'm always amazed when I walk into a supermarket (OK, *any* business) and don't see a "Guarantee" . . . somewhere. Good place—on the right-hand side of the store (because Shoppers tend to walk to the right). Look at your closest mail order catalog for the words. The guarantee can range from "We guarantee everything. Period" to a longer explanation of who you are and why you guarantee everything you sell. Whenever a business tells me, "Everybody knows we guarantee what we sell," I look at them and tell them they are wrong. Everyone does NOT know who you are or what you do. In fact, one out of five Customers, on average, leaves your business every year.

8. Eight out of ten Shoppers say, "All ads (in a specific business) look alike." If you want me to be a Customer, I have to know WHO you are. You must have a "look" before you have an "image." If I took your name off the bottom of your ad and put on your competition's name, would anyone know the difference? If they would not, tear up the ad and start all over again. Can't have people become Customers if they think they're walking into some other business instead.

9. Give a "bounce-back" at time of purchase. Mail order companies do this all the time. They include with your order a special offer good on the next purchase. You must receive some return. And what you receive is far greater than what you lose if you do *not* offer something. Supermarkets do this by tucking coupons in your shopping bag that are valid for NEXT WEEK'S purchase. Try this only because . . . it works!

10. Send "thank you" letters. The day you make the sale. No later than the next day. The Shopper will be impressed and seriously consider becoming your Customer. No matter how much you read about this simple technique, when was the last time YOU received a "thank you" letter for your last purchase? *(And during the past week you bought . . . something!)*

Buyers are impressed, will tell their friends, and subconsciously begin to think of themselves as your . . . Customer.

Part 3

THE CUSTOMER

Introduction to
Customers

———————■———————

Customer / kes-te-mer/ *n. Someone who purchases something from a business.*

Why do people buy? Only two reasons:

1. Good feelings.
2. Solutions to problems.

If you satisfy either of these needs you make a sale. You now have a Customer.

Going to the beauty parlor or buying new clothes gives a woman good feelings.

A husband and wife buy life insurance to guarantee an income for their children.

A man and/or a woman go to a restaurant for an enjoyable evening.

Think of the product or service you have. How can you promote it by appealing to one of the Two Reasons People Buy?

Once you attract a Customer to your business, you will want to sell that Customer again and again. But to do that effectively, you have to realize that there are many different kinds of Customers:

- Customers who buy only one brand.
- Customers who come in only at the start of new seasons.
- Customers who shop ONLY sales.

Why do business owners get upset when a Customer comes to their business "only for a sale"?

Sale Customers are very valuable. They buy quicker, appreciate value, and are consistent in their attendance. You should treat them every bit as nicely as nonsale Customers.

But some businesses treat Customers who buy things on sale with disrespect. A friend of ours went to an airline counter with an upgrade certificate for a free trip to Hawaii. The agent looked at the coupon and said, despairingly, "Oh, you've got one of these. . . ."

"Yes," our friend admitted, "and 'one of these' means I am a very good Customer of your airline."

"Well," she sighed, "I guess I have to fill out the paperwork."

Annoyed, our friend answered, "I don't think you understand the ground rules. Let me tell you what they are. You are overhead. I am profit."

Rare is the Customer who complains about this type of behavior. A government study (conducted by the Technical Assistance Research Program—or TARP for short) says that "half of Customers who experience problems—both individual consumers and business customers—never complain to anyone."

No wonder the average business loses 20 percent of its Customers every year. A study in the *Harvard Business Review* by Frederick F. Reichheld and W. Earl Sasser Jr. called "Zero Defections" said if you could keep just 5 percent of the Customers who leave . . . you could *nearly double your bottom-line profit!*

Or, to say it another way: If you cut Customer losses from 20 percent to 10 percent, the average life span of a Customer doubles from five to ten years and the value of that Customer more than doubles.

How is that possible? Because . . .

- Customers generate more profits every year they stay with you.
- Customers give you free advertising.

- Continuous improvement in service to the Customer is not a cost—but an investment.

Let's talk about "the lifetime value of a Customer."

There was a time in American business when demand outpaced supply. When the point of view was "making every sale." When it didn't make any difference what you sold Customers as long as you sold them . . . something.

The successful business knows the school of "once bought, once forgotten" no longer exists for the profitable company. The thought has to be, "What does this Customer mean to me in terms of long-range business?"

Maryland National Bank says it costs $100 to acquire a new credit card customer. "But a customer we have for five years represents $100 in profit *every year!*"

A supermarket entrepreneur calculated what the average family spent on groceries in their lifetimes. He told us, "Every time I see someone come through my front door, I see $264,000 stamped on their forehead in great big numbers. No way I'm going to let them be unhappy when they leave."

How about the 50 percent of Customers who *do* complain about something that went wrong? About 45 percent complain to a frontline employee who may or may not handle the complaint in a customer-satisfied manner.

What that means: **Only 5%—or one in twenty Customers—complain to anyone in management.**

Conclusion: For every ONE problem where someone has taken the initiative and had the perseverance to complain to someone "at the top," at least nineteen other complaints are not reported or not recorded. In fact, TARP found several companies where as many as 2,000 problems occurred but only one was reported to a corporate-level officer.

Top management doesn't know (1) Customers left and, more important, (2) WHY they left. Why don't Customers complain to top management? Several reasons:

a. "You can't fight City Hall."

b. "Nobody gives a damn anyway."

c. "It's not worth the trouble."

d. "I don't want to spend the time and aggravation."

e. "They don't really care, anyhow."

f. "How do I do it?"

Here's why it is important to have UNhappy Customers complain:

1. By having Customers complain AND satisfying them, you raise those Customers' loyalty as much as 50 percent. What that means: Every time you make an unhappy Customer happy, your revenue increases by half the value of the average Customer.

2. Customers who do NOT complain are the *least* loyal. They don't complain because of reasons A through F listed above. They simply go someplace else instead.

3. Customers whose complaints are quickly resolved are the *most* loyal.

The TARP study says that "loyalty drops by 25 percent among Customers whose complaints were not solved in a timely manner."

Take care of any problems immediately. If not immediately, as soon as possible, and tell Customers when they will hear from you with a solution.

How do some businesses convert Prospects into Shoppers into Customers? Newspapers have come up with a new idea for keeping advertisers. Many of their Customers left to use the more targeted ways of advertising like direct mail. Some supermarkets across the country have transferred a huge chunk (or sometimes ALL) of their newspaper dollars to another medium. How can newspapers fight back?

Here's one way: with new software that preselects the advertiser's target.

In the past newspapers had names and addresses for subscribers and even nonsubscribers. But they used this information only for circulation development. Today, to be competitive, "They offer targeted and efficient marketing programs to their advertising clients," says

Nick Cannistraro, Senior VP and chief marketing officer of the Newspaper Association of America.

And he gives an example: A children's clothing store wants to distribute a catalog through the newspaper. In the past, they sent the catalog to ALL the homes in a specific area. But with new software, the paper can deliver specifically to, say, families with children ages six to twelve.

"And if the store wants to target only families living within two miles of the store they can do that too," says Phil Miller, president and cofounder of Alternate Postal Delivery, which designed this new product.

Newspapers, once famed for not caring about their advertisers because the paper was the only game in town, have seen new and unexpected competition spring up. They have decided perchance, perhaps, possibly they should listen to, take care of, show an interest in the Customer.

This new attitude is a long step for a medium that once prided itself on not promising you placement ANYWHERE in the paper. ("It depends on how the layout person puts the paper together.") But the rules have changed. Today newspapers are concerned with keeping the Customer, not letting them fall back on the Ladder to the rung below.

Converting Shoppers into Customers does not have to be the result of twenty-first-century electronics. The basic, simple, generations-old ideas still work today.

Ira Hayes, motivational speaker and retired award-winning salesman with NCR, said he always carried thank-you cards with postage stamps on the envelopes. Whenever he made a sale, he immediately filled out the card with a personal message thanking the customer for the order and mailed it *that day.*

If only some of the salespeople who sold us merchandise through the years had listened to Ira . . .

One evening, over dinner, we asked the assembled family the name of one salesperson out of the thousands of salesmen and saleswomen who had called on us over more than forty years—one who cared if we lived or died. One who contacted us *other than* the two times a year—

fall/winter and spring/summer—when they appeared to sell us merchandise. One who picked up the phone or dropped a note to say thanks for an order after it was written (as Ira Hayes did). One who called to ask whether everything was selling OK and if not, could he move some of the merchandise to another store? One who told us about special end-of-season prices even if he made only half commission—when we knew the goods were going to the larger-volume department stores.

In the long silence that followed after the meal, not one person's name was given. What an indictment of the selling profession!

If only ONE salesperson had called and done any of the above, his or her business could have increased a minimum of 25 percent with us the following seasons simply because we felt the salesperson cared.

How Not to Treat a Customer

Five years ago we went to a local photography shop where we spent thousands of dollars a year for film developing.

We had received a mail offer from Kodak for a free 8 × 10 photograph if we sent the negative to them before the end of the month. Since our camera shop was a Kodak dealer, we brought it the negative to handle the free offer.

"But you're one day late," said the woman behind the counter.

We looked at the offer and realized she was right. "But we've been out of town for a few weeks and didn't realize we were late."

"Well, you are. . . ."

And so we asked for the owner of the store. The owner came out; we explained we wanted our free picture.

"But you're a day late."

We assured him Kodak would not care. That he shouldn't care either.

"Sorry," he said, "I have to say no."

And so did we. "No" to any future business with him.

When you realize that by not giving us the free 8 × 10 picture, he lost, conservatively, over the next five years, $50,000 in business . . .

No wonder there's an empty store today where his business used to be.

The Japanese have a word for it: *kaizen.* It means "constant improvement." It means Customer Service is NOT as important as Customer Satisfaction (see the chapter on customer satisfaction). Customer Satisfaction means doing the job right the first time.

Most U.S. businesses spend five times as much for a new Customer as they do on the Customer they already have.

Doesn't make sense when you realize current Customers are worth five times more than new Customers.

In their book *Marketing Myths* Clancy and Shulman call this "The Death Wish Paradox." Where a company spends money to find new Customers and not enough money to keep and influence current Customers.

Here's why: For every five Customers who have a problem with you (as THEY define "problem"), you will lose one.

Your future success, your reason for being and for doing more business, is with the Customer you already have. What can you do to bring them up to the next rung of the Loyalty Ladder?

One successful, proven way that works every time (well, almost) is to set up focus groups in your business.

In your day-to-day business decisions you are swallowed up by the physical limitations of your place of work or the mental limitations of what you think works best.

Here's an opportunity to expand your thinking, plans, and direction by simply asking advice from those folks who know best what works in your business: your Customer. And, by listening, you bring them up another rung of the Ladder.

A focus group is nothing more than a cross-section of your Customers brought together to discuss YOUR business.

It's a real-life adaptation of something make-believe we call "The Invisible Cabinet."

The Invisible Cabinet works like this: You mentally picture a group of the people you most respect in business.

Mine includes people like Stanley Marcus, John Wanamaker (yes, the original; since the cabinet IS "invisible," members can be living or dead), Roland Macy (the founder of you-know-what). Those kind of people.

When you are faced with a business decision and not sure what to do, you assemble your Invisible Cabinet and ask them what THEY would do. You KNOW what they would do because, after all, you selected them and know their background, history, idiosyncrasies. And you mentally sit back and listen to them advise you.

One of our first books was called *But Would Saks-Fifth Avenue Do It?* In this book I said that when I was faced with a major advertising decision and not sure what to do, I would simply ask myself that question. And the answer would appear. Like the time the radio salesman offered an eight-foot mechanical bunny rabbit for our store that had the radio broadcast blaring out of the bunny's stomach. The children would come in and have their picture taken with the rabbit while it was broadcasting the station. At first I thought it was pretty novel—an eight-foot bunny rabbit in our children's shop. Cute. And then I asked, "But Would Saks-Fifth Avenue Do It?" And called the radio salesman to say, "Thanks, but no thanks."

See how easy it is when you have someone else make the decision for you?

And so it is with focus groups. Not that they necessarily MAKE the decision for you—but they give you insights and direction you might otherwise not have considered.

What is a focus group? One definition came from *Forbes* magazine: "Six people around a table eating pizza is a party. Six people around a table talking about eating pizza is a focus group."

That works.

So how do you gather the people around a table to talk about YOUR business?

Start with your Customers. Here's a ten-step program to follow:

1. Ask. Tell your customers all about it. How it works. What they have to do. Recruit them with a notice on your business bulletin board. Or stuffers in the shopping bags. Or—as Giant supermarkets did in Washington, D.C.—a full-page ad asking people if they'd like to belong.

2. Get basic information. What's their name, address, phone, age?

3. Limit participants. Ten to fifteen. Make sure they are a cross-section of your Customers by age, religion, ethnic back-ground, income.

4. Mail an agenda. Let them know BEFORE they arrive what they're going to talk about. Conversation is NOT limited to the agenda, but it's a starting point.

5. Begin with who they are. Their jobs, families, how long they've shopped with you.

6. Hire a professional moderator. Don't run the meeting yourself because your emotions get in the way. The local college will recommend a professor from the business department.

7. Have staff attend. Not many. A few each time. Their job is not to offer excuses or give reasons why things cannot be done. They are there to . . . listen.

8. Keep it short. About two hours is fine. After that, people tire or start to repeat themselves.

9. Tape it. You need a record of the meeting. Otherwise you find yourself saying, "What did they say about . . . ?" or "Who remembers the solution to . . . ?"

10. Give gifts. Not money. Gift certificates. ($10 to $20 as a thank you.) OK, everyone's assembled. Great. Memorize these Dos and Don'ts.

Do

Give everyone a chance to talk. Your moderator will encourage the quiet ones to speak by asking questions like, "What's your opinion of this, Jack?" Or, "Do you agree with Margaret?" That's their job. Have everyone become involved.

Meet quarterly. More often it becomes a chore. Less it becomes unimportant.

Have staff attend. Divide them: department heads, clerks, cashiers. And circulate the key points to those who did NOT attend. (Remember the number one reason people want to work with you is "a feeling of being in on things.")

Don't

Don't assume it's scientific. It's not. What it is: a cross-section of your customers telling you what they don't like about your business. One of America's busiest supermarkets begins its sessions with, "Don't tell us what you like about our market. Tell us what you DON'T like."

Don't steer the conversation. Don't ask what you want to ask. Listen to what they want to say.

Don't keep members more than four times. If you do, they regard themselves as fixtures and lose the fresh, objective approach. Tell them ahead of time they are only required to attend three or four of these programs. Give them dates in advance so they can schedule their calendars.

RULES FOR KEEPING CUSTOMERS

If service is the answer to keeping Customers from leaving, are there rules to follow that work? Answer: Yes. There are five. Here they are:

1. **Hire the right people.** Singapore Airlines employs less than 2 percent of the thousands of women who want to become "Singapore girls." They very carefully screen applicants to make sure their staff is customer conscious. Here's why: A recent survey asked 700 major companies the question, "Does your salesman care about you and your business?" And 92 percent said "No"!

American Express gives cash awards of up to $1,000 for great performers. Example: Barbara Weaver cut through miles of U.S. State Department red tape to refund $989 in stolen traveler's checks to a customer stranded in Cuba.

2. **Listen.** One of the main things a business must do is *listen* to its Customers. General Electric wanted to find out why its sales weren't increasing. It asked its Customers the reason they were not doing more business. The most quoted answer: "Your salesmen talk too much." Direct marketers "listen" by TESTING. The number one rule in selling always has been to simply "find out what the Customer wants to buy. And give it to them." You can do that in direct response advertising by "listening" and "measuring results" and "testing."

3. Invest early and heavily in technology to support customer service.

American Express plans to spend $300 million on technology to improve service. One year they followed up 20,000 customer transactions to see how the Customers rated the treatment they received. How important is this? THIS important: Most people do not complain. If they do complain and you respond to the problems immediately, you not only keep the Customers, you increase their sales with you and, MOST IMPORTANT, they become your best salespeople! They tell their neighbors, friends, and business associates to hurry on down and buy YOUR product or service.

4. Keep an eye on the competition. Simply yelling at the competition is not the best way. Yes, see what they are doing. Yes, watch them. But your goal is to have your competition keep an eye on YOU. What do YOU do that is innovative, different, and unusual to enhance your database? *Simply show your Customers you care about them as Customers.* Give them reasons to buy from you rather than from your competition.

One early move in this direction was a 1932 Chrysler automobile ad that was headlined, LOOK AT ALL THREE, meaning Chrysler and the two major competitors. Their reasoning: When you see the difference you'll buy THEIR product. Far more powerful than the company making your decision for you. That's temporary. When the consumer makes the decision, it is far more permanent. A recent Norwegian ad for Mycron computers positioned the firm against two competitors: IBM and Norsk Data. In the ad Mycron gave you THREE coupons to request more information. One had the address of IBM, the second of Norsk Data. The third was theirs! Their feeling: If "you compare all three" . . . you'll buy us.

5. Ask the Customers to rate your quality of service. Stay at most major hotels around the world and there is a note asking you to "rate our service." Housekeepers are given a small reward for every filled-out report they hand in. Hotels then know what the Customer wants (and they also build a database of these names). Embassy Suites does 350 in-depth customer interviews every day. "It's probably the most extensive survey ever in the hotel industry," says president Harvey Feldman.

Every week Fidelity Investor Centers in the United States asks 3,000 customers who recently did stock market trades with them to rate the service they received and to suggest improvements.

Cadillac gathers focus groups of owners and examines repair orders and complaints. Result: Cadillac jumped from fourteenth to seventh place in Customer ranking of best automotive repair service.

With the new competition around us, today's businessperson must look for innovative and different and imaginative ideas not only to keep present Customers but also to have them tell others. This means taking care of the Customer. This means concentrating as much on the Customer you have as on the Customer you do NOT have. "Business is never as healthy," said Henry Ford, "as when, like a chicken, it must do a certain amount of scratching for what it gets."

Four-mula for
Success

Here's a simple little technique to increase your business that will take you about fifteen minutes a day. On the average, it will build your volume at least 10 percent a year or more. We have received hundreds of letters saying it worked (and none saying it didn't). The concept is so simple, so easy, you will wonder why no one ever told you how it worked before.

It involves making four contacts every day. And you have four choices: by phone, by mail, in person, or by reference.

You must commit to do one of each of the four categories. Or two of two. Or four of one. Any combination you're comfortable with. Time required: about fifteen minutes a day.

Once you start you will find yourself automatically performing the routine every day. It might be difficult the first few days developing a habit pattern, but after that, the idea will become as much a part of the day's activities as opening the mail or returning phone calls.

We have described this technique to thousands of businesses all over the world. Some tried the idea right in the middle of our program when taking a coffee or lunch break. Most wait till they return to their place of business the following day and, figuring, "Hey, what do I have to lose?" start the program.

Your efforts will be rewarded instantly. This is not one of those "try this for six months and see the difference" ideas. We're saying, "Try this for *one week* and see the difference." You'll be amazed how quickly your present Shoppers become Customers and Customers become Clients simply because you practice the "Four-mula for Success."

Here's how it works:

Let's begin by picturing a box divided into four parts. We'll start with the upper left-hand corner and call this box:

FOUR PHONE CALLS

You have the phone numbers of your best customers. (And if you don't, start listing those numbers today!)

In addition to their phone numbers, you might list some additional information: What they bought last time. What they like. Key points of your last conversation with them.

Now, when you make those four phone calls, you will have in front of you some basic information to talk about.

Interesting fact: About one of three spur-of-the-moment phone calls you make will prompt this type of response: "Now this is a coincidence. I was going to call you today."

This type of call can be a "thank you," special news for a preferred customer, or simply friendly ("I was thinking of you today . . . "). The first time we received a call like this from a fellow marketing person in Chicago, we waited for him to ask us for something. A favor. A book. A contact. A . . . something. Finally, after a few moments of pleasantries we asked, "Was there something special I could do for you today?" And he answered, "No, I was just thinking of you and wanted to call and say hello."

We thought about that for several days and repeated this story to others (and now we're repeating the story to you). Those spontaneous calls simply make you (or your Customer) feel . . . good.

Keep your calls short.

You are friendly, but not time-consuming.

You are sincere, but not saccharine.

You are interested, but not invasive.

You are informative, but not overbearing.

You are . . . the bearer of good tidings.

Some rules about when you call:

• Say who you are up front. Don't anticipate they'll recognize your voice. (Why should they? This is probably the first time you ever called.)

• Use their name in your conversation. Makes the call more friendly. More a visitor to the home than a salesperson ringing the bell.

• Sign off with a pleasant good-bye.

Above all, be pleasant on the phone. We are proud of how our phone is answered: spontaneous and enjoyable. The immediate feeling is, we're glad you called. Employees at Caplan's Men's Shop in Alexandria, Louisiana, answer the phone, "We're having a great day at Caplan's." Remember: This is the first contact the customer makes with you. Is the person answering your phone upbeat, interested, helpful? Even though they can't see the person calling, we believe there is a 20/20 "vision" tied into telephone calls. Here's why:

If customers dislike the way you talk to them on the phone, their willingness to think nice things about you drops 20 percent. And your ability to "close the sale" drops more than 20 percent.

Story: I called an advertising manager of a large corporation to discuss an upcoming column. I would quote him as an expert. Good publicity for him. I was transferred to his voice mail and received this message:

"The voice mail for this person is full right now. He cannot receive any more messages. Thank you."

I didn't call him back. Or quote him in the column.

"He can't receive any more messages?"

Something wrong here . . .

Story: It was the night before an all-day seminar in Dallas. I called the hotel operator for an early wake-up call. This was the conversation:

Me: "Hi, this is Mr. Raphel in room 604. Can I please have a wake-up call for 6:30 A.M. tomorrow?"

Operator (after a pause): "I'm sorry, the 6:30 wake-up calls are all taken. Would you like 6:45?"

"Yes," I answered quickly. I didn't want to be left out of THAT time slot.

"The 6:30 wake-up calls are all taken?"

Something wrong here. . . .

When *you* call, smile when the person answers. Right: a genuine, happy smile. It will come across in your voice.

FOUR NOTES

What this means: Write four notes to customers every day.

Pretty simple. But (and here's the most important sentence) *hardly anyone does it!*

Any seminar on marketing you attend will tell you of the companies noted for contacting the customers *after* the sale: The Gap, Nordstrom. Even Radio Shack has a very, very strict rule that the salesperson MUST capture your name and address before you leave the store whether or not you buy anything. But the key is not in capturing the name. The key is in following through and writing the note. This can take several forms:

- **The thank-you for buying.** Just received one from our new car salesman, who thanked us for leasing the car and enclosed his card to call him if there were any problems. Ordinary? Not really. In the twenty-three cars we've bought or leased in our lifetimes, *this was the first and only time* we ever heard from the person who sold us the car.

   When was the last time you received a thank-you from anyone who sold you anything this year? Your purchases ran into the thousands of dollars, but the thank-yous received were fewer than a dozen if you are a typical customer.

   If you make the thank-you handwritten, the note becomes even more important.

- **The thank-you-for-being-a-customer note.** This is even more effective. This is the unexpected, unannounced, unanticipated message from you to a Customer simply thanking the person for . . . being a Customer. Great time to do this: Thanksgiving. Something along the lines of, "Seems only natural at Thanksgiving that we give thanks for lots of things that happened to us during the year. And you certainly rate at the top of that list. You've been a Customer with us for a long time and I know we say 'thank-you' whenever you come to visit (I hope we do!), but just wanted to take the opportunity at this time of the year to say 'thanks' again."

You can rewrite the words so they sound more natural and more "you." Above all, the note must be sincere and you must believe what you are writing. Then (and only then) will the receiver be amazed, astonished, and simply unbelieving. And will take the note and show it to friends and family. ("You won't believe what came in the mail for me today. . . .")

• **The "congratulations" note.** Something nice happened to them or a member of their family. A daughter chosen for the cheerleading squad. A son picked for the football team. A son or daughter graduating. The customer is elected to head a local charity group. You carefully cut out the newspaper clipping and put it in a folder with a note: "Thought you'd like to have another one of these. Congratulations."

Remember, sincerity is the key. You must "feel" what you are writing is how you actually feel. If not, the words will come out awkward and the message unbelievable.

• **The "wanted-you-to-know" note.** This note invites your Customer to come to your place of business because of new merchandise that just arrived you think the Customer would like to see.

One of the Customers in our men's clothing shop received a note from the manager of our store telling her that new fall clothing had just arrived for her three boys. She posted the note on the front of the cash register in her diner. Many people would ask what it was doing there, and she replied, "This is the first note I've ever received from any place I've spent my money my entire life." (Yes, she came in. And spent more than $1,000. From . . . a note.)

Whenever our store's business began to falter, we would suggest our staff start doing "the Four-mula." Easy to do and inexpensive. We supplied the notes and envelopes to the salespeople. In their off time, when customers were not around, they simply took the time to write their personal customers about newly arrived items they knew those customers would like.

We even empowered our people to offer certain items at a reduced price to these "special" Customers. They did tell us ahead of time what items were offered at what price so we were aware.

The "wish-you-were-here" note. A surefire way to bring in more business. Here's how it works:

> You are attending a convention. You have your picture taken in front of the meeting hall. You go to the local photography studio and have them print 100 copies of this photograph. You brought 100 of your best Customers' names with you (or 200 or 300—whatever you feel like taking the time to write). You tell them on the card where you are, that you are looking over new merchandise for them, and, in fact, that you have chosen some products for them you know they will like.

Within a few days after you return home, your phone will ring asking when they should come in to see what you wrote them about.

We did this first in Helsinki, Finland. We attended their "Vateva," or annual fashion fair showing what was new and exciting in next year's designer clothing. We took a picture of all of us standing in the snow outside the conference hall, which had the day and month and name of the conference on a big sign. We developed the picture and had 300 copies made, which we used for postcards. We wrote to 300 of our best Customers telling them we bought special jackets just for them.

On our return and through the next few months we would be reminded, "Don't forget to call when my jacket comes in. . . ."

When the jackets *did* arrive, we did call and say, "Y'know there's so many nice ones that arrived, we've lined up the ones we think are best for you to choose from."

They came and bought. Why not? After all, we had gone to Finland just for them!

This promotion cost us about $100 to reproduce photos and postage.

We repeated it for several years. And this simple little mailing invariably brought us between $20,000 and $30,000 in business!

We told this idea to a group of art gallery dealers when we spoke at The Greenwich Workshop convention in Phoenix. One dealer immediately went to the hotel's gift shop and bought fifty cards with pictures of Phoenix and wrote her fifty best Customers: "I just met your favorite artist today and saw his newest piece of art. I bought a print just for you. Sincerely. . . ."

Said Melinda Merrill from Hole in the Wall Gallery in Ennis, Montana, "My sales increased by as much as $1,000 a week since I started using Four-mula for Success."

Another attendee was Mindy Aronoff from Westwind Frameworks in Placerville, California. She said, "Customers came in for eight months after we sent them a postcard."

How about if you're a bank loan officer and a loan application was approved: "Just a short note to say 'thanks' for coming to us for your loan. We are pleased and excited to help you with your new plans for your business (or career or travel or . . .)."

Now, when was the last time you heard of anyone receiving a note from a bank thanking them for coming for a loan?

Think of this: When people come home from work, the first thing they do is ask their spouses how they are and how the children are, and then, "What's new in the mail?"

Hey, there is something new—a letter from you!

The list and opportunities are endless. And it begins with you sitting down tomorrow morning and starting.

FOUR REFERRALS

Damon Runyon tells how he was first hired by a newspaper:

"It was in Denver. I went to the editor's office and told the office boy I was there to be interviewed for a job. About ten minutes later the boy came back and said, 'He wants to see your card.' I had no business card. But I reached into my pocket and pulled out a deck of cards. From the deck I carefully pulled out an Ace and said, 'Give him this.'"

He got the job.

We call calling cards "miniature billboards" because . . . that's what they are. They sum up in a few brief words your name, address, and business.

Calling cards become a vital part of your everyday Four-mula. Here's why: On the average, you meet four new people every day. Think about it. A fellow traveler on a bus or train. The waiter/waitress at a restaurant. The salesperson from whom you buy . . . *anything*. Someone introduces you to a new person at a business lunch.

Give them all your calling card. This tells them who you are and what you do. "And if you can ever use my services, please call me. . . ."

Have *you* given *your* calling card to those folks you see every day? At the newsstand, the bakery, the bagel shop, the day-to-day purveyors of goods you buy?

"Wait a minute," says the skeptic. "Those people know who I am and what I do."

Sorry, most do not. Well, they know WHO you are. They recognize the face. They probably know where you work. But not WHAT you do. Your calling card tells them.

Most people receive calling cards when they take a new job. Question: How many are left in the box of 500 at the end of year? Answer: close to 400 or more. Wrong answer. Give away at least four a day and you'll give away 1,000 by the end of the year. Somewhere, sometime, somehow, someone who received one of those cards will call you and ask for your products or services.

Here are five rules (ideas) to make your calling card work for you.

1. Make it memorable. Do something different. Put your picture on the card. Make it a pop-up. We once designed a card for a salesman by the name of Bob Greenglass and put it into a cardboard package that looked like a glass holder. We also had Bob wear glasses with green frames whenever he called on a client. They might not remember his name until someone said, "Y'know who I mean—the salesman with the green glasses."

The way you know if your card is memorable: The person receiving it looks at it and says, "Can I keep this?"

(We used to answer that one with, "No. I only made one. Please give it back." Then we said we were only kidding. "Keep it. Pass it around. Do you want any more?")

2. Make it relate to your business. When Robert Burchmore was with First National Bank of Winnetka, Illinois, he would drop his calling card at restaurants or meetings and, as he said, "People would nearly break their arms and legs racing to pick them up." Here's why: The card looked like a $5 bill folded in half. When you picked it up and opened it, there was his name and the name of his bank. *Gotcha!*

Hartman Leather, a maker of quality leather briefcases and luggage, prints their cards on . . . yes, leather.

Our local glass contractor prints his on see-through vinyl.

Our paper bag salesman had his tucked in tiny paper bags.

American Sign and Indicator (those folks who make time and temperature signs outside banks) have a calling card showing the temperature. Tilt it slightly and the temperature changes to . . . the time.

Allan Katz runs a direct marketing business in Memphis. His card looks like a miniature business reply card.

3. What's on the back of your card? Watch what happens next time you give someone your business card. They read the front, then turn it over and . . . *you have nothing on the back!* Put something there! Your home phone. A free offer. *Something!*

Blaine Greenfield, who teaches marketing at Bucks County Community College, has his basic information on the front with a note on the bottom saying "see over for telephone number." On the back, he lists his telephone number three times. In boldface. In between each number he also lists the phone number for President Clinton, Boris Yeltsin, Queen Elizabeth.

One of our all-time favorites is from friend, consultant, and writer Jeff Slutsky. Jeff sent us his new calling card with nothing on the back. We sent it back asking why he ignored the back of his card. Didn't hear from him for three weeks. Then received his new card. Same information on the front. But now, on the back, this message: "Rent this space." The Japanese have calling cards with directions on how to find their place of business in Tokyo, since street signs are almost nonexistent.

Another favorite was the one we received from a men's clothing store in England. It was a miniature card. Name, address, and pertinent information on the front. On the back was this message: "The size of this card is made necessary because of the amount of business you've given me lately."

4. Make it unusual. Comedian Henny Youngman, when asked for his card, gives you the standard size calling card. On the front are only two words, "My card." After all, didn't you ask him for "his card."

Another one he uses: When grandparents show him pictures of their "pride and joy" grandchildren, he whips out a calling card that has pictures of cleaning products. Pride on one side and Joy on the other.

If your next trip takes you through O'Hare airport in Chicago, you might meet Chubby the taxi driver. Here's his card:

For O'Hare, call Chubby

The Man With The Plan

Call one day in advance.

Air conditioned. Treats. Coffee. Danish. Stereo. Fun.

Call and wait 15 seconds for a return call.

(and then, this kicker on the bottom)

This card will self destruct in five seconds.

5. Spread the word. When we did bank seminars, we would speak to the middle and senior management in the room and ask, "How many of you print calling cards for your tellers?"

Few raised their hands.

"You print them for the CEO and senior management," we would say, "and they give them to the CEOs and senior management of other banks. Why not give them to the people who are your first best salespeople. The folks who actually meet your customers: the tellers. They can give them out both at work and at social occasions and say, "'Next time you want money, come and see us.'"

Management will be impressed when the teller keeps bringing

new customers over to the side desks, saying, "I met this person the other evening and they want to open an account."

When we do this section at our American Express seminars around the United States attended by businesses in a specific community, we wait till just before the afternoon coffee break and say, "Well, our program is nearly over today and my question to you is, How many calling cards have you given away today? This room is packed with potential customers for your business." I then go to people I met during the day and ask them specifically. "You have a bookstore. Everyone here buys a book sometime. How many cards have you given away? And you own a children's clothing shop. Most people here have children or grandchildren. How many cards have you given away? And you, you have a restaurant. How many people here have cards to your restaurant? And put a note on the back saying their dessert and coffee is free if they come within the month because you met them here. Why, if you gave away your cards to the 300 people here today you will have completed your four-a-day for the next four months!"

There is a mad dash of activity as we break for coffee with people giving away the small number of calling cards they brought with them, regretting they didn't bring more.

Story: A stockbroker drives to Manhattan every day. As he approaches the toll gate he positions his car whenever possible in front of an expensive car—a Mercedes, Porsche, Lexus.

He then hands a $1 bill to the toll collector, who gives him back change. Our friend says, "Please take out for the car in back of me as well." Which the toll collector does . . .

Now the owner of the expensive car stops to pay his toll and the collector says, "It's OK. It's already been paid."

"Paid? By whom?" asks the driver.

"By the guy who was in front of you."

"Who is he?"

"I don't know, but he left me his calling card."

The driver of the expensive car takes the card, turns it over, and on the back reads this handwritten sentence: "If you think this is unusual, you ought to see the way I trade stocks and bonds."

Four AFTO

AFTO is an acronym for the well-known salesman's reminder to Ask For The Order.

The president of a local lumberyard was playing golf with the president of our largest bank.

Halfway through the course, the bank president said, "Y'know Tom, we've been playing golf every Saturday for—what is it now—ten years. How come you don't have any money in my bank?"

And Tom answered, "How come you never asked me?"

Which reminds us of columnist and entrepreneur Billy Rose, who once asked, "Did you ever wonder why so many short, fat, and not good-looking older men marry such beautiful young women?" And he answered, "Because they asked."

Most salespeople do not ask. Fear of rejection. Not sure what happens after they are told "no." Wondering what to do next if the sale is turned down.

You have to Ask For The Order.

Who do you ask? Certainly friends and people you know well who can use your product or service. Remember, if you have a friend and he's buying what you have to sell from someone else . . . you don't have a friend.

You have to Ask For The Order

One great way to start is the old but still successful idea used by insurance agents. Once you make a sale, you ask your new client if they can recommend someone else for you to offer a similar program. Or, if you call on someone new, can you use their name for a reference? Since this new client has committed to signing contracts and paying money, he or she will usually agree.

But you have to Ask For The Order.

Four-mula for Success works! But like any new idea/program/concept/direction . . . you have to do it.

Think of the rewards.

For if you work 250 days a year. And you do Four-mula every day. That equals **1,000 extra contacts** you will make this year.

Will that result in more business?

Will that bring your customer closer to the top of the Loyalty Ladder?

Will that put more money in your pocket?

Sure. But you have to set aside the necessary fifteen minutes every day. A certain time of day is best. Just before your business opens. Just after you close. During your lunchtime. Shut yourself in your office with a Do Not Disturb sign.

And when strangers and those most envious look at your new success and ask, "What secret formula did you discover this year?"

Just smile and walk away, saying, "You're spelling it wrong. . . ."

INTERVIEW
Feargal Quinn

■

The "Boomerang Principle"

Feargal Quinn is a kind, humorous friend who just happens to be Ireland's leading supermarket owner and a member of the Irish Senate. He is also a firm believer in bringing people up his stores' Loyalty Ladder.

He believes businesses should practice the "Boomerang Principle": It's not enough to have shoppers come in the first time. The name of the game is getting the **Customer** back.

Feargal says, "Once you start to think it through, this principle can radically change the way you do business. At present, your approach may be like playing golf, where the idea is usually to get the ball to travel as far away from you as possible.

"When you throw boomerangs, your objective is different, your strategy is different, and the way you judge your results is different."

Quinn says he often had to fight his accountants when he implemented certain customer service practices such as:

- Making all the stores' checkout lines candy-free so mothers and fathers would not have to fight off children who demanded a sweet treat;
- Putting child-care centers in all his stores so children could be entertained while their parents shopped;

- Offering several self-service brands of teas, which were much cheaper than the brands available at his competitors.

Quinn describes what is needed to carry out such policy decisions effectively:

"Make no mistake about it: you sometimes need considerable courage to take the unquantifiable option. This is where *leadership* comes in.

"The person at the top of the business must sometimes be prepared to put his or her neck on the line because of a hunch, a gut instinct.

"Sometimes the role of the leader is to say to the others: 'All right, we can't show this with figures. But I am prepared to take the long view, and my instinct is that we will benefit more in the long run from doing such-and-such.'

"This is what business risk is all about. And, of course, if you want to stay in business your instincts had better be *right*.

"An important part of becoming *successfully* customer driven is honing your instincts so that they give you the right answers most of the time, and all of the time when a decision is critical to the future of the business."

We talked with Quinn recently about some of the things that made his business successful.

Q. You said you want to make your customers "guilty." Why?

A. The "guilty" idea came from a customer at one of our customer panels. A customer said, "I went to your competitor one time but I felt guilty at the checkout." I said, "Tell me about it," because I knew the other store was very expensive and maybe she thought she was spending too much money.

But she said money wasn't the issue. She explained, "One time when I was in Superquinn [Feargal Quinn's Market] I discovered when I went through the checkout and packed everything that I left my purse on the table at home. So I told the checkout operator I had to go home. I asked if they would put the frozen food in the freezer and the ice cream in the ice cream cabinet and I would be back in forty-five minutes.

"The manager came over and said, 'No, no, take it away and pay me next week.' The order was about $150 and I have felt guilty shopping anywhere else since that day."

The woman told me the name of the store manager, and it was someone who had left us fourteen years ago! This customer has felt guilty shopping anywhere else for fourteen years because of one thing the manager did for her fourteen years earlier. It's worth almost anything to achieve that sort of guilt. I was thinking of asking our staff to pick-pocket our customers so nobody has enough money at the checkout.

Q. What can you do for your customers in addition to giving them a good shopping experience?

A. You have to reward your customers.

We relaunched our loyalty scheme in June 1993. It's called Super Club. It's been a huge success. There are now 120 Texaco stations also issuing Super Club points. And there are many other retailers, including a bank, who also issue points.

You earn points by the total amount of your purchase. You get double points if you shop Monday, Tuesday, and Wednesday, and if you buy certain products, you also get bonus points.

The points are good for merchandise and also very low prices on airline tickets. There is a catalog that lists all the things you can receive. It includes goods, gifts, toys, free travel, and a cash discount if you prefer that.

Something like 80 percent of our customers now use these cards. And every time they come through the checkout we have two visual display units on the cash register. One of them is visible to the customer and one is not visible. The one that is not visible to the customer flashes on the customer's name as the customer's card is put through the electronic slot. Now the checkout operator can say, "Thank you very much, Mrs. Raphel."

But the display unit visible to the customer only shows the number. So the customer doesn't actually see her name. Now that is one of the "fuzzy benefits."

Q. What if a customer forgets his or her card that particular day?

A. It doesn't happen very often because our card is a double card. You break off the bottom part and it becomes part of your key ring. Everybody, or almost everybody, has the card on their key ring. The same number on the card is now also in their pocketbook. Since we did that, very few people forget their card.

Q. What do you plan to do with the information you generate about your customers?

A. We have a huge amount of information. We are still deciding what to do with it. The law in Ireland says you have to get your customer's permission before you use that information, and 99 percent of our customers have given us permission.

We believe people really enjoy our program. In fact, we had one customer recently at one of our customer panels say that she is so hooked on receiving bonus points that her dog has been eating cat food for the last three weeks because we had bonus points on cat food but not on dog food.

Q. What do you do for your best customers?

A. Let me describe to you a program we are starting. If a customer spends $75 with us for twenty-five of the last thirty weeks, a little star appears on the screen. The manager will move to that customer as she comes through the checkout and will say, "Mrs. Raphel, you are a very good customer here, you are much better than the average customer, so in the future when you want to cash a check, don't bother using your check card. We'll happily allow you to cash a check for up to $300 and take the change. You use us as your bank."

We've discovered we have no problems with regular customers who shop with us for twenty-five or thirty weeks. Their checks never bounce. We are able to single out those customers who are regular customers and make them more loyal. We also want to give our customers a birthday cake on their birthday with their name on it. When somebody comes through the checkout lane, a light flashes up that it is their birthday. We put their name on a cake and discreetly give it to them at the door.

Q. How do you go about prospecting for customers?

A. We decided that everybody in Dublin who had a tummy is a potential customer. To be fair, when we decided to look for the loyalty system, we decided not to distribute it to every household because we felt if we did that we might devalue it. Instead, the first few weeks we did it privately and quietly only to customers in the shop. We said, "You are a good customer," and we gave them a card and made them feel important. We used word of mouth rather than advertising.

Other customers started asking about our program, so we set up a little stand inside the shop. Everybody coming in was approached, and we would ask, "Would you like a card?" If they said yes, they would have the card before they got to the checkout.

We are now doing general advertising for the card. But we are happy we started it by offering it to our own customers first. It was the right way to go.

Q. What new programs do you have to reward your customers?

A. We have what we call a "goof scheme." In our stores today there is a giant goofy character. Every customer coming in is handed a little card the size of a credit card folded over with that month's name. It says if we goof then here's what you gain. It's very colorful. We have fifteen goofs we list each month. And if we goof you get 200 super-club points, worth a couple of dollars. Examples of goofs are if we give you a shaky supermarket cart, if your birthday cake is fifteen minutes later than the time you ordered it. In other words if you ordered it for 3:00 and you come in at 3:20, if it's not ready you get 200 points. If you are not satisfied with our bag packing, if there are soft things on the bottom of the bag and hard things on top, we give you 200 points.

The whole concept of this is that the customer becomes the quality control inspector. Our customers respect us, and they now know our high customer service standards.

Find Out What
Your Employees Want . . .

————————■————————

and Give It to Them

I used to manage new store openings for the Miles shoe chain in upstate New York many years ago. A week or so before a store would open in a new shopping center or on Main Street, we would come into town, stay at a hotel, and wait outside the competing shoe stores until they closed.

As the personnel came out we would introduce ourselves, tell them we were from their new competition (which, of course, they knew about), and ask, "How much money are you making now?"

Most would tell us, and we would automatically offer them 20 percent more money if they would come with us.

Our object, of course, was simply to start off our business with qualified staff who would also bring some of their customers.

It worked. The main consideration of workers was "to make more money," and we gave them that opportunity.

Is money still the first consideration today? This was the question facing Professor Ken Blanchard when he was at Ohio State University. (The same Ken Blanchard who is the author of *The One Minute Manager*.) He surveyed 10,000 employees, asking what factors were most important in their job. He gave them ten answers and asked them to rank the most important factor, then the next most important, listing them in order from one to ten.

He then gave the exact same survey to managers and supervisors, asking how THEY thought their employees would answer.

Before we go any further, let's stop for a moment and give you the choices. We've left room for you to rank the choices from one (most important) to ten (least important) and to guess how you think the employers and employees ranked them.

	Your Ranking	Employer Ranking	Employee Ranking
Feeling "in" on things			
Appreciation of work			
Higher wages			
Working conditions			
Interesting work			
Job security			
Management loyalty to workers			
Promotion and growth potential			
Sympathetic help with personal problems			
Tactful discipline			

The reason we bring this up at this point is that in order for your business to compete, survive, and not be listed on the obituary pages of next year's financial newspapers, you not only have to **Find Out What The Customer Wants . . . and give it to them.** You must also **Find Out What Your Employees Want . . . and give it to them.**

Which brings us back to the Ohio State survey. Let's take a look at the final results:

	Employer Ranking	Employee Ranking
Feeling "in" on things	10	2
Appreciation of work	8	1
Higher wages	1	5
Good working conditions	4	9
Interesting work	5	6
Job security	2	4
Management loyalty to workers	6	8

Promotion and growth potential	3	7
Sympathetic help with personal problems	9	3
Tactful discipline	7	10

WHAT A DIFFERENCE

Employers said "higher wages" was the number one factor.

But the employees placed that FIFTH on the list.

Now, look at what employees listed as number one: "Appreciation of work." That was closely followed by "Feeling 'in' on things," which employers listed LAST.

Your workers spend an average of 25 percent of any given week at their job. They want to know that what they do with one-quarter of their lives is simply . . . appreciated.

Forget about differences between what women and men want. Writer Christopher Caggiano researched dozens of surveys on "What Workers Want" and concluded that "there was no difference among the desires of the sexes."

Wellesley College's Center for Research on Women concluded that "men and women find similar aspects of the workplace rewarding and problematic."

If your workers complain about their pay, it's usually a sign that something else is missing. And most of the time it is simply "an appreciation for work done."

People need to be able to answer the question "Why am I doing this?" Putting in extra hours to finish a job is frustrating if people don't think they are having a valuable effect.

People want to be recognized for their time and effort. One person's exhilarating schedule is another's intolerable grind unless someone steps forward and says "Good job." Or "Thank you." Otherwise the job makes the employee miserable, and that can, literally, kill the employee. Japan, the word *karoshi* is well known. It means "death by overwork." It is NOT caused by overwork but by the "attitude" of the worker. *Fortune* magazine wrote that "the health risks of hating one's job have been known to medical researchers in the United States since 1972 when a

Massachusetts study showed the surest predictor of heart disease was not smoking, cholesterol or lack of exercise but job dissatisfaction."

I was doing a seminar for Tennessee Grocers in Memphis and walked over to one of the supermarket owners in the audience and asked, "How many people do you have working in your business?"

"I have eighty-four people working for me," he said.

"Hmmm," I said, "eighty-four people working for you. Well, it's a shame that more than half of them will leave you before the end of this year."

Now the supermarket business has one of the highest employee turnover rates of ANY business, but the man was still taken aback.

"What do you mean by that?" he asked.

"Well, didn't you tell me you had eighty-four people working for you?"

"Yes," he said.

"Well, if you had told me you had eighty-four people working . . . *with* you, I would have said that hardly anyone would leave. You see, no one wants to work FOR someone. But everyone wants to work WITH someone. . . ."

The now-accepted (hopefully) premise is that instead of finding something the people working with you are doing wrong—find something they are doing right. And compliment them. You will be amazed how quickly their productivity will rise.

I encourage businesses to use pictures of employees in their advertisements. Show off the butcher in the supermarket, the salesman selling shoes, the sheet-metal worker, the staff plumber. What you are doing: making them feel a part of your business. Instead of something the owner takes annual depreciation for like office furniture or the copy machine.

The success of your business can be specifically traced to a concept I call "the Psychology of the First-Person Plural." What that means: Who comes first in your business, the employer or the employee? We think it is the employee, and here's a simple test to see if it works for your business.

Listen to someone who works with you talk about their job. If they use the first-person singular, you hear sentences with the words "I" and "me," and they refer to the company as "them," you are listening to a problem. The words should be "us" and "we" and "our."

They tell the story of Marshall Field speaking to the wife of one of his employees, who introduced her six-year-old daughter to the owner of Chicago's famous department store. Mr. Field asked the young lady, "And what does your father do?" expecting her to answer with the name of the department where he worked.

"Oh, this is my daddy's store," said the little girl.

The mother, embarrassed, started to apologize, but Field replied, "No, don't apologize. I only wish everyone working here had that attitude and we would be finest store in the world."

He knew his store would grow and prosper only if everyone worked as a team—all the players from the just-hired trainee to the owner in his executive office. They must know they are interdependent on one another.

Now look at what employees said was the SECOND most important category: "Feeling 'in' on things."

The employers and managers put that LAST.

You cannot expect your business to achieve higher earnings and be the envy of the competition unless you involve and inform your staff of your plans, goals, hopes, aspirations, dreams. . . .

Every business is continually swamped with rumors and half-truths that lead to suspicion and insecurity and that result in poor job performance.

There is also a very selfish reason for ongoing communication with people in your business: They will give you great ideas!

A study by the Wyatt Company, an international consulting firm in Boston, found that among employees dissatisfied with the way their job benefits were communicated to them, only 13 percent said they were "satisfied." But among those who liked the way the company communicated and talked about benefits with them, 75 percent said they were satisfied. How many of your workers really know what benefits you give them?

And the benefits don't have to be just health insurance and sick days.

For several years we closed the store for three days and took everyone on vacation!

We ran ads in the paper saying, "We're closed for the next three days because we're all going on our annual vacation!"

(That was the time of the year when we received the most applications. We were asked, "How can I work in *your* store?")

Once we went to Walt Disney World. Another time we hired a special deluxe bus with a built-in TV, lounges, and catered lunches and took everyone on a trip through Vermont to our favorite villages. Still another time we went to New Orleans and had breakfast at Café du Monde and dinners at famous French Quarter restaurants.

Lots of pictures. Many memories. People still talk about them.

The memories of the good times together are *never* forgotten.

We had monthly store meetings in our business. The agenda was very "rough"—only topics of conversation where I would talk about an upcoming promotion, a new line, an advertising campaign, which we would hand out for everyone's comments and suggestions.

There was never a meeting where I did not pick up at least one idea from one employee that I would use to benefit my business.

I would end every session by going around the room, calling everyone by name and asking them if they had anything else to add to what was discussed that day. That way each felt they were included in the decisionmaking simply because . . . they were!

What was I doing? Taking the TOP two categories employees said were most important to them and making them work for the benefit of our business.

It is important you follow through at the next meeting on what action you took on what was talked about at the previous meeting. Follow-through is important for the golf player taking his swing, the baseball pitcher throwing the ball, and you in making sure that-which-you-decided was actually done. Otherwise your actions are thought of as simply condescending and not meaningful.

Jack Miller is president of the Quill Corporation, the giant mail order office supply company. He has 1,000 employees, and he walks the corridors where his people work. He has lunch in the company cafeteria and chats with rank-and-file employees. He says, "It helps defuse some of the bull I get from my managers."

The average business spends many hours working on plans for the future, the purchase of new machinery, the solicitation of business, the concern over personal image in marketing, advertising, and promotion. But the average business's greatest strength is with the person who pours on the coal and makes the engine go round the track. If you don't use these folks, you have wasted your most valuable tool.

There is a classic story about the time a worker in an auto plant was asked by his new foreman if he had any ideas about improving production.

"Sure," said the worker, and he gave the foreman an idea that was brilliant and saved the company many hours and thousands of dollars.

Later he was asked, "You've been working here for twenty years. How come you never came up with that idea before?"

His answer: "No one ever asked me."

Ten Characteristics of Top Salespeople

———————■———————

1. **Work hard.** Promoter Bill Veeck (you remember Veeck—he sent the midget to the plate for the St. Louis Browns!) said of his successful baseball franchises in St. Louis, Cleveland, and Chicago, "I've met a lot of people that are smarter than I am, but I never met anyone that worked harder." And are you happy in your hard work? There is an old Chinese proverb: "He who cannot smile should not own a shop."

2. **Be self-confident.** Your customers will believe in you if you believe in yourself. Dodge supersalesman Stan Smith tells his customers not to worry about anything going wrong in their cars. "You buy me!" Stan says. And his customers know Stan will take care of any problems with their cars.

3. **Have self-discipline.** In his book *How to Get Control of Your Time and Life* Alan Laiken tells people to divide their mail into three piles: *A* (the most important), *B* (the not-so-important), and *C* (the least important). Then throw the *C* pile away. Take the *B* pile, divide it into an *A* and *C* pile, and again throw the *C* pile away. Take the *A* pile, divide it into 1-2-3 priorities, and tackle the number one priorities first. That's self-discipline.

4. **Have perseverance.** A salesman used to call on us with merchandise we felt not right for our store. After a few seasons we asked him how long he was going to call, since we consistently turned down his line. "Well," he said, "it depends on which one of us dies first. . . ."

A McGraw-Hill survey said on average it takes five repeat calls for a salesman to get that first order from a client.

5. Be flexible. If you send out a mailing piece to a test market and the response is low, change the copy. Or the mailing list. Or the product. It is fine to live on high expectations. But if the realities tell you otherwise, you must be flexible.

6. Have goals other than money. Self-made millionaires were once interviewed by Merv Griffin. He asked them if money had been a driving force in their success.

Each said no. One said there was the challenge to make a jet plane for individuals instead of just for airline companies. Another spoke of perfecting a food recipe and selling it to the mass market. Each in turn said they "had this idea," believed in it, and worked for it.

Famed newscaster Bernard Meltzer tells of the time he was trying to raise money to go to college. Though accepted by tuition-free CCNY in New York City, he needed $100 for books. He approached a friend of the family he called Uncle Joe. He told him of the problem. Uncle Joe handed him a check for $100. Meltzer, overwhelmed, said, "I don't know when I can pay you back the money. . . ."

Uncle Joe replied, "You can never give me back the money, Bernard. I will not accept it. However, there will come a time in the future when you will be successful. And someone will come to you for help. You must leave your door open and you must listen, and you must try to be of assistance. And then you can say, 'I'm paying back Uncle Joe. . . .'"

7. Have respect for the buyer's good sense. The con man making a living from hit and run will not obtain true success. His triumphs are of the moment, his success illusory. Only when you know and understand the problem of the Customer will you develop the answer to his or her needs.

We once went with a local real estate consultant to a bank officer for a real estate loan. Our meeting lasted less than five minutes, and we received immediate approval.

"What happened?" we asked in the hallway after the meeting. "Why did he say yes so quickly?"

The learned, older real estate man looked at us and slowly said, "I never ask a question unless I know the answer is yes."

Our real estate consultant had assembled all the critical and necessary information. He summarized it quickly and presented the total package within a few minutes. The loan officer found all the necessary documentation he needed without long explanations and detailed questioning. He gave his approval.

Our consultant simply knew what the Customer wanted . . . and gave it to him. And the sale was made.

8. Be willing to learn from others. My father sold insurance for Metropolitan Life Insurance Company during the Depression. He collected a quarter-a-week premium from customers. One day he told a Customer, "Instead of coming to the door every week, simply leave the quarter in an envelope with your receipt book in your mailbox."

She agreed. He did this for six months. One week he opened the mailbox and saw his envelope with the quarter. And another envelope from the Prudential Insurance Company with another quarter.

He rang the bell. The customer answered the door. "Tell me," he said, "are you mad at me?"

"Why no," she said. "Why would you think so?"

He explained he collected her premium every week for six months. Today he saw a premium for another insurance policy—written by his competition.

The woman looked surprised and said, "Oh. Do you sell insurance? I thought you were just a collector."

From that moment on, my father always told his Customers he was a life insurance *salesman.*

9. Be able to handle big money. People who handle big money use it as a tool the way a carpenter or a chemist uses his tools.

An experienced clothing buyer said, "I know my budget. I am conscious of units. But if I start relating my 'buying dollars' to the dollars in my pocketbook, I would run screaming from the room."

10. Be a perfectionist. Former President Jimmy Carter tells of the time he was a captain in the navy and reported to his superior,

Admiral Rickover, after completing an assigned task. "I have completed the job," said Carter.

Rickover looked up from his desk and quietly said, "Is it the very best you could do?"

"Pardon, sir?" said Carter, not quite sure what the admiral meant.

"Did you do the very best you could possibly do on that job?" said Rickover.

Carter hesitated and then said, "I'll check it out, sir, and report back."

Carter double-checked and triple-checked his work. He came back and said, "Sir, it's the best job I could possibly do."

Rickover did not look up from his desk. "Dismissed," he said. He knew Carter would not come back until the job was perfect.

Good salespeople appreciate the attitude of Admiral Rickover. They are not satisfied until they do the very best they can do.

On Establishing
School Ties

■

Our first customers came from the Italian section of Atlantic City. One told another, and soon they became a foundation for our business. Their lives revolved around their neighbors, their community, and their church.

Their children attended St. Michael's, the Catholic church in their neighborhood. This meant our clothing sales were limited, since the children wore uniforms to school. We knew what our customers wanted: parochial school uniforms. But we couldn't sell uniforms to them because the school was supplied by an out-of-town company specializing in parochial school uniforms.

One day we went to the school and watched the children playing in the churchyard. The young girls wore plaid jumpers and basic blouses. The young boys had navy pants and white shirts. But no ties.

That gave us an idea. A few weeks later we approached the Sister at the school in charge of uniforms. We told her we wanted to talk about uniforms. She began the conversation by saying the school was satisfied with their supplier. We agreed the uniforms were good-looking but noticed that the boys had no ties. The Sister told us the supplier did not make ties.

I then presented a selection of navy blue ties with the school's emblem woven in gold. She asked the price. I showed her my invoice: $1 each. I offered to supply the ties at our cost. No profit.

"But why would you sell them at no profit?" she asked.

"Because, Sister, one day, I will supply uniforms to all the students in your school. . . ."

The first year we supplied the ties at our cost. We also made sure there were a few dozen delivered at no cost for boys who forgot to bring their ties to school.

The next year we offered several styles of boys' pants—all at a similar quality to what the school was using but at a lower cost. "And our store is right here in town. We will alter all the pants to fit properly. We will guarantee all the pants. If they are ripped or torn or don't fit properly, we will replace them at no charge during the school season."

We received an order for the pants.

Within three years we were outfitting the entire student body with uniforms. Armed with the Sister's written recommendation, we visited other parochial schools in our area.

Within five years we were outfitting fifteen private and parochial schools in our area. We set up a separate department in our store and hired as personnel mothers of children going to the schools who were familiar with the needs of each school. We also continued to make sure a quantity of uniforms were given to the schools for pupils unable to afford them.

What this meant: Every year, hundreds of boys and girls came to our store to be outfitted for parochial school.

And if they needed gloves, scarves, a winter jacket, a party dress, a suit, a sport jacket, well, as long as they were in the store anyway . . .

We soon developed a business that brought in tens of thousands of dollars annually simply because we had discovered a need that was not filled: a school tie.

If there is a moral to this story it is this: Stop looking for the big sale. Concentrate on the small ones. One reason: No one else does. The small sale evolves into the larger sale. Edgar Bronfman, who controls the largest liquor company in the world, said, "To turn $100 into $110 is hard work. But to turn $100 million into $110 million is inevitable."

Why Do Customers Leave You?

————————■————————

Why do Customers leave you?

How many times have you played the "Whatever happened to . . ." game. Wondering why a certain Customer who used to buy what you have to sell doesn't buy anymore?

Is there a reason? Or group of reasons? Has anyone ever done a study on this?

Through the years, we've accumulated a group of reports from different sources ranging from *U.S. News & World Report,* the *Harvard Business Review,* and several trade magazines to half a dozen motivational and "secrets of successful selling" articles.

But (and here's the amazing fact) they all have the same statistics.

Now whether this is one person copying what someone else has written or said or simply perpetuating a myth like the Piltdown Giant, we're not sure.

What we are sure of is that the statistics make sense because they worked in our business (and seeing them gave us a reason to develop a new customer-oriented marketing plan) and in other businesses as well.

Here are the numbers as repeated in books, columns, and from the mouths of let-me-tell-you-how-to-succeed speakers:

Why Customers Leave

14 percent leave because of complaints not solved.

9 percent leave because of the competition.

9 percent leave because they moved someplace else.

68 percent leave for . . . no special reason.

In other words: Seven out of ten customers who used to buy from you left for . . . no special reason.

We don't believe that. We think there was a reason. Or a series of reasons:

We think they left because you never told them you cared.

We think they left because you never told them they were important.

We think they left because you never said "thank you" and "please come back and shop with us again."

Many times we have found that owners and operators are so busy minding the business they forget to mind the Customers, and in the immortal words of supersalesman "Red" Motley, "Nothing happens until a sale is made."

How many times have you walked into a store and found no one to give you any help or assistance?

Good friend and writer Ken Erdman tells of the time he and his wife were shopping in a Philadelphia department store. His wife found an item and brought it to the counter—but no one was there. And no one to be seen. And so Ken simply stood in the middle of the room and yelled at the top of his voice, "Help! Help!" Suddenly security people appeared from everywhere demanding to know the problem.

"There's no problem," said Ken. "We just want someone to help us."

The Japanese handle that by having people stationed on either side of the door when you walk into their shops. They bow and say *O-kyak-a-san,* which roughly translated means, "You are a visitor to my home."

Do I feel that way when I walk into your business?

Is one cashier talking to another. Or a friend on the phone. Or busy fixing stock. Or . . .

They are so busy minding the business, they forgot to mind the customer.

A retailer friend proudly showed us his new computers. He could tell us how many pairs of pink socks were sold on any given day at any given hour. His carry-home briefcase was filled with voluminous print-out sheets that he read with the same interest as the newest novel by John Grisham. He would pencil in notes on the margin, make references for future buying patterns, and use the store as an office away from his office at home.

His once-successful business went bankrupt.

He was so busy minding the business, he forgot to mind the Customer.

Now nothing is wrong with cleaning stock, taking inventory, and buying computers. It is a practice devoutly to be wished, admired, and encouraged. But not at the expense of the Customer. Businesses often tend to build fences to hide behind.

We did a series of seminars for banks at annual state meetings across the country. We asked each of them, "How many made more than ten officer calls last month?" ("Officer calls" mean the bank officers had to leave the bank and personally make a call on Customers and potential Customers throughout the community.) Few raised their hand. Yes, it was written down for them to do. Yes, they knew it was important. But there were papers to read and sign and employees to watch and criticize and . . . well, there just wasn't enough time.

We reminded them to "take the time," or the competing bank would be out asking a simple question to the Customer: "When was the last time you saw your banker?"

They were so busy minding the business, they forgot to mind the Customer.

And what of the phone call to a business questioning a bill. And the answer, "Sorry, our computer handles that."

Really? What's his (or her) name? Can I talk to him? If the computer is going to take care of the business, does that mean it takes care of the customer as well? Shall we set up your business like the old-fashioned Horn & Hardart cafeteria? Customers come in, look for the section they want, scan the little windows till they see the quantity and price they want, dial their credit card number alongside the tiny window opening, and click—it opens for them to take what they want.

And those of you that rave about the tremendous success of home shopping on TV, consider this fact: The total sales (while impressive) make up less than 3 percent of the total retail sales in the United States.

People are lonely. They want someone to talk to.

People are critical. They want to kick the tires and touch the fabric.

People are social. They want to "get out of the house" and go somewhere . . . the local mall or business is fine.

The growth of the megamarkets in the supermarket business had traditional groceries shaking with fear of lost business. And, in fact, many suffered and then learned how to compete. Here's what they found:

- Senior citizens didn't like walking around a 250,000-square-foot store. It was too tiring. (Especially when they saw stock clerks maneuvering the aisles on roller skates because of the huge size of the complex.)
- Customers no longer felt like someone. They were . . . anyone.
- The locations were mostly out of the neighborhoods, which meant driving or finding a bus.
- The "specials" this week were often not available the following week because they depended on the manufacturer's overstocked positions.
- The hours were not as long or convenient as the traditional supermarket's.

These new discount giants became huge dinosaurs, and one begat another till it became difficult to tell a tyrannosaurus from a brontosaurus. They blended together into one huge collage until a Customer would use their names interchangeably and no one knew the difference.

And, suddenly, the "alternative store format" (as the supermarket industry euphemistically likes to refer to these competitors) stopped growing. Some, like the giant dinosaurs they resemble, became extinct and simply closed the doors because the one-million-dollars-a-week volume they needed simply to stay open was not forthcoming.

What DID happen was that the smaller retailer rediscovered the reason to survive: He knew and cared about and took care of . . . the Customer.

And so the next time the desk piles up with figures to beat and merchandise to buy and salespeople to hire, make sure it does not take up the greater part of your day. That belongs to the Customer outside your door roaming around looking for help in buying an item.

Take care of your Customer. If you do, you will have a business to take care of.

Dollar for Dollar, Nothing Returns as Much to Your Business as Direct Mail

■

The year was 1964. We had a little children's clothing business in Atlantic City, New Jersey. Our annual volume was so small we could not afford conventional advertising. However, we did have the names and addresses of a few hundred customers. We decided to send them a mimeographed letter once a month about merchandise on sale just for them.

For a very small cost, we doubled our business.

I wrote a story about what we were doing and sent it to *Direct Marketing* magazine. The editor called and said he would buy the story and asked, "Since we believe retail direct mail is the coming revolution, would you like to write a monthly column on retail direct mail?"

"I certainly would," I replied, hung up, and turned to my wife and asked, "What's retail direct mail?"

The "coming revolution" of retail direct mail predicted thirty years ago turned out to be scattered shots by untrained marksmen using ancient weapons. Only within the past few years has there been an attempt to encourage, educate, and embolden small businesspeople to use direct mail in their business.

"Retail direct mail" remains, for the most part, an orphan. Known about, sometimes mentioned, but rarely invited to the party. Look through the program of any marketing convention held in the United States (or anywhere in the world). Trying to find anyone speaking on retail direct mail is searching for the proverbial needle in a haystack. This, despite the fact that more money is spent on direct mail than is spent on magazines, radio, billboards, and advertising T-shirts—all put together!

So who's spending all the money on direct mail? The large catalog companies. The big department stores. Look through your morning mail and see the advertisements from the office supply folks, computer companies, book publishers. But not much from the local small businessperson.

Today small businesspeople still spend only about 2 cents out of each advertising dollar on direct mail. Only about 5 percent of U.S. retailers are using any kind of retail direct mail.

Some revolution . . .

The small businessman or woman contributes up to 80 percent of the employment and a major share of any country's gross national revenue. Who's teaching them, showing them, encouraging them to do retail direct mail—their most valuable weapon to survive and succeed in an increasingly competitive economy?

Now, we cannot, in this one brief chapter, tell you all about direct mail and how it works. That would be like the woman who called me one morning and said, "I just opened a dress shop and I want to use direct mail. Can you tell me how it works in the next few minutes?"

Well, uh . . . no.

The salespeople from the newspaper, radio, TV, and magazines all come in to see you with layouts, designs, copy, jingles. All you have to do is sign on the bottom line and they take care of the rest.

But not direct mail. That's you.

Can you start without a twelve-week college course?

Can you be effective without reading a dozen books on how to do it?

Is there a simple, easy, uncomplicated method that will work?

The answer to those questions is yes, yes, and yes.

Through the years we've received phone calls and letters asking about what works and what doesn't. What's important and what's not. We have narrowed those queries down to the Twenty Most Asked

Questions About Direct Mail (. . . *and the answers*).

You can start by simply building a list of your present customers' names and addresses. When you have a few hundred, write them a letter telling them what's new in your business, what's different, exciting, and unusual that just arrived and, oh yes, you've included some special offers just for them. NOT advertised anyplace else.

Here are the Twenty Most Asked Questions About Direct Mail (. . . *and the answers*).

1. What are the advantages of direct mail over any other advertising?

A: Two big advantages:

Selectivity. You can mail to whom you want. You can't tell the local radio or TV station, "Next time you run my commercial, only run it in this part of town 'cause that's where my customers live. Don't run it anywhere else." Can't do it. Some newspapers do offer some selective zip code mailings for special prices, but you're still surrounded by all those other ads.

Measurability. Ed Mayer, one of the early gurus of direct marketing, said it well: "Direct Marketing is a 'what' medium not a 'why' medium. If I send out 1,000 mailers and 100 people show up, I know 'what' happened—I had a 10 percent return on my mailing list. But I don't necessarily know 'why.'"

2. What's a direct mail piece made up of?

A: Three parts: The list, the offer, and the creative. Of these three, the list is the most important. A "rough" gauge of the importance of each might look like this:

List	50 percent
Offer	35 percent
Creative	15 percent

This breakdown makes the creative people like me very unhappy. But I know it's true. If you have the best offer in the world but you send it to the wrong list, you will have terrible results.

If you have the best list but you send them a bad offer, you will have terrible results.

And if your creative is designed by an award-winning artist on the most expensive paper and sealed with hot red wax and is mailed to the wrong list with the wrong offer, you will have disastrous, guaranteed money-losing results. So, if the most important part of your mailer is the list, then where do you find this "list"?

It begins with the customers you have. Every time anyone spends any money with you, write down his or her name and address and telephone number. If possible, see if you can find more information:

- Birthday (month and day only. People don't want you to know their age).
- Clothing size (if you're a clothing store).
- Favorite artist (if you sell prints).
- Favorite foods (if you're a food store).

Well, you get the idea. The more information, the better your results. Knowing something about your customer is as important as knowing everything about your product.

3. How do I know the people still live where I'm sending the mail?

A: Good question. Especially since one out of five people move every year. If you send something first-class mail, the post office will return your letter with the corrected address at no charge. If you send something out third-class mail, the postage is cheaper, but you pay for each corrected address if you add "address correction requested" on the address side of your mailer.

4. Will I receive better results if I personalize my mailings?

A: Not always. Here's why: If your computer prints the customer's name several times on one page, most people will know it's a computer letter. It's far, far more important to have a *personal* letter than a *personalized* letter. What's that mean? This: Your letter should be friendly, comfortable, one-on-one, as if the customer were in the room and the two of you were having a conversation. That's much, much more believable than printing the name several times in the letter, which can not only be intimidating but feel like an invasion of privacy.

5. What's the difference between first-class and third-class mail?

A: In a word: money. Third class is cheaper. BUT . . . third class arrives much later. You have to figure about ten days. Often more. If you are working on a tight deadline, mail first class. Especially if you have a small list. The difference in postage for 1,000 mailing pieces is only about $100. Not worth the savings.

6. People receive lots of mail. How can I make sure they see and read mine?

A: Your customers will open your mailer because they buy from you. If they are not customers of yours, try something different: Mail in a box, a tube, an oversized or colorful envelope. In the first few seconds your customers handle a mailer, they make the decision whether they will open it. Hand-write the address. Use the BACK of the envelope for one more reason to read what you sent.

What they'll always read: A letter addressed to them personally. Especially handwritten. Great example: a "thank-you" after they have bought something from your business.

7. How fast will I know if my mailer worked or not?

A: Within two weeks after your customers receive the mailer.

8. How often should I mail to my customers?

A: At least four times a year. We discovered that sending mailings to our top 500 customers once a month was not too much. We discovered that sending mailings to our top 500 customers *twice* a month was not too much. Great list. As long as we made it a great offer we would average a 20 percent response!

9. What's the most important word to use in my headline?

A: If I had to pick one, it would be *free*. Use it. Often. Say "free." Then say "complimentary." Then say "no charge."

10. Shall I accept only a check with the order?

A: No. The more ways you give the customer to pay, the higher the response. That means check or credit cards or COD or so much down and so much a month.

11. Are there certain words that make the reader want to keep on reading?

A: Sure. Here are a few: *new, save, guarantee, hurry, wanted, announc-*

ing, easy, offer expires (date), *limited offer, discover,* and *you.* John Caples, direct marketing guru, once examined the most successful ads ever written. He found the word "you" appeared in nearly half the winning headlines. How about "free for you." That's good. . . .

12. I read somewhere that a real stamp pulls better than printed stamps, that a smaller envelope is better than a bigger envelope, that long copy outpulls short copy (or was it short copy outpulls long copy?), that . . .

A: Stop. None of that matters very much. Go back to step 2: the list, the offer, the creative.

13. What percentage of returns should you receive from your direct mail?

A: It depends.

It depends on how much you are spending and how much you are receiving back. If you want to sell a Rolls-Royce and you receive only a 1 percent return on your mailings, it is more than enough to pay for the mailing and make a nice profit because the cost of the item is so high. Lower-priced items need a higher percentage of response.

A rule of thumb is that your business can usually expect a return of around 10 percent if your mailer is going to your regular customers who expect to receive direct mail from you on a regular basis.

No other advertising medium gives you an exact measurement. But when you send out a direct mail piece, you'll know in a few days whether or not your mailer worked. That's why people "test" their mailings.

We once did a sale and mailed out gift certificates. The customers had to fill out their name and address on the gift certificate when they came to the store. We received 15 percent of the certificates back. Next time, we preprinted the names on the gift certificates and the response rate jumped to 25 percent!

I love David Ogilvy's story about the time his brother Francis wrote a letter in Greek to the headmasters of private schools when he was selling cooking stoves. When some wrote back saying they could not read Greek, he sent them another letter—in Latin!

14. Is there a trick I can use to increase response?

A: Here's one that works: involvement. Have your customers fill in something, tear open something, use a "yes" or "no" label. Here's another: Include a gift certificate that must be used on or before a certain date. No one likes to throw money away.

15. Will premiums bring in more business?

A: Yes! Examples are all around you: Look at the cereal boxes and the special "premiums" you can have if you send in box tops. (Anyone want a slightly used Buck Rogers decoder ring? Or am I giving away my age?)

We used to go to Helsinki, Finland, every January for "Vateva"— their annual fall and winter "fashion show." The four of us would usually travel on SAS Airlines. One day I saw a full-page ad in a travel magazine saying that if I took Finnair to Finland, they would give me a notebook computer that would list telephone numbers and addresses and other information . . . free.

We canceled our tickets on SAS and bought tickets on Finnair.

Why? Because of the premium.

Consider offering a premium in your next mailing piece. We were able to increase the return 5 percent on our mailing piece for New Year's Day—our biggest sale day of the year—when we offered a Free Trip For Two . . . to somewhere people wanted to go: New Orleans, Walt Disney World. We made a barter deal with our travel agent ("We advertise your agency in our mailer, you give us a terrific price on the trip"), and our cost was only about $100. But what a dramatic difference in response to our mailer! By simply adding another "premium."

16. What's the first thing people read in a letter?

A: Whatever you put on the upper right-hand part of your letter. That's where your customer's eye goes first. Siegfried Vogele, one of the world's experts in direct marketing methods, is professor of direct marketing in Munich, Germany. He has done extensive "eye" tests on what people look at first, second, and so on when they receive your mailing piece. First they want to know who is writing to them. Then they look at how the letter is addressed. And then their eye jumps to who signed the letter, and the next thing they read is . . . the P.S. (surprise, surprise). They do not go back to the beginning of the letter until they read the P.S. ("Hmmmmmm, I wonder what they forgot to put in the letter that they had to add at the end?") So make sure the

P.S. repeats the big benefit you put up front, which they won't get around to reading until they've read the P.S.

17. When's the best time to mail?

A: January. That's why you receive all those big packages from publishing houses telling you how many millions of dollars you have won. THEY know January is the best month for results. And to answer your next question, the worst month to mail is usually June. Because vacations start or weddings happen or school closes or . . . Another bad time is December unless your mailer has to do with gift giving. Christmas gift giving takes precedence over everything else. Just remember you're fighting the mailbox glut of thousands of other marketers who are also selling gift ideas.

18. Do testimonials work?

A: Yes. If they relate specifically to the product. The BEST testimonials are from people who have used your product. Give their names and their cities to show they are real people.

You should also *guarantee* what you sell. If your product is a good one, the percentage of people who return products is very small. The percentage of people who will buy products because you have guaranteed performance is much larger.

19. What if I get back a terrific response to my mailer? Can I make the exact same offer to the exact same list a few weeks later?

A: Sure. Here's why: On average, sending the same offer to the same list (to those who did NOT buy the first time around) will return *half* of your first-time response. So, add up your costs and your sales. If one-half the response still gives you a profit . . . go for it!

20. How can I start?

A: Two ways:

1. Save the direct mail pieces you receive that capture your attention and copy the best ideas.

2. Call your postmaster. Set up a meeting with him or her. Start off by stating, "I want to do direct mail for my business. Can you help me?"

Acres of
Diamonds

———■———

At the turn of the century, Dr. Russell Conwell, a Baptist minister, traveled throughout the United States and gave the same speech nearly 6,000 times. The effect was so powerful that wherever he went, audiences would pack the halls to hear him talk. He earned several million dollars (a huge amount of money for that time) and donated the proceeds to found Temple University in Philadelphia, named in honor of Conwell's church, Temple Baptist.

His speech was titled "Acres of Diamonds." His theme: "Diamonds are not in far-distant mountains or in yonder seas: They are in your own backyard, if you just dig for them. . . ."

This is the story of how that sermon still works today in any business if you use direct mail—a tool that will prove there are, literally, "Acres of Diamonds" in your own backyards. . . . They are your Customers. Your Customer list is your *best* list.

We call our Diamond (or yours) the "Database Diamond."

Here are the four files that make up the Database Diamond:

1. The Prospect File.
2. The Customer File.

3. The Suppression File.
4. The Store File.

Let's take the files one at a time. . . .

THE PROSPECT FILE

Three key places to find prospects are voting lists, zip codes, and list brokers. Select from these lists the ones that most closely match your Customer profile. These are your best prospects for increased growth.

PART ONE: VOTING LISTS

Leo McGinley & Sons market in Falcarragh, Ireland, decided they would try direct mail, but there were no list brokers and no mailing lists. But there WAS a list of voters in the town—each a potential McGinley customer. And so he sent his very first mailer to the 5,000 voters (households) announcing a special sale on Mother's Day. Since the holiday fell on a Sunday, they received permission from the parish priest to open that day.

The results were more than the store could handle. Nearly half the population of the town showed up for the sale! Not only did the small police force have to come to handle the crowd, but the parish priest had to be called to calm the crowd.

The mailer cost $4,000. Business done: $52,000.

PART TWO: ZIP CODES

The Norman Eton Street Station, a restaurant chain in Michigan, sent a laser mailing to 40,000 customers. They selected zip codes of people with incomes over $30,000 (most retailers would know income levels by where people live) and businesses with more than ten employees. They enclosed a personalized check redeemable for several different reduced-price meal offers. They matched zip codes to income areas of potential customers.

Cost of mailer: $20,000. Response rate: 40 percent, for a business total of $368,000!

PART THREE: LIST BROKERS

Norm Thompson is a catalog company in the northwestern United States. To increase its mailing list, they did an analysis of their customers. The demographic results were matched against a profile of readers of U.S. magazines. They asked list brokers to find a magazine whose readers' lifestyle most closely matched current Norm Thompson customers. The company ran an ad in that magazine offering a free pair of socks (value: $6) to anyone who simply wrote and asked for a pair.

More than 300,000 orders were received. **And nearly 20 percent were converted to full-time Customers!** That's 60,000 orders.

Why? The company simply reached out to build more customers based on the customers they presently had.

THE CUSTOMER FILE

This file is divided into three groups:

a. **A listing** of which customers bought what, where, when, and how.

b. **Where customers live,** how much they earn, what kind of car they drive (demographics, geographics).

c. **All Customers.**

THE LISTING

At one time, our store sent *every* mailing to everyone on our mailing list. Thousands and thousands of mailing pieces. But, what if . . . we had a list of which customers bought what merchandise? And we did! Our computer could pull off, by department and kind of merchandise, specific Customers' names on address labels.

Now, for a cost of only a few hundred dollars (because the lists were in the hundreds instead of thousands), we were able to produce mailing pieces quickly and inexpensively with a high return (20 to 30 percent) because the mailers went to customers with a history of buying the merchandise we were offering.

THE DEMOGRAPHICS/GEOGRAPHICS

MBank Preston is a large suburban bank in the richest area of Dallas, where the average home value is $400,000.

Question: What do high-income buyers look for when investing their money?

Answer: The highest interest they can find.

MBank Preston took these two ingredients—high interest and high income—and combined them in a marketing campaign for Individual Retirement Accounts (IRAs).

They pinpointed their advertising to three zip codes in the Dallas area right in the location of all those $400,000 (and higher) homes.

They promoted the IRAs in general advertising but pinpointed the three zip codes in mailings.

Results: 65 percent of their business came from the three zip codes. The remaining 35 percent came from the other fifty-five zip codes in Dallas.

Each new IRA customer received a personal letter from the bank's chairman of the board.

Total budget was $53,000. The campaign brought in $7 million in IRAs, and 40 percent was from new customers because the banks dug for gold in the hills where it was buried.

ALL YOUR CUSTOMERS

Our store ran an annual sale on New Year's Day. This mailing went to the *total* mailing list.

- No other stores were open.
- We were only open for four hours.
- The sale was advertised only by direct mail.

For twenty-five consecutive years, our store did more business in these four hours on this one day than it did most WEEKS of the year!

By mailing to your Customers, you will soon discover you have, in your own backyard, Acres of Diamonds.

All you have to do is go dig them up.

THE SUPPRESSION FILE

How many names do you have on your mailing list that you shouldn't have on your mailing list? What customers have moved? Where? Should they still receive your mail? What customers have a limit on their credit? What old customers do you want to become active one more time? Here's the three parts of this file:

1. Returned mail.
2. Credit risks.
3. Recapturing old customers.

Let's take them one at a time.

RETURNED MAIL

Nearly one out of five people in your community move every year. Some die. Some are born. Some move in. Some move out. Print the phrase "Address Correction Requested" on your mailer. For a small fee, the post office returns your mailers with corrected addresses of customers who have moved. Now you have the choice of sending your advertisement to the new address or not sending it at all ("Aha, they moved to California. Well, they probably won't come 3,000 miles for my sale . . . ").

CREDIT RISKS

You have customers who do not pay their bills on time or do not pay them at all. You certainly do not want to encourage them to come in and charge more!

"Suppression" means just that: taking these names OFF your mailing list because you would otherwise compound an existing problem.

RECAPTURING OLD CUSTOMERS

Every store has customers who have not shopped for a certain period of time. Surveys show nearly seven out of ten of these customers do not come back "for no particular reason."

Direct mail says you *want* them to come back. One very simple tool is a gift certificate mailed to these customers offering them $5 or $10 off their next purchase. No minimum purchase. No gimmicks. Nothing up your sleeve. After all, you are going to your customers. (No, you would not put an ad in the newspaper saying you will give the first $10 free to *anyone.* You are offering the money to *someone*—your customer!)

For the small cost of printing and postage, you will receive back ten to twenty times your investment (or more) simply because you showed your customers you care about them. As an owner of a children's store in Sweden puts it: "Direct mail is an extension of kindness to our customers."

THE STORE FILE

We use our customer list to find out more information about our store, the departments, which departments are selling what to whom, and when.

The store file has two parts:

1. Loyalty building.
2. Response. Results. Analysis.

LOYALTY

One way for your store to do more business is to have your customers shop more often. If you have customers who buy only a certain designer, why not send this narrow list a mailing piece about that designer's just-arrived merchandise and/or sale? The cost is small. Returns are high. What you've done is pinpoint a very small section of your mailing list with high buying power.

Translate this to customers who buy hi-fi components, vintage wines, lawn care products. Whatever your business, you have a tight cadre of loyal customers who want to be told you have something special for them.

RESPONSE. RESULTS. ANALYSIS

Some supermarkets in the United States give plastic cards to their customers with the customer's name and individual bar code on the plastic.

Now, when the customers come into the store and show their card at the point of purchase, it is passed over the scanning machine, just like the products they buy.

Now the store knows at the end of any given period which customers bought a lot of meat ("We sent you this mailing because you are a good customer of our meat products. And we've enclosed some special coupons on meat products . . . "), or fish . . . or anything. Perhaps you want the computer to give you a list of names and addresses of customers who have not shopped in the past thirty days. You can contact them with a special inducement to make them come back one more time.

Supermarkets Should Treat Their High Rollers Better!

―――――――■―――――――

We have a good friend named Stan Golomb who likes to roll dice.

Stan has a marketing firm in Chicago, but he comes to Atlantic City to gamble. Once every six weeks, a limousine picks Stan up from his house and drives him to O'Hare. He then takes a plane to Atlantic City and stays in a plush casino hotel room for a few days.

Stan's room, airfare, meals, and limousine are all picked up by the casino where he gambles. The casino lets Stan know how much he has to gamble for these privileges, and Stan complies. Sometimes Stan wins, sometimes he loses, but win or lose the casino always wants him to come back.

Casinos like to pamper their high rollers. Someone wearing a green visor has scientifically figured out how much their big Customers are worth to them, and casinos have set aside marketing dollars to make sure their high rollers return.

What do you do for *your* "high rollers," the top 10 percent of your Customers?

What special services are you providing to make sure your best customers come back again and again to your business?

And, most importantly, do you even know the names, addresses, and phone numbers of the 10 percent of your shoppers responsible for most of your profits?

Don Schultz says that in order to survive in business, you are going to have to find your best Customers and cater to them. Schultz is presently professor of integrated marketing communications at Northwestern University. In addition to teaching, Schultz is president of his own marketing, advertising, and consulting firm.

Schultz thinks supermarkets are an example of a business that could learn a lot from how casinos treat their Customers.

"Supermarkets give the same deals to everybody," he says. "They do not differentiate between good Customers and bad Customers. Casinos do differentiate. They bring in their best Customers, give them free drinks and a hotel room."

In fact, Schultz says most supermarkets could not even take better care of their high rollers if they wanted to. Right now, Schultz says, "Most supermarkets do not know who their best customers are. They don't know what they're worth, what their value is to them over time, and as a result, they don't know whether to invest in them or not. They don't even know when customers leave for a competitor!"

The time: Sometime in the future.

Our friend Stan Golomb decides to go supermarket shopping instead of going to the casino. A limousine picks Stan up at home. He arrives at the supermarket where his personal shopping assistant takes him around the store in his electric shopping cart. While Stan's order is totaled and bagged and put in the trunk of the limo, Stan munches on free croissants and coffee in the supermarket's "High Roller" lounge. His purchases are automatically put on Stan's debit card, and when Stan arrives home a Christmas present from the supermarket is waiting.

"You know, I'd rather go supermarket shopping than gambling," says Stan. . . .

Don Schultz

———■———

Don Schultz is a professor, consultant, and speaker on integrated marketing. He believes businesses must keep track of their best customers in order to prosper. We talked to Don specifically about the supermarket industry, which has been a laggard in keeping track of their Customers' purchase histories.

Q. Should supermarkets keep track of their Customers' name and address?

A. The real issue is, should a file be kept on everyone that shops in the store? In the initial stages you need to have some way that will trigger frequent purchasers, people who have high volume—the people who are important to you.

You have to go beyond total dollar count and consider the profitability of a Customer. Initially, what you need to do is capture everything. As you learn more about the Customers, you can drop out the cherry pickers, but for that you need some sort of a screening system that allows you to identify those people.

You need a system that analyzes Customers individually, that says, "These people are worth keeping and these are not." A system that is

dynamic—adds, deletes people, and sees when people become important. It adds them to the database and maintains them.

Q. Suppose a Customer purchases $100 worth of groceries. What system do I have to gather that information?

A. Most supermarkets key data off of a check-cashing card or frequent
shopper program. A supermarket is going to have to have some sort of
an electronic shopper-monitoring system, or they are just going to be
shooting in the dark.

Q. How does the supermarket, once they issue the card to the consumer, know what that consumer is purchasing?

A. They can use a scanning system, which is not that big of a deal
anymore.

Q. The system will have to identify the purchase and key it in back to the Customer in some way with an ID number.

A. An ID number can be looked at in several ways—I can key it back
to a telephone number, specific number that I have, a check-cashing
card, any number of things.

Q. Once we have the information, we'd need some sort of printout that lets me know who my best Customers are in terms of purchases. Is that the next step?

A. You want to go back and look at those Customers and start to identify what they're doing and start to figure out ways to hold on to them.
And then you want to manage their purchases in the store. If they are
a family of four with two kids and they never buy anything out of the
meat department, I want to motivate them to shop in the meat department. I want to manage their purchases in my store that are profitable
to me but are satisfactory to the Customer as well. It's a win-win situa-
tion for both people.

Q. How does the average supermarket do that? How do they know if a Customer is not buying in the meat department?

A. If you're scanning his purchases, you know whether or not he bought meat.

Q. So someone's going to have to analyze all the purchase data that come through the scanner?

A. Yes.

Q. Is that someone on the staff of the store or is that an outside person?

A. I think right now the easiest way to do it is externally. You may want to bring it back inside as you get more sophisticated.

Supermarkets have to understand who their Customer base is. Most of them don't know. They rely on gross sales and Customer counts. That's essentially where they are. The problem with that is they go back in to do averages and get silly things like "the average Customer purchases $13.27 a week." That makes absolutely no sense because you've got people there spending $2.15 and people who are spending $250.00. As long as you work on the averages, you will never be able to understand who your Customers are or your business and what's driving your business. Do you have a few very large Customers, or do you have a lot of middle-sized Customers, or do you have a ton of little Customers? You have to understand who your Customer base is, how they buy, and what they buy and then start to look at how you can manage your business once you understand who your Customers are. There may be Customers coming into the store that cost you money.

Don't advertise to them, don't promote to them, don't encourage them to come in. If they cost you money, why do you want them in the door?

Q. On the other hand, there may be some really good Customers who might abandon you and you don't want to lose them.

A. Absolutely. If you go into the average supermarket, you stand in line at the checkout, which is the biggest hassle. You have little old ladies with a handful of coupons buying $14.00 worth of groceries and turning in $13.98 worth of coupons. You've got a person standing behind them with a $250 order getting all upset and frustrated, saying, "Why am I doing this?" That's what they don't understand.

I would advocate having special lines, but if you're going to survive in the future, you're really talking about reallocating the space in the store. Putting the store together the way the shopper wants it, not the way the buyer has organized it. It all goes back to the focus of the organization. Today, most supermarkets are focused on buying; they are not focused on selling.

I want to figure out the group of Customers I want to serve and I want to identify those Customers and I want to serve those Customers.

Q. Once you identify Customers, do you think direct mail is a more efficient means of reaching them than, say, newspaper advertising?

A. Newspaper advertising is mass advertising, and I'm looking for individualized advertising. I want to talk to specific Customers. I would make the argument that if you have a $250 Customer, your store manager's time may be better spent getting in his car and going out to pick that person up and bringing him to the store and letting him shop than standing around trying to watch people mop up the floor. That takes you back to focusing on Customers and their value. Most organizations don't know what a Customer is worth to them.

Q. We have a good example of an industry that does keep track of Customers in Atlantic City with the casinos. They know the play of all the gamblers who go in there.

A. It makes sense for a casino to send a limo out to pick somebody up at the airport and bring them to the casino because they'll make money off of it.

Supermarkets are going to have to do exactly the same thing.

Q. So the casinos would be a good model because they serve a lot of people but focus on the ones that really count. Are there any examples of supermarkets that do a good job of that?

A. Of course not. If there were, they would already be modeled. It's a herd instinct. The first guy will do this and then everyone will jump in line and try to follow him.

Dominick's in Chicago has identified six types of Shoppers or Shoppers' stores. They've stocked the stores differently, they promote differently, they have different communication systems to the people who shop in those stores. They're only steps away from getting down to one-on-one marketing. I think that's where the supermarket business is headed.

Q. What do you think about frequent buyer programs and rewarding Customers on the amount of their purchases?

A. I think the problem with frequent shopper programs is that you're rewarding them with things that can be replicated very easily. What they have got to do is rethink what a frequent Shopper program is worth. What do people really want? Consumers will tell you they want low prices, but low prices are the standard of the game. The question is, what makes a good shopping experience? People don't mind paying high prices IF they feel like there's a value there. If they're getting something that's a pleasant experience.

The question supermarket owners must ask themselves is, "Can a traditional supermarket compete with the logistical systems that Wal-Mart has created?" Over time, can you really get to where they are? My answer is, I don't think you can.

Q. What part do manufacturers play in this?

A. The supermarket doesn't really care what brand anybody buys. All they want to know is, did Customers buy in the category and did I make any money? What happens is when you get into frequent shopper programs, everybody wants to take it down to the SKU (stock keeping unit) level. That's because it's important to the manufacturer. It is not terribly important to the retailer. All the retailer wants to know is, did you buy in the coffee category and how much did you spend? The supermarket's view of how the supermarket operates as opposed to the manufacturer's view is dramatically different. Part of the problem with frequent shopper programs in the past is they have essentially been built for the manufacturer, not for the retailer. Citi-Corp POS (point of sale) died because they drowned in data.

If the manufacturer looks at it the way the retailer does, who wants to drive up sales in a particular category in a particular store and make more money, then they can work together. But if the manufacturer doesn't care about category sales, but brand share, then there's no real reason for the retailer to cooperate unless the manufacturer puts money in the retailer's pocket to compensate for the difference.

The real issue comes down to this: There are two supermarkets in the same community. Both have the same products, both have the same prices, essentially. How do they differentiate themselves and how do they compete? Do they compete by promoting a particular brand of mayonnaise, when the guy down the street has the same product at the same price, or do they compete with unique marketing programs that are not manufacturer driven?

Q. Supermarket owners may say that since the margins are so low in their industry, they can't afford to spend a lot of money wooing their best Customers. Is that a valid assumption on their part?

A. Supermarkets now are giving the same promotional deals to everybody. They're giving the same service to everybody. They are not differentiating between good Customers and bad Customers. Right now, most supermarkets don't know who their good Customers are. They don't know what they're worth, what their value is to them over time, and as a result, they don't know whether they invest against them or not. But when you look at average margins across everyone and across all categories and across the store, it makes no sense.

Claridge Casino Hotel

——————————■——————————

"There was a time," says Robert Renneisen, president of Atlantic City's Claridge Casino Hotel, "when a casino host kept the names of his best Customers in a notebook that fitted inside his pocket. When he wanted those folks to come back, he simply opened the notebook and called them. All we've done today is automate that system. Instead of a notebook in the pocket, we have a database on computers with nearly 400,000 names. And we know more about those 400,000 than the host did about the few hundred he carried in the notebook in his pocket...."

The art of direct marketing and Customer service reaches its zenith in Atlantic City casinos, where there is a relatively stable number of people who come back again and again and again ad profitum.

Casinos can tell you not only these Customers' names, addresses, and phone numbers but also what games they play, how many hours they spend at each game, how much they wager, and what they won or lost.

One of the most successful direct marketing programs is at work at Atlantic City's Claridge Casino Hotel. They took the handicap of being "Atlantic City's smallest casino" and converted it into their major asset with the slogan "Because smaller is friendlier."

We interviewed president Robert Renneisen in his Claridge office, asking how they track their Customers. Renneisen: "We have a matrix approach. We not only track what they spend, we track what we did to bring them here. It's not enough to simply know how much people spend in the casino, you have to look at what it costs you to bring them here so we can keep our margin in some sort of sequence. If someone comes by bus or car, that's a different cost than sending a jet to bring them here."

Q: Do Customers know how much they have to spend to receive special rewards?

A. No. There was a time when you came in, spent your money, and received goodies that went into a "bank account" you could use whenever you wanted. But that soon became unresponsive to the dynamics of the business. You wound up spending money to reward someone today for something they did a year ago. Today we do *not* tell the Customer what they will receive. But they have a "feel" for how much time they need to play and how much they have to spend to receive benefits. We track them with their personalized CompCard Gold. Whenever they play, they show the card or insert it in the slot machines. They know if they use the card, something good will happen to them. We sort all our data five or six times a month. The Customer might receive an invitation for a free room, for show tickets, for parties, for free drawings. They all have expiration dates. But every offer depends on the cost of the promotion versus the value of the Customer.

Q: But don't all other casinos do what you are doing? They also keep a database of their Customers, what they spend, how often they come. . . .

A. Right. But how do you USE that data? There's a hundred incentives you can use to bring back the Customer. But if it costs you more than it should, you have to change. And if you change, does that affect the Customer's loyalty? You must look at direct marketing as a tool that allows you to spend your marketing dollars more efficiently. The Customer doesn't care what he gets or why. They care if you forget them.

Q: But there has to be a relationship between cost and return.

A. Absolutely. Whether you're talking about a rebate at your car dealer or a sale on peas in the grocery store or a free roll of quarters at the casino.

One worry you always have is, how will the guy down the street compete with you?

I would rather compete with someone who's smart and knows what they're doing than someone who raises the ante so high you know they can't keep it up and it will cost a lot of money.

It's like a gasoline price war. Are we going to let them take away our Customers and then hope they come back? There's a balance involved. As soon as you throw the balance out of kilter, you may capture some business you wouldn't have had—but it's a false assumption to think you bought loyalty. All you bought is business. When the status quo returns, the customer returns to their original decision-making values.

Q: How do you find your Customers?

A. Ten years ago it was as simple as looking for household incomes or buying a gold credit card list. Today it's far more complicated. So we position ourselves as different than our competitors. And we are. We're smaller. So the only way we succeed is to NOT compete head-to-head with all the other casinos. We're the alternative. Now it's true there are only a certain percentage who like that approach. Fine. We say that segment is big enough for us. Then we look at lists for new Customers who are like our current Customers. And not just demographics. We also do geographics, psychographics, lifestyle indicators—different techniques we developed in-house. We put all these new lists through screens to filter out names to make sure we come up with a series of hits that match who we want. We merge/purge these new names against our own list. We assume if we're on the money and in the right geographic market, we should see a high percentage of our present Customers on these new lists. If we don't, we dump the list because it's not valuable.

Q: When you see how successful you are with your sophisticated direct marketing, do you wonder why other noncasino businesses don't use this same approach?

A. Why department stores, supermarkets—any business that has a high volume of Customers and draws from the same universe—why they don't do database marketing is beyond me. It's a lot more cost-effective. I'd rather put coupons in the hands of 20 percent of my best customers than buy four pages of the local newspaper every Sunday.

Q: Since every casino has its own databases and sophisticated marketing, what makes the Claridge different?

A. You have to carve out a special niche. You might have the best deal. Or you might have Customers who want to go to a specific hotel like the Taj Mahal or Caesars because they want to play where the high rollers play. Or they like the restaurants. Or it's easier to park their car. What you need is a trade-off between value and quality acceptable to the market niche you want. We believe that service and friendliness—how you treat the customer—are more important than mailing incentives.

Q: When the Taj Mahal first opened, the experts said the first place to go out of business would be the Claridge because you were smaller and therefore weaker.

A. That's right. But we said our goal was to go after those who *wanted* a smaller, friendlier place. It simply didn't make sense that we would be hurt by the Taj Mahal opening when you think about it. If people wanted to go to a bigger, fancier place they already had ten other choices in town. The bigger casinos already here were the ones that should have been worried. The year the Taj opened we were only one of two casinos in town that increased market share. The media wrote about the Taj being the biggest—but, in the same story, they wrote about the Claridge being the smallest. If there were eight column inches about the Taj, there were sixteen column inches about the smallest place in town. We got a million dollars' worth of free press. It was the David and Goliath story all over again. . . .

Q: It's one thing to have a slogan that says "smaller is friendlier"—but how do you have your staff believe in this philosophy?

A. Our research said Customers like the Claridge because we're friendly. We're smaller. But we're friendlier. Once we established that positioning statement we had to live up to it. You begin by telling the staff that we know what our Customers want. We know they want a homier, friendlier atmosphere. They want a place where they're greeted by name. People normally expect good service from a hotel or casino. Now when you tell them you're friendlier, you raise the expectations. You made a promise. If you don't deliver, it's far worse than never to have made the promise in the first place. We have a three-point program. One: honesty. We tell our staff that friendliness is a way of making sure their jobs will be there for them tomorrow. Two: We invest money in training programs—even if we have to take money out of our marketing programs. Three: We treat our employees the same way we expect them to treat our guests. Honesty, training, reinforcement, and one more: the Golden Rule. Soon it becomes self-policing. We have less turnover. We have a higher percentage of employees here from the day we opened than any other place in town. The employees themselves won't tolerate substandard performance. When that happens, you've got an engine cooking.

"You have to look at your data as a tool that allows you to spend your marketing dollars more efficiently," says Renneisen, "because that's all it is. The Customer doesn't care how he gets what he gets or why. What he cares is that he does get something and in a way that makes him feel good."

Can't do that with a notebook in your pocket. Can do that with the accurate database marketing like Renneisen uses at Atlantic City's Claridge Casino Hotel. Where "smaller is friendlier."

CASE HISTORY
The Greenwich Workshop

———■———

"We are not in the limited edition art business. We are in the art and visual entertainment business."
— DAVE USHER, CHAIRMAN, THE GREENWICH WORKSHOP

Suppose your company makes widgets.

You receive an order for 70,000 widgets at $325 apiece.

You are ecstatic. You rush in to your boss, and he compliments you on getting the order. But then he says, "I know you received an order for 70,000 widgets. But we are not going to make 70,000 widgets. We are only going to make 57,500 widgets. We are not going to fill the other orders. In fact, we are going to destroy the widget mold so we can never make another widget in the future."

What is your boss doing?

Well, if your boss is Dave Usher and your product is not widgets but limited edition art prints, he may be making a shrewd strategic marketing decision.

Dave Usher is chairman of The Greenwich Workshop, a leading publisher of limited edition art prints. Greenwich takes original art from its more than thirty artists and makes state-of-the-art print reproductions in limited editions, each signed by the artist. Greenwich specializes in representation and narrative art. Most of its artists paint western, wildlife, aviation, and other realistic scenes.

"There is a definite niche that we have," says Dave Usher. "It is heartland America."

Usher believes that in the case of limited edition art, less might be better. "If I had a crystal ball and could see what the total market demand was for a particular print, then I would print 80 percent of that total. That means there is another 20 percent of prospective purchasers who want the image and are probably willing to pay more for it."

In the case of an upcoming print by popular Greenwich artist Bev Doolittle, Greenwich is printing a limited edition of 57,500 prints even though Usher envisions demand for another 10,000 to 15,000 of the print. Because the demand for prints from a popular artist can exceed the supply, Greenwich runs the risk of disappointing gallery owners who want to meet the excess demand. But Usher says that Greenwich has to accept the possible wrath of some dealers to ensure continuing demand for its products.

Partly because of this pent-up demand, the price of the prints of many Greenwich artists in the secondary market (the market created after the initial printing) has greatly appreciated through the years. But Greenwich doesn't promote the fact that its prints may appreciate in value. Usher explains that advertising "print appreciation" is a two-edged sword:

"In the art market prices go up but they also come down. If you have people who buy prints because they feel that they are going to appreciate significantly, they become disenchanted if the prints don't rise quickly in value, and they don't want to deal with you anymore. We want someone who looks at the print, really likes the image, and puts a frame on it, hangs it up, and enjoys it. These people are not going to become mad at you. They are going to want to have more product and more information about particular artists."

Today, The Greenwich Workshop sells limited edition prints through a network of 1,100 independent retail galleries in the United States and Canada. And business is booming. Greenwich is expanding into Europe and looking at the possibility of selling its prints in Asia.

But business wasn't always this good. When Dave Usher started

The Greenwich Workshop with two artists and a car in 1972, the total retail sales of the largest print publisher at the time were $2.7 million. Today, Greenwich can achieve $12 million in sales at wholesale on one print alone.

Greenwich achieved this success the old-fashioned way, satisfying one gallery owner at a time. Dave Usher says, "One of our gallery owners had a flood in Kansas City several years ago with eight feet of water in his gallery. We helped him replace his inventory."

The Greenwich Workshop communicates with its gallery owners through sales representatives, letters, dealer conventions, and employees on the road visiting the network of galleries. "We just finished a seminar and people came out feeling they were a part of a family," Usher says.

In addition to maintaining a good relationship with its artists, Greenwich also believes in giving substantial amounts to good causes. In recent years it has supported projects that benefit American Indians, the Smithsonian Museum, the National Wildlife Federation, and Paul Newman's Hole In the Wall Gang Camp, among others. The Greenwich Workshop also contributes to local causes through its dealer network. To date, Greenwich has raised more than $3 million for charitable causes.

Although Greenwich started out as a limited edition print company, it recently has expanded its product line as well as geographic horizons. Greenwich is now producing books, posters, furniture, videos, and porcelain. Usher explains why Greenwich has expanded its product line.

"If you look at the walls of a home or an office there are only so many spaces you can hang two-dimensional prints. But there are a lot of other places you can put books and you can put figurines and you can put furniture." Usher says the furniture and porcelain and some of the books Greenwich produces will be in limited editions.

He says that The Greenwich Workshop has to expand its product offerings to grow as a company. He cites an example given by Ted Levitt from Harvard University: "The railroads in the 1950s and 1960s ran into problems. They were looking at trucks transporting goods and they didn't do anything because they said, 'We're in the railroad business.' Then they looked at aviation and they said, 'That's not us. We're in the railroad business.' They should have realized they were *not* in the railroad business. They were in the transportation business.

"Similarly, I look at what has built us a business over the years and it has been the limited edition prints. We still have a lot of tracks and a lot of engines in our limited edition print business. I look at us today as in the art and visual entertainment business. We present the dealer and ultimately the retail Customer an environment of an artist's work. If you want to have the original, if you want to have a book, if you want to have a print, poster, a porcelain, furniture, video, we are going to be able to provide that whole artistic environment to you."

Usher believes the main difference between the 1990s and the 1980s is that in this decade "You can't survive if you are mediocre. You need to do new things, you have to be in touch with your Customer." He sees difficult times ahead for retailers, but believes The Greenwich Workshop will be a "flag" his dealers can rally around.

What is Dave Usher doing?

He is making sure *his Customers* (the retailers) become his Advocates. They sell all the products he brings to them.

In turn, the retailer's Customers become Advocates. They return again and again to buy quality artistic products, and they also tell their friends about The Greenwich Workshop.

By concentrating on keeping his retailers at the top of the Loyalty Ladder, he gives those retailers the tools to bring their Customers to the top as well.

Ten Ways to Convert Customers into Clients

—————————■—————————

1. **Advance notice of . . .** *everything.* You mail much of your advertising third class because of the money saved. Not to these folks. They receive everything first class because they are your first-class Customers. Their names are separate and apart from the rest. When a sale is coming up, they are mailed not only first class but also earlier. (*And yes, you tell them. Otherwise, how do they know?*)

Having a fashion show? They're the first to know.

A new line arrives at your business? They're the first to know.

You make changes in store layout, departments, personnel? They're the first to know.

2. **Special promotions for them alone.** Everyone expects you to have sales at sale times of the year: Washington's Birthday, the Friday after Thanksgiving, fall and winter closeouts. But these folks have SPECIAL sales. For them alone. Unscheduled. They just suddenly . . . happen. And you tell them, "This is a special sale for special Customers. We are not advertising or promoting this to our entire mailing list. Only to certain customers."

Your response will increase dramatically because everyone wants to feel they are "special." And you tell these folks they are because . . . *they are.*

3. Things you normally charge a small service fee for are theirs . . . free. If you mail purchases, you usually charge.

If you gift wrap, you usually charge.

If you send something overnight, you usually charge.

Not for Clients. They receive services you normally charge for at no charge.

(*And yes, you tell them. Otherwise, how do they know?*)

4. Gift certificates from noncompeting stores. This is a very special treat for your Clients and very easy to find. You go to other businesses in/near your own business and tell them you are willing to send a gift certificate for their merchandise to your Customers. It must be good value, however. You will not accept the "Take $50 off on your next $500 purchase." It must be given with NO strings.

If they are not willing, they don't understand how to do more business for their business. Cross them off the list. Move on to the next. What you are doing: providing them with excellent Customers for a small consideration. If they don't understand that, don't worry. Someone else will be renting their place in a year or so.

5. Free gifts at unannounced times of the year. This is very effective—and cannot be overdone. In the morning mail, your Client receives a gift certificate for some wanted item. Free. All the Client has to do is come to your business and pick it up by a certain date.

We gave away canvas carry bags with our store's name that sold for $10. Free—if our prospective Client came to the store within the next week. We gave away more than 100.

BUT . . . here's what happened:

a. We had "traveling billboards" throughout the community. Whenever our Clients went shopping, there was our name prominently displayed on the canvas shopping bags.

b. Almost without exception, they bought something else when they picked up their free bags. Remember, these are very good Customers (they're on the way to becoming Clients). They don't want to take advantage of you. They appreciate the gift and "While I'm here, I thought of something else I could use . . ."

When we added up the cost of the 100 bags against the additional, unexpected, would-not-have-been-made purchases, we were way ahead. And the Customer was reaching for the Client rung of the Loyalty Ladder.

5. What they want is what they get. Most Customers feel there are limits to what they can ask for. Overnight alterations. Same-day delivery. A prompt return call from the person not available. Customers don't expect any of these service because they don't receive them. But Clients—ahhh, what they want is what they get.

Most requests CAN be honored by simply ignoring the rules that say they can't be honored. Douglas McCellant, a behavioral scientist, says, "An integral aspect of the nature of a high achiever is they respond to contingencies and adapt their style." That's you. If you want Clients.

The more glaring error is when you promise but don't deliver.

We went to the Hyatt in Chicago, and employees wore "Yes, I Can!" buttons. We were hurrying for a plane and asked the receptionist if the hotel would mail some slides for us. They were packaged, addressed, ready to go. She said they would ("Yes, I can!") and asked me to take the package to the bell captain. We did. The person in charge said to me, "We don't do that." I said the receptionist told me they did and I was in a hurry and . . .

"Sorry, that's not our job," he replied.

I suggested he take off his "Yes, I Can!" pin and replace it with another saying "No, I Can't!"

(P.S. We did bring the package back to the receptionist, who apologized and said she'd handle it. She did.)

6. You're available when they want you. I like the fact that my insurance agent lists his home phone in the telephone directory. If I need him for an emergency (which always occurs after business hours), I can call him at home. We returned to our store after hours because someone had forgotten to pick up a pair of altered pants needed for an important meeting that night. This occurred rarely, but in this instance we automatically transformed a Customer into a Client.

8. The "extra" service that sets you apart. Not much different than advertising expert Rosser Reeves's USP—Unique Selling Proposition. If all quality hotels are alike, what makes the difference?

When I travel to Switzerland and stay overnight in New York, I book a room at the Drake hotel. They are tied in to a Swiss hotel program, which means they take my bags and put them on the plane! A friend told me of this on my last trip to Switzerland, and you know where I booked my overnight room in Manhattan. I became an INSTANT Client.

9. They know who I am. It was Dale Carnegie who first wrote about the importance of calling people by their name, saying that the average man is more interested in his own name than in all the other names on earth put together. Makes you feel important. When I check into the Four Seasons hotel or stop at the Halekulani in Honolulu and pick up the phone, the operator says, "Yes, Mr. Raphel, can I help you?" Yes, I know my name must appear on a computer somewhere, but I'm impressed.

Supermarkets try to impress on their checkers the importance of saying thank-you to Customers and saying their names, which they know if the Customer paid by check or credit card. Most Customers are amazed to hear their name. They don't associate the fact they gave you the identification themselves.

I left Harry's Bar in Florence, Italy, and as I walked out the door, the bartender called out, "Have a good day, Mr. Raphel, and please come back again."

I was startled. It took me a few minutes to realize my waiter had given my credit card to the bartender who rang up the check. But how many people have I told THAT story to?

10. Loyalty Programs (step one). Converting Customers into Clients means giving them special recognition. One way: Establish a special club for them alone. They qualify by the number of dollars they spend with you. This gives them very specific benefits.

Once they become VERY special Customers, you take them into Loyalty Programs. (*See "Ten Ways to Convert Clients into Advocates" at the end of the "Clients" section.*)

Part 4

THE CLIENT

Introduction
to Clients

—————■—————

Cli-ent / kli-ent/ *n. Someone who regularly shops at your place of business.*

What makes a Customer a Client? How do you have Customers climb up to that rung on the Ladder where they "buy everything that you have to sell that they could possibly use"?

One-sentence guideline: Make Them Feel Important.

Of the thousands of hotels we've visited through the years, one of our favorites is Honolulu's Kahala Hilton. One story tells why:

We had checked into a competing hotel and were very unhappy with the service and the room. We called the Kahala, said we were unhappy with our accommodations, and asked if they had a room available.

"Just a minute, Mr. Raphel, and I'll give you a reservation," said the operator.

It seemed only a few seconds later that the operator came back and said, "We'd be happy to accommodate you, Mr. Raphel. I know you usually stay in room 318." (I do? How did they know that? Mighty fast computer.) "And that room is not available, but will 418 be all right? It's the room right above."

"Uh, you bet, sure, and how. Terrific."

She quoted me the rate and we taxied over.

On arrival, a few minutes later, the registration clerk said, "Mr. Raphel, the reservation clerk made a slight mistake. She forgot that the room she offered had a lanai [balcony], which is $25 more."

"Oh, well," I said.

"But we quoted you the lower rate, and that's all you will pay."

We went to the room, and there was a tray of assorted island fruits—pineapple, guava, mango, papaya—and a message from the manager: "Sorry your vacation did not begin well. From now on you'll have a great time!"

Wait, it's not over yet.

And, every day of our stay, there was another fresh fruit plate, ensuring we would have a good time that day.

I skipped a rung and quickly went from a Customer to a Client.

A Lands' End catalog customer called for a last-minute Christmas present for her brother. What was his shirt-sleeve size? The customer was not sure. The operator suggested that perhaps he had ordered from them before. She checked the records and there was the size. It was shipped the next morning. Customer became a Client from that moment on.

One of the best stories we know about a Customer becoming a Client was told to us by Feargal Quinn, whom we interviewed earlier in this book. He practices what he calls "the Boomerang Theory," claiming, "It's not too difficult to bring in the Customer the first time. What you have to do is have them come back again."

Here's what gave him that idea: As a young man he worked at his father's holiday camp called Red Island, just outside Skerries on the coast of north County Dublin. The time was post–World War II, and people were looking for a good—but inexpensive—vacation.

When they bought their week's vacation at Red Island, they paid a bill that included everything: travel, meals, accommodations, entertainment—everything. From the moment they arrived till the moment they left, the Customers paid . . . nothing.

Feargal quickly learned that "no matter how hard we worked to give them a good time, we would not increase our profit from their stay. So we had to work our tails off to create the best holiday experience they ever had because *we wanted them to come back next year!*"

What was he doing? Bringing the Customer up to the next level of the Ladder to be a . . . Client.

If a Client is "someone who buys everything you have to sell that they could possibly use," how do they know what ELSE you have to sell besides that which they came in to buy?

You have to tell them.

You have to practice AFTO—which means Ask For The Order.

If a Client calls or comes to your business and asks for an item and you sell the Client only that item and then stop, you are a clerk. Not a salesperson. Not a consultant. Not a trusted adviser. In fact, you have done your Client a disservice. You have not completed the sale. You have not encouraged the Client to consider other items to use in addition to or in fulfillment of that which they asked for initially. *But you have to Ask For The Order.*

Feargal writes, "When a Customer asks for a half pound of bacon we say, 'Will you have a few sausages and a black pudding to go with that, ma'am?'"

We found that when someone bought a suit in our stores and we suggested a shirt, tie, and socks, he bought more often than not and was pleased we made the suggestion.

Consider the alternative: He goes home and suddenly discovers he does not have the right shirt or right tie or right socks. Is he happy you did not suggest these items? Or mad?

A caveat about Clients: They cannot be lumped into one demographic, geographic, or psychographic pile. Your business carries high-priced merchandise. You want to promote a specific credit card. Obviously it is American Express. But when American Express asked its cardholders where they most wanted to use their cards, it was surprised to find K Mart and Sears atop the list. A recent Gallup poll found that more than half of Customers surveyed nationwide said they shop at both discount stores and conventional department stores.

Said one person, "The perfect mall has Nordstrom at one end and Wal-Mart at the other."

Whatever the type of business you own, you will really prosper only when your Customers become Clients. And the way to start that process is by establishing rewards.

Reward!

———■———

"The rewarded customer buys, multiplies, and comes back."
—Dr. Michael LeBoeuf

You can have the best merchandise, the nicest personnel, the most comfortable environment, and you will have a steady flock of Customers. But when you take the extra step, when you find the special "hot button" that really appeals to your Customers, when you give your Customers something extra, then you're on the road to developing Clients.

Story!

There's an old joke about two friends, Bill and Pete.

Bill goes to Pete to borrow some money, and Pete turns him down.

Incensed, Bill says, "How can you turn me down? When you were having troubles with your wife, wasn't I the one who brought the two of you back together? When your daughter wanted to get into college, wasn't I the one who wrote the best recommendation? When you wanted an introduction to sell your product to the biggest firm in town, didn't I set up the appointment and you made the sale?"

Pete thought about that for a while, nodded his head in agreement, and then said, "But what have you done for me lately?"

WAYS TO SAY "THANK-YOU"

For forty years, we owned and operated a retail clothing mall named Gordon's Alley in Atlantic City.

Every Thanksgiving we gave away a present to everyone who shopped in our store.

The reactions varied. Some said, "What's this for?" Or, "Did I buy that?"

We answered, "It's Thanksgiving. It seems the right time of the year to say 'thanks' for shopping with us. I'm sure we say 'thank-you' every time you shop. I hope we do. But it just seems right at Thanksgiving that we tell you again how much we appreciate your business. This is just a small way of saying thanks."

In our buying trips for the store we would look for a great little gift item with perceived value. "How much do you think this is worth?" was the question we asked ourselves. If the answer was ten times more than the cost, we chose it.

We made sure it was *not* merchandise we sold in our store. Otherwise Perceived Value became Real Value.

Example: A supermarket ran an ad giving away violets to every customer at Easter. Good move. Until you opened to an inside page and found you could also buy the violets in the store for 99 cents. Does that mean the customer was only worth 99 cents?

A reverse of that is what we did on Memorial Day. We contacted a local florist and placed an order for 500 miniature clay pots with two-inch-high baby trees. Everyone who shopped in the store received a tree to take home and plant. The cost of each tree was under a dollar. The value received from the astonished Customer was impossible to measure. How much was the plant worth? One dollar? Three dollars? Five dollars? Answer: Whatever the Customer *thought* it was worth. Which was always much higher than our actual cost.

One Christmas, through a friend, we contacted the mayor of Norfolk Island in the Pacific Ocean nearly two thousand miles from the nearest point in Australia. Norfolk is famous for three reasons:

1. Its postage stamps. The worldwide sale of these collector items to philatelists pays for municipal services in lieu of taxes. (Now that's an idea!)

2. The final home of the descendants of the *Bounty*. (Remember Fletcher Christian and his mates throwing Captain Bligh overboard?)

3. The origin of the Norfolk pine, thought by many to be the ideal Christmas tree.

We had the mayor of Norfolk Island write a note to "The Customer of Gordon's in Atlantic City" in which he told the history of the Norfolk pine.

We reduced the letter and placed it in a small pot with a miniature Norfolk pine purchased from our local florist. We placed an advance order for 1,000 trees for the Christmas season. We felt this would last us the five selling weeks from Thanksgiving to Christmas.

We ran out the first week!

Everyone wanted the miniature Norfolk pine tree. We had to airfreight a special shipment of a few thousand more trees to meet the demand. Friends told friends who told friends, and all came to shop in our store because of the free little Norfolk pine Christmas tree.

We never told anyone we were giving away the trees. We never advertised the fact. But the word quickly spread. And more and more Customers arrived simply because of the "free tree."

The Customer who continues to buy from you is the Customer who knows you appreciate their business. Because you tell them. And reward them.

THE GREATEST BUSINESS SECRET IN THE WORLD

Remember the scene in the western movies where the camera panned to a close-up of the poster of the bank robber? At the top in big black letters was the word WANTED! Then the name. And then, in even bigger and blacker letters, the word REWARD!

The reason was simple: Offer someone a reward for doing something and the response will be far greater than if you simply tell them you want something.

You want your salespeople to bring in more sales? You'll have them bring in more sales if you give them a **reward!**

You want more Customers to come to your store or buy your product? They will come and buy more quickly if you give them a **reward!**

We call this sales technique the Psychology of the Second Interest. Here's what it means:

You can have someone buy something you want them to buy if you **reward** them with something else they want to buy.

It's far easier to make a sale if you stop concentrating on the product *you* want to sell and, instead, offer something else *the customer wants.*

Which is why there are toys in Crackerjack boxes.

Which is why new business openings feature a free Jeep and a Caribbean cruise on the front page of the ad just below the words GRAND OPENING.

Which is why Procter & Gamble will give you $5 toward the latest Disney videotape if you buy one of its products and send in the box top.

People buy better, faster, and quicker when you offer a reward.

THE FIVE REASONS PEOPLE DO NOT BUY

What are some of the reasons people do *not* buy? If we knew them, would they help you come up with a reward that would make them *want* to buy?

Here are the five most common reasons why people say they do *not* buy what you have for sale. In these difficult times you hear them used more often than before.

Your assignment is to Free the Negative Five! Break their chains! If you know what they are and how they work, you can cast them aside.

1. No need.
2. No money.
3. No hurry.
4. No desire.
5. No trust.

Let's take them one at a time and see how we can overcome these no-no-no-no-nos.

***1*. No need.** Joe Karbo took in $10 million because he answered his Customers' needs. He offered them a book titled *The Lazy Man's Way to Riches.* Most people figure you have to work hard to make a million dollars. After all, less than one-half of 1 percent of the U.S. population are millionaires. But look, here's advertising copy that said if (1) you were lazy and (2) you wanted to be rich, read this book.

He offered his Customers a reward.

2. No money. We once sold clothing door-to-door. When Customers told us they had no money, we said, "No problem. Just give us a dollar a week on your bill and we will pick it up from you every week." This doubled our volume the first year. We no longer picked up just the $1 on their account, we sold them new merchandise as well. And we told them what we would offer them in a weekly mailer with the items we would bring them *next* week.

It is a proven, guaranteed, never-fail fact that the more ways you give Customers to buy, the more they will buy. Cash. Charge. Credit. Layaway. Having "no money" is one of the easiest not-to-buy reasons to eliminate. Your reward: You don't pay for everything at once. A little at a time. Affordable.

***3*. No hurry.** Franklin Mint offered a limited number of reproductions of classic books bound in leather and numbered. When that number was reached, too-late Customers received their money back with a "Sorry, you didn't order in time" note. Will they order *faster* next time? Oh, yes!

The Greenwich Workshop offers signed, limited-edition prints from famous American artists to their 1,000-plus distributors across the country. In the past, as soon as a new print was made available, it was oversold. Now dealers no longer write in what they want. They call and fax their orders. They know if they don't hurry, they have no inventory. No inventory, no sales, no reward.

I just received a pop-up calendar in the mail from a company that wants to see if I'm interested in pop-ups. They were very clever to make sure I didn't take advantage of them, since the calendar they sent me was for last year. Their thinking: If I wanted calendars for this year, I'd have to order them. My thinking: I threw out the calendar. But if the sample had been for *this* year, I would have kept it on my desk because it was current. However, no calendar was on my desk because they offered me no reward.

4. No desire. Dr. Ernest Dichter, head of the Institute of Motivational Research, said that when people come to a restaurant they are hungrier for *recognition* than they are for food.

Writer Robert Ringer says the best-selling headline he ever wrote was to promote Douglas Casey's bestselling book, *Crisis Investing.* Wrote Ringer: WHY YOU WILL PROBABLY LOSE EVERYTHING IN THE COMING DEPRESSION.

The book sold 400,000 copies and was on *The New York Times* best-seller list for fifteen weeks.

But when you create the desire, you must also supply the answer as he did in his book.

Another way to create desire: Offer a reward. One of the above-mentioned Greenwich Workshop retailers put together a Member-Get-A-Member program—a $25 gift certificate for every new Customer a present Customer brought to the store. In the first month, five of the new Customers made purchases totaling $9,204. Cost of the gift certificates and printing: $300.

Story: German submarines were destroying Allied ships in World War I. The Allies called in a consultant. He said to heat the ocean to 180 degrees, which would force the Germans to surface the submarines and they then could be attacked.

The navy thought this was a great idea and asked the consultant, "But how do we heat the ocean to that temperature?" Said the consultant, "I'm a consultant. I gave you the answer. You work out the details."

One way to create a desire is to appeal to someone's city, country, or favorite sporting team. Any kind of tie-in generates increased bottom-line results.

There is a classic story of the Polish veteran from the town of Dryna who returned from World War II and, because of the strain of combat, was mute. No one could get him to talk. One day he was in a veterans' hospital listening to a radio broadcast of a soccer game between his hometown Dryna and a traditional competitive city. At the end of a hard-fought battle, his team scored the winning goal. At that exact moment he jumped out of his bed and yelled, "We won!"

And never said anything again until the day he died.

5. No trust. Ringer also says the "most unsuccessful ad I ever wrote" was headlined AN OPEN LETTER TO HOWARD HUGHES. But the product had absolutely nothing to do with Howard Hughes. No reward for reading.

It was a gimmick to have someone read the ad. And after they read the ad and found nothing in the ad that dealt with Howard Hughes, they stopped reading and stopped trusting.

A company in Dublin sent out a direct mail piece offering laundry service. The company's reputation was good, its service excellent, but it received a pathetically small response to its letter. Oh, the name of the company was "Swastika Laundry Ltd.," with a swastika symbol on their stationery. No amount of explaining that a "swastika" means "good luck" and is merely "a symbol in the form of a Greek cross" could develop trust in their readers. The symbol was stigmatized.

By Freeing the Negative Five you will be better equipped to reward your current Customers. Says Roger A. Enrico, president of Pepsico Worldwide Beverages: "If you are totally Customer focused and you deliver the services your Customers want, everything else will follow."

Free the Negative Five!

Offer a Reward!

Added Value

———■———

We persuaded the owner of the Ethan Allen furniture store in Maryland to have his delivery people make one more trip to the truck after the furniture was in place. If it was a dining room set, they returned with a dozen roses in a vase. If it was a lounge chair, they brought back a magazine rack. If it was a bedroom set, they brought back two pillows. All at no charge.

Soon they became known as the furniture store that delivered more than expected. They were practicing Added Value.

Added Value is the unexpected, unadvertised, unasked-for "extra."

It is the little "extra" given to the Customer as a thank-you after the sale is completed. Unexpected, unadvertised, and unasked for . . . but often remembered longer than the purchase of the high-ticket item.

I recently bought a few thousand dollars' worth of carpet. I felt what I bought was fine and attractive. (Well, I did have to vacuum the little pieces left over. . . .)

BUT . . . what if the installers had left a couple of bottles of carpet stain remover with a thank-you note?

Would my reaction be that I was pleased and satisfied and that I must tell someone?

Every automobile I bought in the past thirty years has never (that's N-E-V-E-R) resulted in a thank-you note from the salesman. (Except for the one I leased. Why is that?) Why not a gift certificate with a note saying, "The first washing and waxing is on me!" *Something* . . .

Why doesn't the mail order company where I buy my hundred-dollar shoes toss in a can of polish?

Why doesn't the barber who cuts my hair (a $20-plus tab) offer me a bottle of shampoo sold only in barber shops? The first one is free. And if I like it and want more, where is the only place I can find and buy it?

Why doesn't my travel agent have flowers waiting in my cabin for my expensive week's cruise?

Why didn't the appliance store where I spent thousands of dollars for a new refrigerator and stove deliver the refrigerator stocked with gourmet foods?

Why didn't the landlord have a bottle of champagne for my nephew when he moved into his new apartment?

Why didn't the TV store send over a couple of free videos when they delivered my new VCR?

Why didn't the salesman who delivered my new copy machine bring a dozen reams of paper with the thousand-dollar-plus machine?

Why don't lawyers send me attractive folders for the will they just drew? (OK, OK, forget the lawyers giving something free. . . .)

The list goes on and on. Whatever your business, there is something that relates to your business you should give away free to your Customer at the time of the sale. All they will do is make a decision to buy from you again in the future and tell their friends as well.

On the other hand . . .

I went to a restaurant and ordered dinner with some friends. Two of our entrées were not hot enough. We told the waitress, who apologized and reheated the food to our satisfaction. At the end of the meal she said, "I'm sorry for your inconvenience, and we want you to have complimentary coffee and dessert."

Yes, we have brought our friends there time and time again.

We had lunch at the American Express office in New York City. They ordered lunch from a caterer for just the four of us. It arrived soon after with a big selection of homemade cookies. "She always does that," said our hostess. "Every order comes with something free."

Why don't restaurants include something "free" when they deliver takeout orders? A piece of fruit. A sample of the cake they bake daily . . . *Something*.

I like the fact that the place where I buy my seafood includes a half-dozen lemons.

I like the fact that the place where I buy my annual firewood includes three boxes of kindling.

I like the fact that the place where I bring my photographic film gives me a mini-album with the finished prints.

When you consider that customers think all supermarkets are alike—they all sell food.

All banks are alike—they all sell financial products and services.

All clothing stores are alike—they all sell clothing.

All furniture stores are alike—they all sell furniture.

The thinking is as deep as the listings in the yellow pages.

BUT—what if one of these businesses did something different, separate, apart, and in front of the competition? Would you consider going back again and again not just as a Customer, but as a Client?

You bet. And how. Of course.

Try it. It's called . . . "Added Value."

"But Doesn't Everybody Do That?"

────────■────────

They tell the apocryphal story of the time Schmidt's beer wanted to capture a larger share of the market. The ad agency sent an account executive to tour the plant. He saw the huge vats, the raw ingredients, and then, in a separate room, men dressed in rubber suits using live steam to clean bottles.

"What are they doing?" he asked

"Why, they're cleaning the bottles with live steam," said his tour guide.

"Why?"

"To make sure the bottles are hygienically clean."

"Wow!" said the account executive, quickly scribbling the information down on his notepad.

"Why are you writing that down?" asked the guide. "Everybody does that."

"Really?" said the account executive, smiling. . . .

A short time later ads appeared in national magazines with the headline: WE CLEAN OUR BOTTLES WITH LIVE STEAM. The copy explained that this way the beer you drank came from these extra-clean bottles.

Soon, a competitor's ad said they *also* cleaned their bottles with live steam. And the beer drinker in the bar said, "Sure. After Schmidt's showed you how. . . ."

A visitor from Mars might think all people on Earth look alike. After all, they have two arms, two legs, two eyes, two ears, a nose, a mouth. . . . But each has individual characteristics that make them separate and apart from one another.

Each of us has individual strengths that we are not quick to use or talk about, or are even aware of. You may have an excellent memory, be an expert on Elizabethan literature, have an in-depth knowledge of baseball statistics. But because you enjoy doing what you are doing, you might think, "But doesn't everybody do that?" No, they don't.

No matter what product or service you sell, you are doing something that you think is ordinary, taken for granted, and "everybody does that"—but the customer doesn't know this. You have to tell them. And when you do, you position yourself as the maker or seller of the product or service that uses this unique technique.

I met a book dealer while doing a seminar and asked him the reason for his dramatic growth and success despite competition from the major chains in his town. "I guarantee the books you buy."

How's that again?

He has a sign in his bookstore saying he guarantees you will enjoy what you buy to read. If not, bring it back for a refund.

"But no one does that with books!" I said.

"Except me."

"And how many people bring books back?"

"Hardly any. But it makes them very comfortable making up their mind whether or not they should buy in the first place. From the day we started this, sales increased dramatically."

Another story: We were walking through the showroom of an Ethan Allen furniture store in Maryland and noticed a room where carpenters were working on furniture.

"Do you make the furniture here?" we asked.

"No," said owner Jim Mahler, "those are carpenters doing repair work on Ethan Allen wood furniture."

He explained that Ethan Allen gave a lifetime guarantee on all their wood pieces. The quality and workmanship were so good that if anything happened, the company would repair any defect.

"Wow," we said, remembering the beer story as we wrote it down on our notepad, "that's terrific."

And, on cue, Jim said, "But all Ethan Allen stores do that."

"Really?" we said, smiling, visualizing the ad that soon appeared saying, "Every piece of Ethan Allen wooden furniture is guaranteed for your lifetime!"

Yes, yes, yes, soon a competitor ran the same guarantee in its ad as well.

But the customer said, "Sure. After the other store did it first. . . ."

We're talking Perception here, folks, versus Reality. If you can position customers to perceive something about your store, they will accept it as reality.

Take the time one day to sit down and write down all the little services you do for your customers. You'll soon come up with a list you can use in your future advertising.

"Here's our 6-point Guarantee" (or whatever the number) and list them.

Yes, yes, much of your competition will then do the same thing. But you did it first!

What happens when you buy food at a supermarket, bring it home, and are not satisfied? The melon is too ripe, the meat has an unpleasant odor, the fish is too dry—whatever. You bring it back, and the owner/buyer/courtesy desk quickly takes it back and gives you credit for new merchandise.

BUT WHY DON'T THEY TELL YOU THEY WILL DO THAT?

"Because everybody does that," said one supermarket owner.

And then we tell the story of Publix supermarkets in Florida and Georgia, which run their guarantee in the store, on their bags, in their ads, and on their calling cards. Here's what it says:

OUR GUARANTEE

"We will never knowingly disappoint you. If, for any reason, your purchase does not give you complete satisfaction, the full purchase price will be cheerfully refunded immediately upon request. We have always believed that no sale is complete until the meal is eaten and enjoyed." And signed by the president of the company.

And so I call my mother vacationing in Florida and ask her where she does her food shopping.

"Publix," she says.

"Publix?" I ask. "But Mom, you have to go past three other super-markets to shop there. Why do you go the extra distance?"

"Didn't you know," she answered, "Publix guarantees all the food they sell."

"But Mom," I said, "ALL the food stores guarantee all the food they sell."

"Really?" she said. "So how come they don't say so?. . . "

And Publix winds up with a major share of the total food market in Florida. Just because of this guarantee? No. But, as an uncle once told me, "It couldn't hoit. . . ."

Positioning yourself as doing something "different"—even a per-ceived difference—can bring customers to you.

Good example: Saturday was a good day for our retail business, Gordon's Alley, to advertise, since most of our shops sold clothing and Saturday was a day off for many people, especially children. And so our advertising theme for the Saturday ad was, "If it's Saturday, it must be Gordon's Alley."

What did that mean?

Nothing.

Except in the Customer's mind.

After hundreds of exposures to this simple phrase, our Saturday business soon doubled that of any other day of the week.

Were we doing anything different on that day? No.

Were we offering something of great value on that day? No.

Couldn't someone say the other stores in town were also open on Saturday and "But everyday does that?" Sure.

But they didn't. We were the first to tell everyone that "If it's Satur-day, it must be Gordon's Alley."

And where did many Customers start their shopping each Saturday?

Right!

"Customer Service Doesn't Work Anymore . . . "

—————■—————

We had just finished a seminar in Phoenix for art gallery owners stressing Customer service. One of the businesswomen came up to us and said, "You know, Customer service doesn't work anymore."

"What?" we said and asked her to explain.

"Well, it used to be the answer, but no more," she said. "You see, Customer service brings the Customer in the first time. But Customer satisfaction brings them back."

Here's how it works:

Customer service is doing all the things you promise you will do. Delivering the deli tray on time, having the alterations finished when you say you will, not having to wait endlessly for the doctor when you come in for an appointment. Poet Robert Service said it well: "A promise made is a debt unpaid." That's service.

Customer satisfaction is making Customers so happy with your goods and services that they run around the community and bring more people to buy your goods and services. This satisfaction is a critical link to repeat and future business.

Richard Silipigni, vice-president of sales for CBS radio, examined the pants he picked up at his dry cleaners and noticed that a spot was not removed. He took the pants back. The clerk said, "All complaints have to be made within twenty-four hours. If you want the spot removed, you'll have to pay again." They gave him good service but no satisfaction.

Consider this fact: This year you will lose about 20 percent of your Customers. That's the national average.

One out of five customers are so upset with their present business they'll do business with someone else (anyone else) if they can find a reasonable alternative.

And why did they leave? Find out. The most important reason for finding why a Customer left is to find the *reason* they left. Here's why: It could be the exact same reason others have left. Good service. Lousy satisfaction.

And did we mention the free advertising you receive from the satisfied Customer? (We did? Good. It's worth repeating.)

Management consultant Pete Tosh said, "More and more Customers are deciding to do business with businesses that satisfy their requirements rather than just talk about it."

In order to stay in business you need 20/20 vision:

- Cut down the wandering 20 percent who leave you because of poor service.
- Add to the 20 percent of your customers who give you most of your business by having them find you more Customers.

A Cambridge, Massachusetts, survey asked 1,500 people, "How well do service companies satisfy your needs as a Customer?" Only one in ten said "excellent." They provide service. But they don't give satisfaction.

If you don't climb aboard the Satisfaction Express you might find your competition has already left the station. *Advertising Age* wrote, "Customer satisfaction research has grown to an estimated $100 million industry in the U.S."

"Satisfaction research is one of the fastest-growing areas of research," said Simon Chadwick, CEO of Research International in New York. His company's business jumped 100 percent in one year, and he plans to double it again the next year. Why? "It's a lot cheaper to regain Customers than acquire new ones."

Which brings us to our oft-repeated axiom: "'Tis far, far easier to sell more to the Customer you have than to sell a new Customer."

Echoes Maritz Marketing in St. Louis, "Customer satisfaction research accounts for 35 percent of our $54 million revenue. Last year it was only 10 percent." That quote is from Marsha Young, director of Customer Satisfaction. (Read that one more time: a *director of Customer satisfaction.*)

GTE Telephone Operation collects customer satisfaction information by making 250,000 calls a year. They tie in executive compensation by basing one-third of executive pay on Customer satisfaction.

Remember all those seminar notices you received in the mail on Customer service? Watch for the ones on Customer satisfaction. The Xerox corporation ran a seminar in Sydney, Australia, with the title "Using Customer Satisfaction Measurement Systems to Improve Customer Service Quality."

Included in the program was a half-day workshop, "Keys to Designing a Customer Satisfaction Measurement System." Satisfaction . . . not service. Other titles included "Measuring Customer Satisfaction" and "Actioning Customer Satisfaction."

Something's happening out there, folks. . . .

Need a place to start? Consider using an acronym suggested by Barry Urquhart, Australia's foremost consultant and public speaker on handling customers. In his book *Serves You Right* he emphasizes that successful businesspeople have pride in their work. The word PRIDE to Urquhart stands for "**P**ersonal **R**esponsibility **I**n **D**elivering Excellence."

Not just in service. But in satisfaction.

Make Sure the Story Isn't Better Than the Store

———————■———————

Vrest Orton owned The Original Country Store in Vermont. He left the journalistic jungles of New York City where he worked with H. L. Mencken on the *American Mercury* magazine. He returned to his family roots in the tiny town of Weston (population 400) to open a shop in the tradition of a turn-of-the-century general store. His inventory was much the same merchandise of that time long ago: *McGuffey Readers,* jumbo metal hairpins, Lydia Pinkham Herbal Compound, Ovaltine, and candies with the nostalgic names of Mary Janes, fireballs, and jawbreakers.

As visitors shopped with him, they asked Vrest if he had a catalog to order from when they returned home.

This intrigued Vrest, the writer turned retailer. Wanting to have the best direct mail catalog he could put together, he traveled to Freeport, Maine, to meet successful mail order cataloger L. L. Bean for advice.

Bean listened to Orton's plan, agreed with his ideas, but gave him a parting warning: "Make sure, Vrest, that the story isn't better than the store."

What was he saying? This: Don't overpromise. Don't make the product sound so appealing in what you write that Customers are disappointed when they receive the product.

When you write your advertising copy, ask yourself, "Would I believe this if I had not written it myself?" Truthful copy never needs later explanations.

The developer of the GE Answer Center, N. Powell Taylor, says, "You have to exceed the Customer's expectations."

One sure, positive, guaranteed way to make Customers happy is to give them something "extra" they did not expect when they ordered from your catalog or walked into your store.

Most retailers feel they have to list every single reason, every single feature, every single benefit customers will receive when they order or arrive. Not true.

When the Alley Deli restaurant in Atlantic City started a delivery service, it put something "extra" in each package: a piece of fruit, a slice of cake, a minicandy assortment. Customers called and said thank-you. *And they told their friends.*

Customers feel they are receiving something "extra" they had not planned to receive when they committed to buy.

What is their frame of mind when this "something extra" arrives? How do they feel about you and your business? Will they *tell their friends?* You bet. And how. Positively.

What happens if you offer more and deliver . . . less? This: Customer *dis*satisfaction, unhappiness, and passing the word to everyone they know *not* to do business with you.

We recently saw an advertisement to lease a Cadillac for a low $299 a month. We went to the dealer. The salesman sighed (he had obviously gone through this before and wanted to shortstop the objections he saw coming). He said, "Did you read the small print?"

We looked at the ad again and found, in tiny 4-point type, that we needed to have the first and last months' payment up front plus an additional $1,500. The $299 suddenly turned into almost $2,400!

Which brings me to my current example of promising a lot and delivering less: hotel room rates.

Why do hotels advertise a low rate and then, in tiny print at the bottom of the ad, inform me this rate is for "per person, double occupancy"? In other words if the advertised rate is $69, the REAL rate is $138.

Or an ad in a recent issue of *The New York Times* for a "special" rate at a Catskills resort for only "$89 a night." The small print says it applies only to "per person, double occupancy." Now the $89 is REALLY $178.

But wait, keep on reading and you'll find this "special" rate applies to a three-night minimum stay. Now the $89 is REALLY $534.

It's no wonder a recent survey said that 5 percent of Americans don't associate the word "trust" with the word "business."

What an indictment.

But wait—what if the reverse were true? What if I trusted you? What if this trust came about simply because you promised a lot but delivered more?

Would I tell my friends? Oh yes. And how. You bet.

So when you plan your next promotion, advertise your next sale, write your next mailer, be careful of what you promise to deliver. Make sure "the story isn't better than the store," or you will find yourself in the embarrassing position of Ethel Barrymore in 1906. She faced an unhappy audience at the end of the play *Sunday* and gave this now-famous curtain line: "That's all there is, there isn't any more."

DWYPYWD

—————■—————

A survey of American consumers asked the question: "Why Do You Buy Where You Presently Buy?"

They wanted to know why you used the insurance salesperson you used. Why you chose your present bank. Why you shopped for food in a specific supermarket. Why you bought your clothing at a specific store.

Here is the one major, overriding, specific reason clients come back again and again to your business. It is best explained with these letters: **DWYPYWD.**

Whenever we write them down, show them on a slide, or put them on a blackboard, someone invariably asks, "What does it mean?"

We make them wait by saying, "Well, it means the same backwards and forwards." (And it does.) And then say, it stands for "Duwypee-weed."

"Uh, okay," they answer, "but what's it REALLY mean?"

"This," we say. "Do What You Promised You Would Do."

And that is what makes the difference.

Think of the successful retailers, businesses, doctors, lawyers, architects—name the business or profession. How many in each can you rave about, would, in fact, be an Advocate for? Very few. But the

ones you have chosen fill the primary characteristics of Doing What
They Promised They Would Do.

The architect we use, and are Advocates for, has done a dozen or
more jobs for us, giving us an up-front approximation of the final cost.
And he is consistently accurate.

The bank we use, and are Advocates for, brings papers to our office
to sign so we don't stand in line.

The dry cleaner we use, and are Advocates for, tells us "the shirts
will ready Thursday before noon" and has them ready Thursday
before noon.

The clothing store where we shop might say, "The pants will be
altered for you by 8:00 A.M. tomorrow." And they are.

Make sure what you say is what you do.

PROBLEM: What happens if you can't? An emergency comes up.
Or the person responsible for doing the project was sick, didn't show
up, or was late.

SOLUTION: Call your customers and tell them.

They invariably will say, "Thanks for calling."

Then . . . tell them the new time the product or service will be
available.

One of the worst violations of this technique is to make a promise
and then not deliver.

• We know of a speaker who agreed to appear at a charity benefit.
He then received an offer for a paying job the same evening. He
canceled the first commitment even though his name and photo
were already printed in the program.

Within a few hours, most of the members of the charity knew of
his withdrawal. Many were potential Customers for this speaker
in the future. Result: lost future business. More important, loss of
credibility. Difficult for anyone to be HIS advocate.

• We had a photographer we needed for a distant city shoot. He
agreed to the time and the price. One week before the event he
called to say he would not be there because he had a higher-
paying job, "But I've arranged for a substitute so you won't be
stuck." But we were stuck. We chose him. We did not want a sub-

stitute. What gave him the right to make the decision for us? We were so astonished that we called him back a few minutes after we hung up and said, "I can't believe you are not showing up because someone offered you more money after you promised me you would appear."

His response was that he couldn't understand my attitude. After all, wouldn't anyone do the same thing?

Uh, well, no. And we stopped being his Advocate and are aware of thousands of dollars in business he lost because he "had a better-paying job."

• Another photographer (yes, we do work with some good photographers, too, but these *are* true stories) we sent on assignment to a local car agency. The dealer had a 1920 Chevrolet, and we asked the photographer to take his picture with one foot on the car's running board. We would use this for a used car ad in the local newspaper.

He brought the photo to me the next day. The car was black. The owner was dressed in black. All you could see was his face and his hands. The rest blended into the black car.

"This won't do," I said. "You'll have to go back and take it over and have him wear a light suit for contrast."

"Well, that will be an extra $50 charge," said the photographer.

"Why?" I asked

"Well, it's a new job."

"But you didn't do the job right the first time. You knew this was a picture for the newspaper and it's totally unacceptable."

He disagreed. So I took out my checkbook, wrote a check for $50, gave it to him, and said, "OK, here is your $50." I took the photograph from him and said, "And now the picture is mine."

He nodded approval and stood in shock as I promptly tore the picture into several pieces and threw it into the wind.

"WHAT ARE YOU DOING TO MY PICTURE?" he asked.

"No, no," I answered, "it's MY picture now. And that's what I think of it."

Now imagine a creative person in any endeavor seeing his or her work dismissed—no, not just dismissed, destroyed. He was shocked, then chagrined and said, "Well, okay, I'll do it over."

"Sorry, too late," said I. "You just don't understand. . . ."

He not only did not understand he had lost his professionalism, he also, as of that moment, lost an Advocate.

• But on the other hand . . . there is the story of Tom Haggai, CEO of IGA supermarkets—more than 4,000 in North America. Before he took on this awesome responsibility, Tom, a Baptist minister, was nationally known as an inspiring messenger with his motivational programs for many and varied groups across the country.

At one time he was involved with the national Jaycee movement. One day he heard from Bill Suttel, a Jaycee member from New Jersey who had run for the national presidency and lost. His campaign had a debt to overcome, and his committee planned a fund-raiser. But they needed a great speaker. Tom, who was the chaplain for the North Carolina Jaycees, was approached and agreed to be the keynote speaker for the fund-raiser.

At the same time, Tom was working with Mayflower Moving Company. One of the spokesmen from the public relations division called Tom all excited to announce he was able to book Tom on the Johnny Carson show!

What an opportunity for Tom to give his message to millions of Americans at one time. What was the date?

The same night as the fund-raiser.

"Sorry," said Tom, "I can't do Carson's show. I have another commitment."

The PR man was astonished. What could be more important than being on Johnny Carson?

Tom explained he had committed himself as the speaker for the fund-raiser. "Have the committee get another speaker, Tom," said the PR man. "I've pulled every string I have to get you on this show because I respect you and [the not-so-subtle reminder] after all, you are under contract to Mayflower."

Tom said, "I want you to know I do appreciate what you have done. But I gave my word to appear at this dinner."

The PR man fumed some more, saying, "They'll never invite

you back. They don't like people who turn them down."

For days afterward Tom heard from other people who tried to dissuade him from honoring his original commitment, asking, "Do you know what you are doing?"

And Tom answered, "Yes, I do. You see, I made a commitment. . . ."

It is difficult in this increasingly competitive commercial world where entrepreneurs are quick to seek the high ground and any advantage over another.

But throughout this country there are many, many Advocates of Tom Haggai. Simply because they know he would Do What He Promised He Would Do.

INTERVIEW
Tom Haggai

■

Tom Haggai is CEO of IGA, Inc., the largest alliance of independent supermarket owners in the country. Tom is a firm believer in bringing his customers to the top of the Loyalty Ladder.

Q. I think you have really come up with a winner with your Hometown Proud slogan for IGA. I wonder if you had any thoughts on how that slogan relates to Customer loyalty?

A. Loyalty, such as my generation knew as a young person, is not the loyalty that we have today, but I think that loyalty can be built.

The independent grocer is more prominent in the smaller-populated counties. And for many years a grocer could say, "We went to school together, our families grew up together. I'm the local person, and you owe me because I've been in town, I grew up here, I have a family business." Maybe such loyalty did work in the forties and fifties. But that approach does not work today.

We have learned that loyalty is not something we could presumptuously claim. We had to earn it and not take the Customer for granted. **We have to be better-than to be as-good-as.**

What I mean by that is if you go into a chain store and the store doesn't look good, you say, "I bet this manager will be chewed out and they'll make a change here and they'll get this store on target."

If you go into an independent store and the store doesn't look good, the immediate reaction is, this is an independent store and they just can't afford to keep up and be as-good-as. So my statement is that we have to be better-than to be as-good-as, because we are sort of judged with a little harsher set of standards.

I think to be fair it's always easier to talk about good old days than bad new days, but I think loyalty is harder to come by simply because our culture isn't as loyal. It's little things we miss. I don't think a public school should be a sectarian school, but I think that when I went to school and we stood up and quoted the Twenty-third Psalm out of the writings of David, and then did the "Pledge of Allegiance" and sang a verse of "America," that had a very positive effect on every kid in that school in Massachusetts. Today we don't have those automatic loyalties that were taught when we were very young and impressionable. Loyalty now has taken on a little bit of a different meaning. I think people feel good when they feel they are cared about. But because of all the formats we will never have the easy loyalty and we'll never expect it. We expect people will shop at other stores and get certain things that they can get there better.

Q. Your top 20 percent of supermarket shoppers in recent studies spend fifty times as much as the bottom 20 percent, and the profit margins on your best customers are higher. Should IGA be treating their best Customers differently?

A. Those studies focus more on the metropolitan market where there is not as much loyalty. I don't think the differential would be as much for our stores.

I think there is a danger of the airplane seat syndrome. No matter what discount you give the Customer, he sits in the seat unhappy because when he sees someone across the aisle grinning he's convinced they got a better deal than he did. And so we have to be careful. The trouble with buying loyalty is when you reward beyond your ability to financially support it.

I think that shoppers are loyal mainly because they got what they wanted at the store. Then loyalty rewards can come as a pleasant surprise.

You can tell your customer something like, "Here's what we want to do for you because we are grateful for this amount of business that you gave us." I think if you do it privately through direct mail you avoid the airline syndrome.

I think another way you gain loyalty is when your son or daughter is out on the ball field with the local IGA name on the back of his or her uniform. The people in the stands realize that store is buying the uniforms for the ballplayers. Price is basic, but price isn't the end-all.

Loyalty is not something that can just be announced by the owner of the company or the manager. There has to be weeks of training during which you teach employees how they can make the customer feel that they are glad the customer is in the store.

High turnover in a store is the most deadly thing for loyalty. We start first with recruiting employees, having an employee training program. One of our retailers who employs high-schoolers has an orientation session with the new employees *and* their parents. He explains to the parents what he expects of their youngsters when they come to work for his store.

The grocery market is different from fast-food establishments. You have to have a good benefits program for your employees.

It is important to remember that your "Customers" are also the people that report to you. They are your primary Customers. Because the people that buy the groceries, they are the Customer of your Customer. Owners and managers must treat the person carrying out the bags of groceries to the car as graciously as they treat the person who paid for the bags of groceries to be successful.

Q. How should supermarkets work with manufacturers in devising a loyalty program?

A. Here's where I think we caught ourselves in a trap. On one side we think the manufacturer is ripping us off. I don't personally, but that's the general consensus out there. At the same time we get so involved with the manufacturer that he begins to run our store. I buy the idea that loyalty programs that are designed for the store and controlled by the store are the programs that I think are going to build loyalty.

You can't let manufacturers totally control your loyalty program. There have to be some ground rules, and I hate to see our stores be at the mercy of anybody who has a deal for them.

Telephone Marketing

—■—

Reach Out and Sell Something

Question: Where are most advertising dollars spent?

( ) Newspaper
( ) Television
( ) Radio
( ) Direct mail
( ) Telephone
( ) Magazines
( ) Yellow pages
( ) Billboards

If you answered anything else besides "telephone". . . you're wrong.

More than $70 billion was spent annually on telemarketing in the early nineties. This is a form of advertising you should at least think about using.

In this chapter we are talking about using the telephone as a marketing tool that works with your present customers: when they call you or you call them.

Consider this fact: it costs *at least* five times more to get a new Customer than to keep a current one. And one way to keep your present Customers is to call them.

When you call your present Customer, you are talking to a specific target: someone who knows you and has spent money with you and will appreciate your call because you are bringing them information. Your phone call is to someone rather than to anyone.

Why is so much money spent on telephone marketing?

1. It is interactive. (You and the Customer talk to one another.)

2. It is responsible. (The Customer finds out up front, at once, if you can fulfill their needs and wants.)

3. It is synergistic. (You can "open the door" for sending a catalog, merchandise, or having a salesperson call.)

4. Almost everyone has a phone. (Everyone does NOT subscribe to the paper or listen to the TV and radio at the time you want them to listen.)

5. If you call someone after you have mailed them something, you can increase the results from your mailer five to ten times!

Telemarketing has not grown because it is cheap. It isn't. An overwhelming majority of the phone calls you place (outbound) don't reach the Customer the first time around. Telemarketing has grown so quickly because the Customer wants fast, convenient, and economical ways to buy what you have to sell.

Limit your calls to people who are current Customers. It's less expensive than cold calling and will result in more sales. And your Customers won't complain about intrusive and annoying phone calls from strangers.

Selling by telephone works two ways: inbound and outbound.

Inbound means someone calls you.

Outbound means you call someone.

Here's some information on how each works, followed by a list of rules for telephone marketing. Let's start with inbound. That's when you hear the phone ring.

*   *   *

INBOUND

When you pick up the phone, you start selling. The Rule of First Impressions begins when someone answers your phone. What does the person "sound" like? What does the person on the other end want to hear? This: That the caller reached the right place. And the name of the person they are talking to.

Nothing is a problem. Many times Customers will call with a problem they have with one of your products. Not delivered. Not performing. Not what was ordered. Most people are uncomfortable calling to complain. They're preconditioned from a previous experience or the horror stories they read or heard and are convinced you will give them a difficult time. What a shock (and surprise) to have you say, "We'll take care of that for you. What would you like?"

Think about it. What real difference does it make to you anyway? A refund, a replacement, even a loss of money? What you have to think about is the "lifetime value of the Customer." Is this telephone marketing? You bet it is!

George Walther, in his excellent book *Phone Power*, suggests you eliminate certain negative phrases when you're talking to a Customer and substitute positive phrases.

Do NOT say, "I can't." Say *when* you *can.*

Do NOT say, "I'll try." That means you may or may not.

Do NOT say, "I'm not sure." DO say "I'll get back to you with an answer." And then, "If I call you within an hour, is that okay?"

Many calls are made to ask if you have a special item or if you can deliver or mail a product. (Yes, yes, of course you can. *"Tell us what you want and the answer is yes."*)

After taking the order, suggest something else. But make that something "special."

We once helped create a food catalog for a retailer. When we received the catalog, we called for an order. They were polite, accurate, and thanked us. We then called the owner and said, "Every time someone takes an order, suggest something ELSE for them to buy. Something NOT in the catalog and specially priced for this week only. You will sell that extra item to one out of ten who call."

He called us back a few weeks later and told us we were wrong. One out of five bought.

OUTBOUND

Each of your salespeople has a list of his or her favorite Customers. (And if they don't, start that today!) This little black book has the Customer's name, address, telephone number, and the kind of merchandise they like.

Simply calling them up and letting them know **what they like just arrived** will be flattering and will automatically produce sales.

Simply calling them up and letting them know about **a sale ahead of time** will be flattering and automatically produce sales.

Simply calling them up and **reminding them about a birthday or holiday** will be flattering and automatically produce sales.

The big advantage for your business is that all these calls are made by people presently on your payroll. They make these calls during "down" time, when they are not taking care of Customers in your business.

The bigger advantage: You are giving a specific message to a specific Customer for a specific item you know they want.

The best advantage: more business!

SIX RULES FOR ANSWERING CUSTOMER SERVICE CALLS

1. **Answer the phone quickly!** If you let it ring more than three times, the person calling you is annoyed.

2. **Say who you are.** Speak clearly. Say your name easily. Most people talk too fast, and the listener, hearing an unfamiliar name, doesn't quickly associate who you are.

3. **Say who you're with.** Like this: "Good morning. This is Tom Jenkins from the Gordon's shops."

4. **Don't keep me on hold too long.** Most people are annoyed to be put on hold. More people are further annoyed by listening to canned music. Try to answer the person's question immediately or offer to call back with an answer. They'll appreciate the fact that you honor their time. How long is too long? Longer than a minute is too long. Holding onto a phone for a minute equates into five minutes in the customer's mind.

5. If a Customer is complaining, don't interrupt. Let Customers finish what they want to say before you offer a solution. You should, however, let them know you're still there with little phrases like "I see" or "I understand" or a simple "uh-huh." That way the Customer will feel you're concerned. After you hang up, drop them a note to confirm what you promised. Boy, will they be impressed.

6. Use the Customer's name. A quick and easy way to build a comfortable relationship is to mention the Customer's name while talking to him or her. This personalization will diffuse anger.

FOURTEEN RULES FOR TELEMARKETING

1. **Give your staff an outline.** The 1-2-3 key points they should use when talking to Customers. Here's why: You are condensing a selling story into the fewest possible words with the most possible benefits. Doing this "off the cuff" will not work. You must prepare ahead of time. Bob Hope once said, "The best ad-lib is the rehearsed ad-lib."

Some of your salespeople may say they are not "actors." Remind them they use certain phrases all the time in their everyday face-to-face selling.

Don't use a written script salespeople have to memorize because it will sound like a written script they have memorized. Just give them the key points and let them take it from there. They must have the option of changing words or phrases that "sound more like me." The important goal is to make it sound "natural."

2. Tell. Don't sell. When you sell, the person on the other end of the line hears the "sound of selling" in your voice. When you sound friendly on the phone, the person listening to you is more receptive to what you have to say. Relax. Remember: Everyone likes to buy. But no one wants to be sold.

3. Use the four Cs. Be Clear, Concise, Conversational, and Convincing.

Okay, the phone is ringing and your potential buyer picks up the phone. . . .

4. Say who you are and what you want up front. When you call a Customer, do NOT say you are a salesperson for your company.

Instead say, "Hi. This is Murray. Is Mrs. Walsh there?" Most of the time you'll get Mrs. Walsh. If the person asks, "Who's calling?" THEN say who you are, where you're from, and why you're calling.

5. QUICK! Give a benefit! "I'm calling to tell you about the winter sale we're having at Gordon's, and since you're a good customer, I wanted you to know about it before it's advertised." Yes, yes, of course, your telephone call IS an advertisement. But not in the "accepted" newspaper/radio/TV tradition of advertising.

Now you've told them you're from a store they know. Where they shop.

Now you've told them a special reason they should keep on listening.

6. Explain the benefit and give a cutoff date. That creates desire and immediacy. "We're offering 20 percent off everything in the store during this sale. The sale starts on Monday and will last only one week. That's why we wanted you to have this advance notice."

7. Deliver the entire message quickly. Don't waste your Customer's time. Come to the main selling feature right away.

8. Ask questions. Don't just keep on talking. The magic word is "involvement." Can't do that unless you ask a question: "I know you like Calvin Klein clothing. Would you like to know what's on sale in your size?" Rare is the person who will turn down THAT offer. And then . . . LISTEN! Many salespeople feel they have to keep on talking, like background music in a movie. But with silence comes orders.

9. Ask for the order. "Would you like me to put one aside for you today? Oh yes, they also make a marvelous gift."

10. Offer add-ons. "In addition to the 20 percent off sale, we're having a half-price sale on six-foot wool scarves. They normally sell for $20 but you can have them on sale for half-price. Only $10. They come in five colors." They will immediately tell you if they want the scarf and will ask you the colors. Great. You've established a dialogue.

"The colors are navy, white, brown, camel, and black. Which color do you prefer?" This is the "not if, but which" technique. Give the customer a choice between something and something. Not something and nothing.

11. Handling objections. If the customer isn't interested in the half-price scarf (or other great buy you offer), accept the turndown gracefully and ask, "Is there anything else you would like me to put aside for you to look at when you come to the store? There's no obligation to buy. We just want to make sure our best Customers have the best choices."

12. Read back what they ordered. Customers will appreciate that you are confirming what they said to you, especially since they can't see and sign the sales receipt.

13. Guarantee. Tell them they must be satisfied or you will take the merchandise back. This makes the Customer feel more comfortable when buying.

14. The close. Sign off with a pleasant good-bye and a thank-you, whether or not the Customer bought anything. Last impressions count almost as much as first impressions.

Ben & Jerry's Ice Cream

———————■———————

Ben & Jerry's story shows how one company turned Customers into Clients and Advocates by turning inward. Ben & Jerry's decided to be true to themselves, to create a product and a company that fit their personalities.

They succeeded so well that *Time* magazine cited them for having "the best ice cream in the world." They were named the Small Business Persons of the Year by the Small Business Administration and Retail Entrepreneurs of the Year by *Chain Store Age Executive.* Their operating slogan is, "If it isn't fun, why do it?"

Even when it comes to picking a new CEO—"Tell us why you want to be Ben & Jerry's CEO in 100 words or less"—Ben and Jerry manage to put humor and fun and receive enormous publicity from a process usually kept quite close to the corporate vest.

Ben and Jerry never hesitate to inject their personal, social, and political values into their company—and their Customers love them for it.

Here's the recipe for making a successful ice cream company:

1. Start with some market research. Find out what your customers want. Find out how much ice cream they buy a week.

2. Flavor your ice cream similarly to that of your successful competitors. Price your ice cream competitively.

3. Package your ice cream in half-gallon and gallon containers because the more ice cream your customers buy, the more money you will make.

When it comes to Ben & Jerry's, one of the most successful ice cream companies in America, that recipe is:

Wrong.

Wrong.

Wrong.

The real key to Ben & Jerry's success, according to cofounder Jerry Greenfield, was making ice cream to fit the unsubtle taste buds of cofounder Ben Cohen. According to Jerry:

"Ben happens to like big chunks in his ice cream. At the same time he can't taste very well. I was initially making the ice cream and he was tasting it. I kept flavoring the ice cream more and more strongly until he could tell what it was. He also liked big chunks of nuts and cookies and candies in his ice cream, so we put more and more of those in the ice cream. Ben was the taste buds of the company."

And because of Ben's taste preferences, you'll find fragments of Oreos, KitKat bars, fudge brownies, etc., in abundance in Ben & Jerry's ice cream. Yummmmmm.

Ben and Jerry were two undistinguished students who started business in the late 1970s with very little money and a shared appetite for ice cream. They took a $5 correspondence course on how to make ice cream and then just overflavored the ice cream until Ben liked it. It turns out there are lots of people who share Ben's taste in ice cream, and Ben & Jerry's grew rapidly.

Today, Ben & Jerry's is a large company with more than 500 employees and over $140 million in annual sales. They have achieved this growth by providing ice cream their Customers want and not through elaborate market research.

In fact, Jerry is not sure how much ice cream his best Customers eat. "I guess our average user is eating about a pint a week," Jerry says. "But if somebody told me, hey, no, that's not right, it's actually two and a half pints a week because we did research, I'd say 'Ohhh, really?!'"

Ben & Jerry's niche is in the superpremium end of the ice cream market. "Our business is entirely through pints, which is the upper end of the business," Jerry says. Even though Ben & Jerry's main competitor, Häagen-Dazs, has been marketing a quart-size product for several years, Ben & Jerry's still has resisted the urge to go to bigger packaging.

It's been tough to resist bigger packaging, because there is logic in selling bigger packages of ice cream. "One theory says that people eat more ice cream when they have it in their freezer," says Jerry. "If you can get them to buy more at a time and keep more in their freezer, they will eat ice cream more frequently."

But that's a theory that Jerry doesn't believe. "We believe people are flavor driven. And if you are out of stock at the store with their favorite flavor, they won't purchase or they will purchase somewhere else."

They also know that people's tastes change, and so they listen to their Customers. "We had Customers who wrote and said the chunky ice cream was fine, but how about some smooth flavors," says Jerry. "We thought that was a good idea not only for our present Customers but also to attract new Customers." And so Ben & Jerry's put out a whole new line of smooth flavored ice cream.

They also listen to the 100 owners of their franchise scoop shops. A few years ago, "The scoop shops told us they were losing business to yogurt shops and that we had to come out with yogurt. We did. It is extremely successful."

After talking with Jerry for a while, you come away with the feeling that this is a company trying to connect with their Customers by staying true to their own ideals. It's as if their Customers will recognize that this is a company devoid of phoniness, dedicated to making the best possible ice cream and supporting social causes that will result in a better world.

Jerry says, "I think for a lot of companies, consumers or Customers are merely statistics. The fact of the matter is there are actual people you are relating to and interacting with. You have to put yourself in the mind-set of the person in the street and think about what is important to your Customers."

In addition to listening to their Customers, Ben & Jerry's occasionally leads its Customers into causes they believe are good and right. "We are working with the Children's Defense Fund to establish a grass-roots network of citizen voters who can be contacted when laws or bills before Congress come up which involve children's issues," Jerry says. The company's goal is to have a list of 100,000 names that will work for the Children's Defense Fund. All the company's containers have an 800 number (1-800-BJ-KIDS-1) that Customers can call to listen to a recording from Ben and Jerry explaining how it works.

Ben & Jerry's has supported many charities and environmental causes through the years. In fact, as Jerry explains, "The opportunity to use our business and power of our business as a force for progressive social change is exciting."

They give 7.5 percent of pretax profits to the nonprofit Ben & Jerry's Foundations. In 1993, they gave away $808,000 in 142 grants to such groups as the Vermont Clean Water Project, the Brattleboro Area AIDS Project, and the Massachusetts Coalition for the Homeless. Cofounder Ben Cohen explains, "Corporations which exist solely to maximize profit become disconnected from their soul."

But Ben and Jerry do not only look outward when trying to institute change, they also look at their own company. They have generous employee benefits, employee empowerment programs, and for many years a rule that the highest-paid employees could receive only seven times the salary of the lowest-paid employee. (This salary cap has not survived their recent search for a new CEO.) But they have tried to combat the feeling, as Jerry says, that in "corporate America the salaries at the top were hugely out of line."

This concern with doing the right thing not only for their company but also for the world has helped Ben and Jerry connect with a lot of people in our society. And it also has the by-product of helping the company and its cofounders receive a lot of good publicity.

"We certainly understand that when you are doing things that are different and unconventional it's newsworthy," says Jerry. "But we have always tried to connect directly with our Customers. That was very easy to do because Ben and I are average people on the street. We didn't go to business school. We learned how to make ice cream from a correspondence course. We fixed up our first store ourselves. We did everything ourselves, and we try to make a company that we would want to relate to."

This involvement by the owners, the intimate connection with the Customers, is what makes Ben & Jerry's Customers climb the Loyalty Ladder. "We are a very human scale and relationship-oriented company," Jerry says. "We are not some nameless, faithless conglomerate who only looks at how much money we make every year.

"And we think that's what people want. They want a relationship with the products they are buying or the company they are buying from."

With Ben & Jerry's you get both.

Ten Ways to Convert Clients into Advocates

—————■—————

1. **Loyalty programs.** We did a program for the staff at the Kahala Hilton in Hawaii. They said they gave a Kahala Platinum Card to their very best Customers—people who booked at least fifty nights in the hotel. They received free pickup and return at the airport via limousine, late checkouts, room ready whenever they arrive. "But what about the ones that haven't reached this level?" I asked. "How about twenty-five room nights entitling me to a Gold Card? Half the benefits but more than someone arriving for the first time."

Next morning they had a card and letter in my box. The letter began: "Dear Mr. Raphel. Congratulations. You are the holder of the Kahala Hilton's #1 Gold Card."

They listed all the extra benefits I would now enjoy. Not all the advantages of the Platinum Card—but now I was personally committed to staying the extra nights so I could have all the extra benefits of a Platinum Card member.

What were they doing? Making me work to become an Advocate.

2. **You're Number 1.** There are many who believe we are still encased in the "Me" generation. The old "but what have you done for me lately?" school.

A recent *New Yorker* cartoon showed people standing in line in a supermarket. The ones with the fewest items in their shopping cart waited in traditional lines. The big spenders had a concierge greet them, sofas to lounge on, TVs to watch. Why do the people who spend the most have to stand longer in line? Why do the best Customers of the airlines (or any business) have to pay more than anyone else?

As an Advocate, whenever I check into your hotel, my room is waiting. Checkout for the other folks is noon. For me it's 6:00 P.M. And there's fresh fruit and wine in my room with a "Thanks for coming" note from the manager.

There is the unexpected gift that arrives in my home for no special reason from the shop where I buy my clothing. Special savings arrive unannounced in the mail from where I spend my big dollars, waiting for me next time I shop there with NO minimum purchase needed to enjoy the savings. Know why? Because I'm a good Customer. Don't believe that? Just ask me. . . .

3. In-depth surveys. When you apply for an American Express Platinum Card, you have to fill out many pages about your background, history, likes, dislikes, ranging from the wine you drink to the novels you read. The more you know about me, the more selective you will be in contacting me for future purchases. You will make available to me only that which I enjoy wearing, looking at, possessing.

4. Call. Don't write. If a Customer has not shopped for a while, you call to find out why not. Is everything okay? Have you done anything wrong? Is there anything special they need?

A few years ago an innovate marketer in Sweden began the SELMA program. The letters were an acronym for **Sel**ective **Mar**keting. The name came because, as the originator said, "In olden days, when you shopped the local store, the owner knew what you bought and when. And since a common name is Sweden is Selma, we called our system that name. Today, we know, through computers, what Selma stored in her memory a century ago."

5. You remember . . . Not just what I bought when but also my birthday. And yes, my spouse's birthday as well. It is not just the giving of gifts, it is the retention of loyalty.

In our store we sent our best Customers a $15 gift certificate on their birthday. And another on the birthday of their spouse. They came, they saw, they bought. Because . . . I remembered.

6. Special privileges. Back to the American Express Platinum Card, where you can participate in a backstage reception with the star of a Broadway show. Or down-front seats when the opera opens. Or special places at the major golf tournament. Yes, you pay for them, but they are otherwise unavailable.

Belong to the Intercontinental Hotel's Six Continents Club for a small fee and receive an automatic upgrade when you check in. And every-once-in-a-while special benefits like the use of the conference room ($50 an hour) for an hour . . . free.

And when I come to shop with you, I let you know when I'll arrive and look for your valet outside waiting to park my car.

7. Special handling. Today a Japanese manufacturer of bicycles offers totally customized products, produced and delivered to the buyer within a week from order. What a difference from Henry Ford's original dictum: "Give them any color they want, as long as it's black."

Which makes us wonder why airlines don't have plugs for PCs next to the seats.

Which makes us wonder why real estate agents don't have a history of homes I'm considering buying.

Which makes us wonder why "banker's hours" are for the convenience of the banker and not the Customer. Let's establish "Client Hours."

Which makes us understand the "Special Shopper" program inaugurated successfully by department stores. Tired of shopping? Don't know what to look for? Look: The store offers your own "special shopper" who first interviews you, finds out your likes, needs, wants, and then can best deliver what you like best.

8. Exclusive phone numbers. When I want to call for a reservation for a room, a meal, a ticket, an order, I am not put on Muzak hold. It is an exclusive number that works twenty-four hours a day! They take my name, my reservation, my request—

whatever. I don't have the same number available to a regular Customer. I have a *special* number.

9. Unlimited guarantee. Norm Thompson does this in Oregon. Their mail order company has trademarked their special guarantee, which they call their "You Be The Judge" Guarantee. What that means: You decide if you are happy with their merchandise; you are the sole judge of when that time should be. Not thirty, sixty, ninety days, or even a year. If you're unhappy at any time, just return the merchandise for a full refund or exchange. Your choice.

When we started a small publishing business we looked to see what other book dealers offered as a guarantee. We couldn't find any. ("What?" asked one when we queried. "You're going to let them read the book and then return it! Ridiculous.")

We went one step further: We told the buyers we offered a "12-month guarantee." Buy the book. Read it. Anytime, during the year, if they wanted to send it back for an exchange for another book or a refund, that was fine with us.

In the first few years we sold close to 100,000 books with this guarantee. *And had none returned.*

Now, if you don't extend this warranty/guarantee to everyone— at least do it for the advocates!

10. **Ask them what they want.**

Write them at least once a year. Tell them they are "very special" (simply because they are). Send a list of the benefits they receive that are available to this unique group alone. (Most will not know or remember, and they will be amazed at what is available from you to them.)

What else would they like?

Remember these are the Best of the Best. They rarely, if ever, will take advantage of you. They will like the fact they are treated as special (wouldn't you?) and they might make a seemingly small request you never thought important enough to consider.

But now that they mentioned it . . .

Part 5

THE ADVOCATE

Introduction to Advocates

—————■—————

Ad-vo-cate/ad-ve-ket/ *n. Someone who tells everyone how great your business is.*

The leading brand in cameras today is Kodak. In canned fruit, it's Del Monte. Chewing gum, Wrigley's; crackers, Nabisco; razors, Gillette; soft drinks, Coca-Cola; soap, Ivory; and soup, Campbell's.

Not surprising? Only when you look at the names of the brands that led each of these categories back in 1923.

They were exactly the same.

Not just because they were good quality. *(Important, but not enough.)*

Not just because they have always been among the top advertisers. *(Important, but not enough.)*

Not just because they had detail men out in the stores building displays and setting up point-of-purchase units. *(Important, but not enough.)*

All of that is important, necessary, and had-to-be-done. But the overriding factor was this: One satisfied Consumer told another who told another who told another down through the generations ad profitum.

Each of these brands has Advocates preaching each brand's Sermon of Superiority. Nordstrom department stores have dozens of apocryphal stories about their service. (Remember the oft-told one of the person returning tires for a refund? He got the refund. Even though Nordstrom does not carry tires.)

But other stories are true and repeated daily: You're shopping and a button falls off a shirt or jacket. They sew it back on. A recent story in *Forbes* told of a woman who owns a suburban Los Angeles real estate agency. She bought Easter gifts for her children who lived in other parts of the country. The gifts arrived the Monday AFTER Easter. She called and complained. Nordstrom refunded the $150 for the gifts and sent an apology note with flowers. And how about having diaper-changing tables in the rest rooms. Not that unusual? WELL, when you realize they are in the MEN'S rest rooms . . .

What is an Advocate?

You find Advocates by "going out and finding out what your Customers want and providing it," says Warren Blanding of the Customer Service Institute in Silver Spring, Maryland.

As simple as holding in-person focus groups. Or as complex as Xerox's system of monthly surveys from 10,000 Customers.

Or GE's Answer Center, which responds to more than three million calls a year to handle Customer complaints or give advice on malfunctioning appliances.

In the burgeoning mail order catalog business, Advocates want what they want . . . fast! You have to answer the toll-free phone within three rings. You have to mail what they ordered within twenty-four hours. L. L. Bean sends packages Federal Express *at no extra cost.* And enclose a return goods address label in case you are not happy with what you ordered plus the phone number of your local UPS driver, who comes and picks it up at (ready for this?) *no cost to you!*

Gone is (or soon will be) the time when a postcard saying your merchandise is back-ordered was *de rigueur.* Today someone calls you and tells you the new delivery date and asks, "Is that OK with you?"

Why do they do this? Simply practicing Feargal Quinn's "Boomerang Theory." They want the Advocate to spread their word. They are aware of the "lifetime value." Listen to Mike Gillispie, director of customer service at Lands' End. "Our investment in our people never stops. Our greatest challenge is to maintain this investment as we grow—upgrading training, making the system easier to use, and providing backup." That means little (and important) techniques like having customer service representatives spend a year—or more—in training before they can answer the phone.

What this means as the fabled Information Highway opens for use:

• Your airline targets a message to you depending on your age. (Fort Lauderdale for the college group. Boca Raton for the parents.)
• Your clothing shop informs you when the clothing from the designer you like arrives in the store.
• Your gallery keeps a record of which artist an Advocate buys, and when their scarce supply of limited-edition prints arrives, guess who knows first?
• Your magazine wants renewals—but different strokes for different folks. One letter for charter subscribers, another for first-time renewals. And the focus changes depending on the sex.

All good, desired, and to be imitated. But don't keep me waiting on voice mail with minutes-long instructions on what number to push for which service. The greatest news we heard recently was of a few major companies that said, "We want people answering our phones—not machines." Probably because the CEO called and couldn't get through. . . .

How Do One Million Customers Feel About Your Business?

———————■———————

In the immortal words of Andy Rooney, "Didja ever wonder . . . ?"

We refer to those weekly polling reports from *The Wall Street Journal, ABC News,* or the bottom left-hand corner of *USA Today* and wonder how accurate they are.

If you look at the tiny print at the bottom, most say they are based on interviews with about 1,000 people and have a plus or minus factor of 5 percent.

One thousand people? To tell me if we should have a health plan, how the president's doing, how many Diet Cokes are sold in one day, and how many angels fit on the head of a pin? (*Only kidding.*)

How can that be?

And so I always look askance at the results of this small sampling.

But then I ran across a survey taken by Brit Beemer and America's Research Group, summarized in the *Parascope* newsletter. What made me sit up, take notice, and read everything very, very carefully was this sentence: "The statistics are based on over a million interviews giving valuable insight into consumer behavior and how stores match the needs and values of customers."

Whew! One million interviews!

Now is the time for all good merchants to come to the aid of their business by knowing what the customer *really* thinks of your business—well, at least one million of them. . . .

Because . . . if we know the attitude customers have about your store, then we will know how to bring them to the top of the Loyalty Ladder.

Let's take a look at what one million interviewees said makes them shop (or not shop) your business:

The first eight seconds of their experience determine whether the customers feel comfortable enough to buy from you. The Japanese know this. They have greeters on either side of the front door as you walk in who bow and say, *O-kyak-a-san.* Which, translated roughly, means, "You are a visitor to our home."

Now, that's impressive.

Much different than walking in and (choose one):

Being ignored.

Listening to two salespeople talk over personal problems.

Watching salespeople prove they can chew gum and talk at the same time.

The old "you never have a second chance to make a first impression" works in your business as well as in personal relationships.

Here's a bottom-line figure that will ring your register: "People who enjoy shopping will spend 20 percent more." That number is from a survey of supermarkets, where shopping for food has always been at the top of the things I like least list.

Now, what if you were the supermarket that made shopping enjoyable?

What if you were the clothing shop whose staff made customers feel like they were the most important people in the world simply because . . . they are!

American Demographics magazine found that out in a recent survey that asked this question: "Do you agree with this statement: 'I am an important person.'"

In 1940, 11 percent said "yes."

In 1993, 66 percent said "yes."

Something's happening out there, folks. Customers no longer want to be anyone, they want to be someone. They want to be recognized, taken care of, and thanked. They want you to appreciate the fact that they are spending *their* money in *your* business.

One way to do that: Make customers feel comfortable when they arrive. I still remember the conversation I had with an elderly woman shopping at a local pharmacy. I asked why she didn't go to the nearby chain drugstore, where prices were lower. Her response: "Because they say 'hello' to me here. . . ."

Hmmmmmmmm.

But wait! This is all AFTER they have entered your place of business. How about BEFORE they come in. Back to the survey:

Four of ten customers form an opinion about who you are by the exterior appearance of your store. If you have a parking lot, is it a clean parking lot?

If you have signs on your windows, can I see the Scotch tape marks from the old signs?

If you have window displays, are they clean, neat?

When I was managing a shoe store for a national chain, the district manager paid me a visit, first looking at our window display. He came in and said, "You don't have a price tag on the dead fly in the front of the window."

Think of your windows as "silent salesmen." They convey a look and an image and an impression before the customer walks through the front door. They identify who you are and what you sell.

We once went shopping for a new car to lease. At one of the large dealerships the showroom floor was dirty, ashtrays were full, and the imitation wall paneling was scarred with tape marks and holes from previous notices. We were reminded of Tom Peters's observation that when you lower the luncheon tray in the airplane and it is covered with coffee stains, do you wonder about the quality of the engine?

Four out of ten customers judge how much you know by how professional you look. We left the automobile dealer mentioned above and went to the next one down the road. As we walked in the salesman approached us wearing a sweatshirt with several stains and drinking soda from a can. "Yeah?" he said. We didn't answer. We left. . . .

Herbie Berger was a salesman who sold us boys' clothing. He said the secret of his success was that he traded in a new Cadillac every year and that his father loaned him $100 to buy a new suit, shoes, shirt, tie, and pocket handkerchief before he want out to see his first customer. "People feel if I look successful, my product is terrific," he said, "and so they buy from me. Everybody wants to do business with a winner."

Most customers know very little about the product you sell. Yes, today's customer is smarter than yesterday's.

Yes, today's customer comparison shops.

Yes, today's customer reads labels on clothing and canned goods and reads *Consumer Reports*.

But they still know very little about the product you are selling.

We recently shopped for a VCR. We asked the salesman in the appliance store, "This VCR is $199. The one over there is $249. What's the difference?" He said, "Fifty dollars."

The salesman in the next store sold me because of this simple technique:

"Here, take the remote control clicker in your hand. Ask me what you want to do and I'll tell you the buttons to push."

Involvement. The key word to having the customer become part of the selling process. In a short ten-minute lesson (with me doing all the work) he taught me all I really wanted to know. How to turn it on. How to turn it off. How to record.

He explained everything in simple, easy-to-understand language. No "inside" technobabble. No shorthand phrases known by the audiophile but foreign language to the couldn't-care-less me.

Your job is to educate customers because knowledgeable customers will buy more and come back more often. They have confidence in you because of your knowledge. They will return to shop with you and bring their friends.

Most customers say all consumer ads look the same. Your ad should make people know who it's from by the illustration, typeface, layout.

The original Volkswagen ads had an identity stamp so you knew who they were just by looking.

We once did a mailer for a local candidate running for public office. Most of the people who received the mailer thought it was an ad from our store! We quickly changed design, layout, colors for his future ads.

Lord & Taylor's loosely sketched fashion ads in *The New York Times* convey a specific identity.

Does the Marlboro man need anything more than a cowboy's face or horse on the range to say they are a brand of cigarettes?

They're bringing back Elsie the Cow, Speedy Alka-Seltzer, Charley the Tuna, and RCA's dog because people still remember them and associate who they are with the product they sell.

The next time you do an ad for what you sell, show it to friends and others NOT in your business. Without your name. "Whose ad is this?" is your question.

When they answer "I don't know" or (worse) name your competition, it is time to go back and start all over again.

A private-sale flyer must scream value. Retailers have negatively impacted between 25 percent and 40 percent of their core customers by sending false-pretense private-sale mailers. Many businesses are mailing more often . . . but giving less value.

Does your customer see through this? Oh, yes!

Gone is the time a store could triple the cost and then mark it down "on sale."

Gone is the time when customers mobbed the twice-a-year winter or summer sale because today, every day seems to be "sale" day.

Gone is the time when the customer is ready to spend one price one day and find a lower price for the same product the following day.

Gone. Gone. Gone.

A bookstore in our shopping complex sent their customers a "private-sale" notice. Then, afraid no one would come, ran the exact same ad in the newspaper. Their results: so-so.

Their reaction: "Direct mail doesn't work. No one showed up!"

But wait! You told your customers it was a "private" sale for them alone. Then they saw it advertised in the paper to everyone. How do they feel, will they feel, what do they feel whenever you advertise a for-them-alone promotion in the future?

Would you believe disbelief? Believe it.

The word "FREE" in an ad has the greatest impact. People find it hard to dismiss, ignore, or pass over the word *free*. It implies something-for-nothing, and though they know in their heart of hearts that nobody gives anything away, perhaps this is the first time . . . ?

If you advertise something for "free"—make sure it's FREE. Especially if you are advertising to your core customers.

There was a court case that decided a furniture company had to stop advertising "free delivery" because it meant they really gave "free" delivery only if you bought furniture at their store.

People are skeptical, wary, and wonder "what's the gimmick?" when they see the word "FREE"—even though it is still a powerful word to keep them reading.

Do NOT advertise "$100 FREE if you buy $400 worth of merchandise." That's not free. You have to buy a certain amount first.

Do NOT advertise anything "free" unless you put the caveat in the same headline or at least the sentence that follows the headline. What this does: makes your ad more believable.

Dust on merchandise or shelves costs retailers 6 to 12 percent in sales every year. What this does: gives the signal, "This is old!"

Why do you think supermarkets stack the newest canned goods in back of the ones already on the shelf?

Why do you think automobile dealers pay the extra cost to have someone shine the showroom cars daily?

Why do you think clothing stores replace tickets on last season's merchandise with crisp clean new tickets?

Right. Because the customer expects that what they buy has just arrived, is the latest available. (Reason why: One out of six customers will buy a product if they know it's state-of-the-art.) **Three out of four customers go to stores because of "sales."** This is a 10 percent jump in just one year.

Why? Because customers expect you to have sales. Check the local department store. They have a sale every week.

Somewhere, in some department, there's a "sale" going on. It is a magic word (next in importance to "free"), and it brings in customers.

There's a feeling among customers that if they pay "the regular price," somehow they have paid too much money. They'll "wait for the sale" because they know it's coming down the road and will be advertised, promoted, mailed within the next day, week, certainly less than a month.

Here's some other powerful offers according to the survey:

"No down payment."

"Low interest rate."

"Zero interest the first year" (which is expensive unless it's just a one-day promotion).

Here's what customers like best (according to the one million asked) in order: REAL lower prices. Free delivery. Free gifts. First choice for the sale.

That's when the customer feels important.

How much attention should you give to all this survey information? A lot. Remember, the basic rule in selling is only one sentence: "Find out what customers want . . . and give it to them."

There's an old saying that "fifty million Frenchmen can't be wrong."

If that's so, seems we should pay attention to 100 million Americans.

Then they'll know you're serious about moving them up to the next level of the Loyalty Ladder and making them . . . advocates.

Testimonials

■

Advocates can be your best source of future business. They go around telling everyone how great your business is and will proudly give you a testimonial.

When you open Harvey McKay's book, *Swim With the Sharks Without Being Eaten Alive,* the first fifteen pages are filled with ... testimonials.

Not a foreword. Not acknowledgments (they come later). But ... testimonials.

Not on the front or back of the jacket cover but *the first fifteen pages!*

What he was doing: Making you feel you made one of the wisest decisions of your life. You are so excited to start the book after reading testimonials from President Ford, Lou Holtz, Norman Vincent Peale, Abigail ("Dear Abby") Van Buren, Billy Graham, and yes, Robert Redford (among the many) that you have already justified making the purchase.

That's what testimonials are all about: other folks telling you what you bought—or are about to buy—was one of the wisest purchases you ever made.

Which reminds us of the story of the car salesman approached by one of his recent customers and asked, "Are you the salesman that sold me my car?"

Salesman answers, "Yes."

Buyer: "Well, would you mind telling me again why the car is so wonderful? Sometimes I get so discouraged."

Surveys tell us that ads for a product are read ten times as much by people who own the product. Why not? You want to be constantly reinforced that the decision to spend the money was a wise one. Look, this ad says so!

We are also very impressed with what our peers tell us. What movies to see, what clothes to buy, what car to own. Life insurance companies have grown by teaching new agents to use the same technique that has worked through the years: asking the person just sold for names of others who might be sold.

When you realize the strength of testimonials, you wonder why they are not used by more businesses. Look at the full-page ads in this morning's paper:

Automobiles: no testimonials here. Okay, automobile salesmen are consistently rated lowest in the "who-do-you-trust" surveys, but that could be overcome to some degree with pictures and comments of satisfied customers.

Supermarkets: no testimonials here. We're talking about bringing in one new customer—worth close to a quarter of a million dollars in their lifetime investment in food. Why not have testimonials from current, happy Advocates?

Department stores: no testimonials here. Why not testimonials from customers who shop different departments within the store?

Look at the morning mail. Offers to sell you the latest computer equipment, publications, office supplies. Where are the testimonials of satisfied customers to make me read, believe, and order?

Testimonial givers are easy to find. They are live, in person, and visit your place of business every day. Here are some rules to Make It Work:

• **Make it believable.** If Boris Becker recommends a tennis racket, I pay attention. I subliminally think, "If I buy that racket, I'll play as good as Boris."

If Michael Jordan recommends a basketball sneaker (even after he's retired), I'll pay the extra dollars for Air Jordans, dreaming I can float as high as he can.

But when a sneaker company paid millions of dollars to Michael Jackson at the height of his fame to promote their sneakers, consumers shrugged their shoulders and said, "Who cares? Don't need a special sneaker to moon-walk."

- **Make it used by the testimonial giver.** When Joe Namath promoted pantyhose, the consumer said, *"Whaaaaat?"* Other makes-no-sense endorsements by celebrities caused the government to issue rules that the testimonial giver should also use the product. Makes sense to me.

- **Make it honest.** Sounds simple, but a rule often stretched or avoided because the testimonial user figures, "Who cares?" We did. A salesman brought us one of his copy machines. We asked for testimonials before we made a decision. He supplied us with a list of "current satisfied users." After he left we called the first half-dozen names. Their comments ranged from, "We gave it back the day after it came in" to "He used our company's name? We threw the machines out a week after they were installed."

When the salesman came back with the order filled out, ready to be signed, we told him we called his testimonial givers and they all said his product was inferior.

He was amazed. "Wow," he said, "you're the first person to actually call the names on the list we give out."

- **Make it easy for your Advocate to give the testimonial.** "But who do I ask?" says the businessperson.

You know who to ask ... customers who like you and your business. They are quick to say good things about you to their friends. You know who they are. Ask them directly if they would be willing to give you a testimonial. The overwhelming majority will say yes simply because they DO like you and your business and the way you have taken care of them.

Recent surveys say testimonials given by satisfied customers are far, far more effective than testimonials given by celebrities. The customer-to-be KNOWS celebrities are paid for their endorsements. Unless the product is directly related (see "Make it believable"), they'll trust/believe/have more confidence in the words of a satisfied customer than the person in the headlines.

We used to supply a couple of "sample" testimonials customers could change any way they wanted. But we soon discovered that if we let Advocates say what *they* wanted, the words were more real, believable, and full of praise and testimony. Words we would never have had the courage or conceit to write ourselves!

Don't forget to have simple, short release forms for them to sign saying you can use their picture and quote in your ads. When we originally asked our lawyer for a "release form," he gave us (literally) a five-page single-spaced document! That would scare any potential testimonial giver no matter how much they liked you or your business. We handed it back and said, "Go back and try one more time. And make it just a couple of sentences." He did. We do recommend you obtain legal advice to make sure you have crossed the *T*s and dotted the *I*s. Most laws demand some kind of "token" payment for permission to use another person's words and/or picture in your ads.

• **Make it spontaneous.** Some of our most effective testimonials came at the start of a sale. The first arrivals were those who received a "private" sale notice. This meant they were our best Customers. We taped interviews with those most satisfied as they checked out, telling them we were making a tape to use in the future and asking if they would tell us what they thought about the sale. They all said "sure," signed releases, and received gifts for doing the testimonials.

We used these tapes as our only radio advertising all week long. Very, very effective.

• **Make sure you respect privacy.** "What does THAT mean?" you may ask this late in the chapter. "You say to use testimonials but honor privacy. How can you do that?"

Here's how: Do NOT give addresses of people you use. The names are fine—or, if you want to be extracareful, their initials—and the city and state in which they live.

Testimonials are the ultimate aphrodisiac for your business. Everyone likes to be complimented, said nice things about, recommended to the family and friends of strangers they meet on the train, across the card table, or introduced to at lunch. You will find that people are anxious to share their discovery of you with others.

What you have accomplished: people who spread your gospel by telling everyone they know, meet, come in contact with who asks about a product or service available from you. You have cloned a group of disciples to spread the word. They have reached the top of the Loyalty Ladder.

They are ADVOCATES!

The Twenty Rules
of Promotion

---■---

Whatever rung on the Loyalty Ladder people are, they always respond to promotions.

More than 4,000 came to our store in the 1960s to see Clarabell the Clown (a popular children's TV personality from the fifties and sixties).

That was topped by the 7,000 who came to see Mickey Mouse.

Each promotion we ran for our business was a single event that resulted in wide recognition in our community.

Promotions can be as large as these or as small as an annual sale.

There are certain steps that seem to work when planning your promotion. Here are twenty guidelines to follow.

1. **Come up with the idea.** This is easier than it sounds. Ideas are all around you. If you doubt this, put together a brainstorming session with your staff. Sit down and talk about an upcoming holiday sale or event and ask, "How do we promote this?"

Someone in the group writes down all the ideas.

No one is permitted to be negative. You'll be surprised at the great ideas they'll give you.

2. **Make it unique.** For example: Running a Grits Festival is unique. Grits is ground cornmeal and a southern breakfast staple.

A Piggly Wiggly supermarket manager in St. George, South Carolina, the heart of the "grits belt," saw they sold more grits per capita than the national average—four pounds verses one pound. Hey! Why not have an annual "Grits Festival"? They have a Grits Eating Contest, floats, and bands, and the highlight is picking "Miss Grits." She is chosen by being weighed and then rolling in a tub of grits for a few minutes. She is then weighed again. Person with the most grits sticking to her body—wins.

Laugh if you will—but the small town of 2,500 now has 50,000 folks visiting every year for the annual Grits Festival.

3. Ask Customers what they think of the idea. An idea that sounds good in conversation or a winner on paper may often simply not be interesting to the customer.

4. Make an outline of what has to be done. List everything from all the advertising to who buys the balloons to who makes the phone call to who's in charge of exterior and interior displays to who's supervising the copy, art, handling the printing. Your outline will soon cover several pages.

5. Make a checklist. The outline of what has to be done is further broken down into specific tasks to be done by specific individuals.

6. Delegate authority. Who does what? This can start out on a volunteer basis ("OK, who wants to find out the cost for silk-screening fifty posters?") or simply assigning jobs. What you're REALLY doing: involving everyone in the process.

7. Keep everyone in your business informed. The number one desire of people working in your business is "a feeling of being in on things." When someone is in charge of something, it becomes THEIR project rather than the project of your business. And since they are coming back on a weekly basis to report progress, their pressure to accomplish is self-imposed.

Next: Tell your Customers *first*. Before you advertise in the regular media. Mail them an advance notice of what's happening when.

8. Have a timetable. What has to be done by when. This way each person is working on a specific deadline.

9. Have weekly meetings. And when you are a couple of

weeks away from the event, have daily meetings. Meetings are good not only because they provide a structure but also because they give you the opportunity to exchange ideas and solicit help from others in the group working on other projects. If someone is unable to make the contacts or find the information they need, someone else will know another way to approach the problem.

10. **Issue weekly press releases.** To the newspaper, the radio, the TV station. Think of a different "news" lead for each release. The opening paragraph must be different, but that which follows can be a repeat of basic information.

11. **Line up speeches at civic clubs.** The local Rotary, Kiwanis, Exchange, Elks, Moose, and other civic groups are always looking for a twenty-minute guest speaker at their weekly lunches. Call them all. Volunteer to come and speak about your upcoming event and the behind-the-scenes story on what goes into this kind of promotion to make it all happen. (And give them theirs-alone rewards when they come in for the promotion.)

12. **Share your promotion with other businesses in your town.** You've come up with the idea, the details, the planning. Why not invite noncompeting businesses to share in the fun? (And also share in the expenses.) You mention their store in all the advertising done for the promotion. This accomplishes two basic purposes: Cuts down your costs. Makes the promotion "bigger" because more businesses are involved.

13. **FREE!** See what you can do with the most powerful word in the English language. Sure, the promotion is the big draw, but what *else* are you doing to make the Customer want to come? Some might not know or even be interested in the sports celebrity but will come if there is some special item at some special price. Or, better yet, give something away . . . FREE!

14. **Run a sweepstakes.** Running a sweepstakes or giving a premium will automatically increase response. That's a good enough reason for you to add either one for your promotion. Remember how when we gave away a free trip for two to New Orleans or Disneyland during a promotion, our traffic increased. Work with other businesses to promote what they have to sell by bartering. "You give me the trip, I give you the advertising."

15. Use testimonials. This is an excellent time to have quotes from your Customers on why they enjoy coming to your business. We had a salesman from the local radio station on hand to interview people about why they enjoyed shopping with us.

Picture the scene. It's celebrity time. Or it's special-event time. The business is packed and everyone is having a great time.

Nine out of ten will give positive statements on why they came. Think about it: If you speak to people who just bought a specific brand of car, they will tell you all the reasons that car is the best. If they did not, they would be saying they had poor judgment. A promotion is an excellent time to line up testimonials about you and your business.

16. Keep the promotion to a very specific time. The narrower the better. One of our most famous promotional failures was our Irish Fortnight Event. We copied the idea from Neiman-Marcus, which was tremendously successful with this idea. But they were a huge department store, we were a small specialty shop. Two weeks for a promotion for them was fine. For us it was a near disaster. If we had held it for one day—or perhaps a two-day weekend—fine. But the longer the time period, the less excitement and desire to be there. After that experience we made sure our celebrities arrived and left within a few hours. Our annual New Year's Day sale, *which increased in volume every year for twenty-five consecutive years,* started as a four-hour sale and was MORE successful than a three-day sale. The drama was intensified, the crowds lined up were bigger, the purchases were faster and larger.

17. Have one last meeting with your staff just before the event. It can be the night before or the morning of. Recheck who's responsible for what. By now the adrenaline will be almost uncontrollably gushing through everyone's veins and they will be hyped up and ready to go!

18. Added Value. Add one more UNANNOUNCED event at the last moment. Entrepreneur Bill Veeck believed in this philosophy strongly. He would attract you to his ballpark with many announced specials and happenings. But somewhere, sometime during the game something "extra" happened—someone popped out of a cake in the middle of the field.

Or . . . "Lift up your seat to see if you have the lucky number for a free drink." Remember to always give Added Value.

19. Include something to bring the Customer back. Mail order companies call this a "bounce-back." You order something in the mail, they send it to you and include another offer for you to buy something again! My wife bought something from Spiegel; they sent the order and included a $20 gift certificate for her *next* purchase. She went though the catalog, couldn't find anything she really wanted, but bought a pair of jeans anyway. Didn't want to lose the $20.

And so: When all those folks arrive at your business for the promotion, make sure they have something in their hands to bring them back again.

Supermarkets do this by having ads about NEXT week's specials tucked into the grocery bags as your purchases are packed.

20. Review. No longer than one week after the promotion is over, all the participants sit down and have a brainstorming session along the lines of "If we had to do it over again tomorrow, what would we do differently?"

Loyalty
Programs

---■---

You've brought your Customers to the top of the Loyalty Ladder. They are now Advocates. Terrific! Now how do you keep them there?

Reward them.

Let them know they are the most important people in the world to your business, because . . . they are!

But how do you "reward" your Advocates?

Give them something special for them alone.

It might seem to you that there's a new Award program or Frequent Buyer or Frequent Flier program appearing in the mail or on the cereal box top every day and that they have been around forever.

Not really. The first Frequent Flier program dates back only to 1980, when American Airlines came out with their "Aadvantage" program. The naysayers (read: competition) said, "It can't work" and "It will cost too much" and "They'll be out of that program within a month or two."

And, of course, within a few months—or, at the most, years—all the other airlines followed quickly because American began to pull away their customers. What American did was follow the by now well-known philosophy of Vifredo Pareto, the Italian economist and sociologist known for his application of mathematics to economic analysis. In the late 1800s, Pareto developed what we know today as the 80/20 philosophy. Translated into economic terms, it means that 80 percent of your business comes from 20 percent of your customers.

Fund-raisers and those folks who run political campaigns have known this for years. Concentrate on the big-buck givers and the smaller ones will come along eventually. You need the latter for perception of support ("Everybody shops there!"). You need the former to stay in business.

Back to reward programs . . .

They have two goals. Continuity: to bring you back again, and Rewards: to make you feel good about the company.

Continuity: Remember the Sesame Street books or dish sets at the local supermarket? The first purchase was a fraction of each subsequent purchase. But now you had the first book or cup, so you had to keep coming back to complete the set.

Rewards: They go back in American merchandising to the Buck Rogers decoder rings, Orphan Annie mugs, and Tom Mix membership clubs. All available if you bought the product, tore off the top (before bar codes were invented), and mailed it to the company with some small change for your reward. In some cases you paid nothing extra. The best example was stamp programs. S&H's Green Stamps were imitated with stamps in every color of the rainbow for different businesses all over the United States. Paste the stamps in a book. When you fill X number of books, pick the prize you want from their catalog. What you were doing: joining a club. Being a member. Belonging.

Dr. Abraham Maslow recognized the importance of "belonging" when he established his Hierarchy of Human Values.

On the bottom rung is **Survival.** Everyone wants know they will stay alive. So they first need food, water, and shelter.

Next rung is **Safety.** You want to know that when you're flying 35,000 miles above the earth, your spouse has steel-belted radials on the car. You want locks on the doors and alarms in your car and/or home.

The next rung is **Belonging.** Americans love to belong to everything from civic clubs to programs that sell goods and/or services. In my wallet I have thirty-seven different cards (and another dozen at home that won't fit and are rarely needed—but, just in case . . .)

Their purpose: to give me something "extra" when they are used.

What American Airlines began in 1980 was quickly followed by their competitors—and copied two years later by Marriott hotels. And again, quickly followed by every other top hotel chain in the next four years. The purpose: to have their Advocates stay at the top of the Loyalty Ladder and bring their friends along as well. They wanted them to buy more, more often. Or, as the term has become known, Frequency Marketing.

Richard Barlow, president of a company with the same name—Frequency Marketing—gives this definition: "Frequency Marketing is the strategy which seeks to identify, maintain and increase the yield from your best Customers through long-range interactive value-added relationships"

How do you do this?

Start a club with special benefits only for those who belong.

This gives you a database (names of Customers with addresses, phone numbers, and any special quirks you can find out about them) and the ability to communicate with them on a regular basis.

Today, Frequency Marketing is found in almost every industry.

There are three basic elements:

1. Benefits. If you belong, you are entitled to something that others who do not belong cannot receive.

2. Database. To hold, relate, and apply the information you receive from the Customer.

3. Communications. How you talk (and, as important, how you listen) to your customers.

There are two kinds of clubs for any business to start: the Closed Club and the Open Club.

The Closed Club means you pay to belong. So anyone can shop Wal-Mart, but if you want to go into their Sam's "wholesale" Club, you have to pay an annual fee. The Open Club means either (*a*) anyone can join or (*b*) certain people are invited to join.

Here's a cross-section of different industries and how they make a Loyalty Program increase their business.

THE HILTON AND SHERATON STORIES

THE HILTON HONORS PROGRAM

We mentioned Marriott starting the program in 1983 with their Honored Guest program. Hyatt jumped on the bandwagon in 1985 with their Gold Passport. By 1987 the Hilton chain realized they had to do something to protect their market share and also build brand loyalty.

Here's why: In the previous ten years there had been a 23 percent increase in the number of hotel rooms in the United States but only a 10 percent increase in volume. How do you have the best customer—the business traveler—choose Hilton over all the others?

Hilton began by sending questionnaires to their IBTs (International Business Travelers). They account for only 15 percent of Hilton's room nights but 60 percent of their revenue. They invited these best customers to join the Hilton Honors program in a special "sweepstakes" mailing.

Nearly 350,000 joined "practically overnight," said Perryman Maynard, vice-president of Hilton Hotel Marketing Programs.

These charter members received points for each overnight stay redeemable for future rewards—free hotel rooms, savings on rental cars, and more.

Membership jumped to one million in one year.

Result: Hilton Honors members almost doubled their room stays from 2.5 percent of the chain's business in 1987 to 4.5 percent in 1988.

Hilton's theme for the program was "Opportunity Cost." Translation: "Here's what you lose if you stay someplace else." (Remember that fear of loss is far more powerful than promise of gain.)

Next: To create excitement and, yes, do more business, Hilton offered these members a "double point" program in partnership with American Express. Use your American Express card when you pay your bill and receive double points.

Result: They doubled room night reservations.

They soon realized that a certain number of the newly joined were not using their new card. This group received a special mailer offering them upgrades the next time they stayed at a Hilton.

Result: Nearly 13 percent responded.

Today there are more than three million members in the Hilton Honors program.

Room nights used by these members jumped from 700,000 to 3.5 million, or 16 percent of all the rooms available—up from the 2.5 percent when they first started.

Return on investment was ten to one when they first began the program. Now it is thirty-one to one—or, for every dollar they spend, they receive $31 back.

Hilton was able to trace $423 million in sales directly back to their Hilton Honors program.

THE SHERATON CLUB INTERNATIONAL

Sheraton was among the hotels-come-lately to the Frequent Buyer program. They had a membership of 800,000 that was not growing. They decided to find out what their customers REALLY wanted and to redesign their program accordingly. They started with a customer survey and discovered the offers made by most hotels involving the hotel itself (free weekends, upgrades, late checkouts) all came in second to their customers' preference: air miles.

Sheraton quickly signed up as partners with United, Thai, Air Canada, Continental, and Delta.

They set three objectives for themselves

1. A total of three million members by 1995.
2. Create the most competitive program in the hotel industry.
3. Maintain the financial viability.

They then created three levels of membership:

1. Basic level. Join for free. Must have a minimum of two stays a year to remain active. Members earn two club miles for every dollar they spend. (If the room costs $100, the member earns 200 air miles.) Newsletters mailed periodically.
2. Gold level. Make four separate reservations and you are auto-

matically elevated to their Gold Level, giving you a 50 percent bonus on miles (three miles for every dollar you spend).

3. Fee level. This was the original program—$25 gave you automatic Gold membership with special privileges: Upgrades. Guaranteed 4:00 P.M. checkout. Morning newspaper. Express Fast Program. (Check in and out in thirty seconds or less.) Suite guarantee. (Call forty-eight hours before you arrive. If there's a suite available, it's yours for the rate you originally booked.) Special gift booklet with premiums that include two nights for the price of one. Two dinners for the price of one. Room upgrades . . .

"Remember, that was one of our goals," said Ed Stahl, VP and director of advertising and marketing for ITT Sheraton, "to make sure our program was equal to or better than any other hotel Frequent Customer program."

Even with this new enlarged program they continued to enroll as many people paying as not paying. Members wanted the extra benefits and figured they were worth the small extra cost.

They soon found out the best advertising was word of mouth. "Nearly 75 percent of our new members came from people staying in our hotels," says Stahl.

Now, armed with this database, they could put together specific promotions. When Hawaii's Sheraton marketing department called Stahl for help because they found out planes coming to Hawaii would be off 10 percent (which meant room rentals would be correspondingly less), Stahl mailed 600,000 packages to members around the world. He offered a 35 percent discount on room rates, food, and beverages, inter-island airfare, and a rental car.

Result: $4 million in room revenue.

Would they have had some of that anyway?

Sure.

Would they have had all of that anyway?

No way.

This year Hawaii said, "Let's do it again."

But now they had statistics. They discovered that 75 percent of the business came from two countries and seven states. So they cut back the mailings to only 250,000—where the customers came from in the last promotion.

Results: Same revenue with a lot less cost.

THE DR. OETKER BACK CLUB (BAKING CLUB)

The Dr. Oetker baking products company in Germany received some startling news when they analyzed a survey of their customers.

Their Customers were growing older. Average age was over fifty. And the potential new Customers—the younger women—"didn't know how to bake."

Their solution: a "Dr. Oetker Back Club" (Baking Club) aimed at the eighteen- to thirty-eight-year-old women with children whose only familiarity with baked goods was buying them at the local bakery.

Reiner Blau, management supervisor of Team Direct in Hamburg, put together the club with the slogan "Baking is fun." They offered membership for $25 that included:

- Recipes on a regular basis (survey said this was the number one request). '
- A magazine six times a year.
- Samples of products, table decorations.
- Special discounts on travel with Movenpick and Holiday Inn at rates below posted prices.
- A hotline to their "Test Kitchen" for any baking problems. They average 650 monthly "How do you bake . . . ?" questions.

Can older people join? Sure. "But that's not our primary market."

Recipe contests are proven attention getters, and they have them for grandmoms and children.

One of the most exciting programs was "Bake with Barbie"—Mattel's well-known doll. Children were encouraged to write for "Barbie's favorite recipe." More than 4,000 did. The company knew that today's young child is tomorrow's target market.

Membership today: more than 100,000.

Said Blau, "The key to success is pampering your club members."

Where there were once few future customers, many now appeared. Created by . . . a membership club.

SEARS BEST CUSTOMER PROGRAM

This idea came from a meeting of Sears store managers in 1991, who asked, "Why don't we reward our best Customers?"

Their reasoning: It costs more than $100 to replace one best Customer with five new ones. But it costs only $3.50 to keep one. So the math is very favorable from a marketing viewpoint.

Management jumped on the idea, knowing they already had a database of their customers—but did not have any program for using it.

They started off with a simple objective: retain their best Customers, which became the name of the program: "Sears Best Customer."

They rolled the program out in 1992, but it did not really take off until Sears sent videotapes on how the program worked to all their associates and their spouses. All staff members were also mailed a preview of each promotion a week before they were mailed to the Best Customers.

"We come from a culture of 'everything's on sale,'" said Al Malony, senior manager for customer marketing. "Here was an opportunity to relate to the customer on a one-on-one basis."

They realized this was a long-term commitment. "We knew it wouldn't increase sales overnight. Maybe not in six months. But eventually . . . "

Malony said there are three ways to create loyalty:

1. Customer satisfaction
2. Convenience
3. Recognition.

Sears does all three

The Best Customers are selected by past purchases. They are requalified every fall. They receive a letter from the manager of the store nearest them saying they are a member of this new club and enclosing a membership sticker to attach to their Sears charge card.

Each letter has more than 800 variations, so the manager can tailor the letter to his or her area—even writing about something happening locally.

"That's the piece that was missing from our other marketing programs," said Malony. "They didn't have the local 'press-the-flesh' information."

The immediate (and unexpected) reaction was letters from customers to the manager saying "thanks for this program."

More than 95 percent of the correspondence and calls were positive. The few that were not gave the manager the opportunity to contact customers and make them happy.

They include a survey with every mailing. ("What can we do better?")

When you're a Best Customer, you are at the top of the list. If your air-conditioning breaks down in the middle of July, the repairman sees you first.

Sears knows that 72 percent of what Customers buy is made at their first stop, so the Best Customer program brings the customer shopping the mall to Sears FIRST.

Originally they wrote to their Customers six times a year. Then eight times. Now they are up to once a month. Customers love to have previews of sales before anyone else. To be the first in.

"The more you communicate meaningfully, the better the program works."

Another result: The more the Customer spends, the more they spend. They shopped departments they never shopped before.

At Christmas the manager sent a simple "Thank you for shopping with us" note and asked the Best Customer to come in during the holiday season for a special present—a box of chocolates embossed with the words "Best Customer." They never expected the response. Nearly 40 percent came for the gift! "We were hustling for chocolate all over America," said Malony.

Customers who came in from the offer spent much more than the average store customer.

Malony says, "The main success tactic is recognition. The Customer is 'special.'

"We have two million chances a day to screw up," he said. "This program helps us make sure it doesn't happen . . . ."

MINI-STORIES: PROBLEMS AND SOLUTIONS FOR FREQUENT BUYER PROGRAMS

The Casa Buitoni Club
Problem: **How to take low customer loyalty to a pasta brand and make it high customer loyalty and increase sales.**

Solution: **Start a Casa Buitoni club.**

The pasta market in the UK is more than £110 million a year, with most of the sales in private label (58 percent). Nearly 25 million households in the UK use pasta—but Buitoni was bought only by 3.6 million households.

The name comes from the Casa Buitoni home in Tuscany, central Italy. The company, established in 1827, is one of Italy's oldest pasta makers, acquired by Nestlé in 1988.

Italian food names are confusing to customers. Recipes are confusing. What this meant: an opportunity to educate customers.

They established the Casa Buitoni club to build a one-to-one relationship with Italian food lovers and offered a free, easy-to-understand recipe booklet in newspaper ads.

Customers had to pay for the call. ("This meant they were really interested," said Buitoni's Duncan MacCullum.)

More than 200,000 called. They were mailed the booklet with an offer to join the Casa Buitoni club. And also tell their friends. (One-third recommend friends.)

Result: 20 percent joined.

They received their first eight-page color catalog newsletter in October 1993 with a questionnaire. One out of five answered.

Members also receive a telephone number to call for any information they want on Buitoni products. The call is now toll-free because they belong to the club.

Future plans: sell Buitoni products directly to club members.

"Consumer loyalty takes a decade or more," said MacCullum. "It's an evolutionary process."

Best response: From a British couple that had a two-month-old daughter about to be christened and they wanted her second name to be Italian. Could they call her "Buitoni"?

"Now, THAT'S brand involvement," said MacCullum.

The Scripps Howard News Card

Problem: **How to increase subscriptions to the** *Rocky Mountain News.*

Solution: **Make new subscribers members of the News Card.**

In the five years between 1986 and 1991, seventy-four daily newspapers in the United States went out of the business. Circulation dropped two million in less than five years.

In the 1940s, the average household took 1.3 newspapers.

Today the average is 0.5 (or two households = one newspaper).

Advertising also decreased.

So how do you increase subscriptions, which means more advertising?

In 1991 Scripps-Howard spent $5 million for 850,000 subscribers. *There had to be a better way. . . .*

They launched the News Card in Denver with their paper, the *Rocky Mountain News.*

They contacted twenty retailers who covered the marketplace broadly—fast-food restaurants, dry cleaners, video rentals, drugstores—places you would go to often. If you prepay a subscription to the paper for three, six, or twelve months, you receive the News Card with a brochure listing businesses where you save money just by showing your card. Participating stores would have extra business and, as an inducement, one-quarter-page weekly ads on a space-available basis . . . free!

A win (for the paper), win (for the business), win (for the new subscriber).

The initial goal was 80,000 new subscribers by December. They had 90,000 in October.

As important: The retention rate was 75 percent and improved monthly.

Bottom line: By offering the News Card, the cost for each new subscriber dropped from $5 to $2.

The Waldenbooks Preferred Reader Club
Problem: **A bookstore is a bookstore is a bookstore. How do you make yours stand out from all the rest?**

Solution: **Start a "Preferred Reader" program.**

To increase their business and maintain a strong customer base, Waldenbooks started their Preferred Reader program. There were two parts:

1. Pay a $10 annual fee and receive 10 percent off every purchase.

2. Establish a reward program for best customers. Spend $100, Waldenbooks sends you a $5 gift certificate. They mail three million certificates a year to their 3.5 million active customers.

What they discovered: These members spend 40 percent more than nonmembers.

In some of their stores, members are 40 percent of the business—or more.

They keep an accurate database on the type of books their members buy. You receive information and newsletters based on your reading preference: science fiction, mystery, children. . . .

In December they mail some of their customers a thank-you letter, signed by the chairman, thanking them for their business and including a $10 gift certificate.

More than 90 percent were redeemed.

The number of loyalty programs designed to keep Advocates at the top of the Loyalty Ladder are in the thousands and tens of thousands. And growing even as you read this.

In reviewing more than 100 clubs from retailers to airlines to gas stations to hotels to pet owners to retired persons (the list is almost endless), we discovered there are certain "musts" each include. Here they are:

1. **Membership card.** (Remember Maslow's "belonging." Makes someone feel . . . special.)

2. Newsletter. (To ensure communications between organization and member.)

3. Luggage tags. (Offered by almost every hotel and airline.)

4. Toll-free numbers. (In case you have questions you want answered.)

5. Special offers. (Not only from the club itself but also from noncompeting businesses as well.)

6. Pins. (Where it works: Civic clubs. Political committees.)

7. Advance notice. (You know about this information before anyone else.)

8. Special privileges. (Dine in the museum's members-only restaurant. Participate in activities peculiar to a specific business like tours, guaranteed lowest prices, insurance coverage. . . .)

9. Be patient. (Success doesn't happen overnight. There must be a long-range commitment and if you build it, they will come.)

What about the future?

First, remember that all programs are NOT successful.

The GE Rewards card as a value-added idea never really captured the imagination. Customers knew they would receive rebates from other stores, but despite mass media promotion, acceptance reached an early plateau, according to Bruce Brittain, a bank industry consultant based in Atlanta.

The GM Card with its offer of accumulating $500 a year for seven years for a new GM car signed up nine million customers in seventeen months. When Ford/Citibank entered the competition, they doubled their members over a five-month period from 500,000 to one million— but much of this increase was simply renewals by people who were already Citibank customers, says Brittain.

Dick Hodgson, one of the world's leading direct marketing experts and the accepted guru of catalog marketing, said there are at least five advantages of customer clubs, including:

1. You change the buyer–seller relationship to a much closer organization–member relationship.

2. You have your best and most loyal customers pre-identify themselves.

3. You can develop much more focused promotions.

4. You can afford to market products or services that might otherwise be unprofitable.

5. You have a built-in source for quick and easy market research.

One of Hodgson's favorite stories is about the Peter Hahn Company outside of Stuttgart, Germany. They needed to build a larger warehouse but did not have enough funds. They formed a Customer Club and sold shares. More than 6,000 Customers joined. The benefit to Customers was a 10 percent discount on all purchases. They were oversubscribed by one-third and built the warehouse. Hahn held an open house when he opened the warehouse, *and 5,800 of the 6,000 club members came from all over Germany!!!*

"Unfortunately," says Hodgson, "most Customer clubs have short lives."

Why is that? He believes the people who create the original idea receive all the credit. The people who follow—the maintenance crew—receive little or no credit for their effort. No ego gratification. So they look for other things to do.

Hodgson says that when he develops frequent buyer clubs for companies, his first advice is "the absolute necessity of making a long-term commitment—not just months, but years—to establish the club, maintain it, improve it and add exciting new elements."

He also favors having the Customer make an up-front commitment like Sheraton's $25 joining fee for the extra special privileges they will receive.

Other experts wonder if there will soon be too many clubs. Will the proliferation present the dilemma of no advantage for anyone, since there is a similar advantage for everyone?

Not so, say most futurists. They maintain that the Frequent Buyer clubs we now see are only the beginning. That you will learn not only more about what your Customers buy but also (ready for this?) what they *might* buy! Steve Cone, past president of Epsilon, a subsidiary of

American Express, says there is information available right now that tells you if your Customer might buy a special product or own a business or simply stop being a Customer. All this comes from their actions, which are measurable and predictable based on their history, which you can store in your database. Cone also sees the development of an Ultra Customer Program—beyond the 80/20 rule. He says there is a new 5 percent rule: About 5 percent of your customers can bring you nearly half your business,

What do you do for THIS group? Cone belongs to the Hyatt exclusive club-within-a-club program available to Hyatt's top 1,000 frequent guests. One of the extra benefits: You never make reservations. There's ALWAYS a room waiting for you when you arrive at any Hyatt.

OUR FAVORITE PROMOTION: THE GORDON'S GOLD CARD

I was about to leave for a series of seminars in Australia.

I was excited about going on the trip not only because of seeing friends in Australia but also because I had received two round-trip first-class tickets for my wife, Ruth, and myself . . . free!

I had these free tickets as a *reward* from an airline for flying so many miles with them. I was one of their valued Frequent Fliers. The airline was rewarding me for being a good Customer.

But how was I rewarding *my* Customers for being good Customers?

If I could think of a way that would not only reward them but also have them spend more money with me, I would do more business.

If the airlines made it work with Frequent Flier programs, why not make it work with a Frequent Buyer program at Gordon's?

I collected literature from the airline Frequent Flier programs. I belong to five, so their material was available. Marriott was just beginning their Honored Guest program for their hotel chain, so I wrote for information. Their success, by the way, prompted almost *all* the hotel chains to copy the idea. My wallet is full of cards that tell me I belong to Inter-Continental's Six Continents Club, the Adam's Mark Gold Mark Club, the Hilton Honors Program, the Hyatt Platinum Passport. . . .

I also picked up the latest material from the major credit card companies (Diners gives their best customers gifts!) and what the gasoline companies offered.

I read every brochure, pamphlet, letter and picked out the sentences that appeared in most of them. Why take the time to create a new selling package when it was already done?

Here's one of the great sentences that almost *every* Frequent Buyer/Flier program uses. Copy it for your future reward program for *your* business: "Your association with Gordon's and your annual volume of business with us places you in a unique group which requires and appreciates special recognition."

How could you not continue reading that letter?

We then went through our Customer computer printout and set an arbitrary number of $1,000 as the minimum amount of purchases you had to make in our store in one year to receive a Gordon's Gold Card. We selected nearly 500 Customers. We now had 500 Customers that gave us nearly $2 million in business every year!

Yes, yes, I know that 500 times $1,000 is $500,000. But remember, that was the *minimum.* Some of the Customers spent $2,000 or $4,000 a year with us. One Customer the previous year spent $12,500 on clothing. (We would have given her *ten* cards if she asked.)

It was the 80/20 rule staring at us. In fact, fewer than 20 percent of our Customers accounted for 80 percent of our volume!

We printed attractive gold-on-white plastic cards with each Customer's name in gold. We mailed them a complete package, including a letter, a free lunch at the Alley Deli restaurant (once a month), a gift certificate to say "thanks" for being a Gold Card member, and the all-important questionnaire to find out more about each Customer.

The letter said they would receive the following:

1. Instant recognition.

2. The Alley Deli free lunch every month.

3. Advance announcements. First-class mail for all store mailers instead of bulk rate.

4. Birthday presents for them *and* their spouses.

5. Unadvertised special offers. We began a monthly mailing only to Gold Card Customers with outstanding specials. Cost: $500 a month, or $1 for each one mailed. Our lowest sales return from these monthly mailings was $4,000. The highest return was $23,500!

6. Gift selection and complimentary mailings. No charge for postage and handling when they mailed gifts.

7. Bonus points. (More on that in a few paragraphs.)

8. A questionnaire that customers filled out and returned because it asked for their birthday—and their spouse's birthday—which we needed to send them a gift on that special day. They also gave us other valuable information, including what designers they bought. What they liked best about the shops. What they wanted us to carry that we did not. Where they read, heard, or saw our ads.

We quickly discovered that 75 percent of our best Customers listened to *one* radio station. Since there are twelve radio stations in our area and we never knew which one to choose for advertising, our Customers told us! And since future Customers would be listening to this same station, that's where we put our advertising dollars.

We found out that by rewarding our Customers, they rewarded us!

We added a P.S. to the bottom of the letter saying, "Since we always like happy endings, we'll add one to this letter. We've enclosed a $15 gift certificate in your name to use in any of our shops. . . ."

No minimum purchase. No, "If you buy, you get . . ." The fifteen dollars was **free.**

We have consistently found out your best Customers will *not* take advantage of you. We were not surprised to discover that our average sale was $50 when the $15 gift certificate was used. Translation: a profit on *every* gift certificate used.

The Gold Card was directly responsible for giving us a big increase in business.

BONUS POINTS

We kept track of our Gold Card customers' sales from their sales slips. They received a gift certificate at Thanksgiving (naturally) for holiday shopping. The gift certificates amounted to about 5 percent of their purchases. But we didn't say that. We said, "Each dollar is one bonus point. If you earn 250 to 500 points, you receive a gift certificate for $25. If you earn 501 to 750 points, you receive a gift certificate for $50." All the way to a maximum gift certificate of $100.

The first year we gave away about $5,000 in gift certificates.

Which was responsible for $50,000 in business.

Would we have done part of this "extra" $50,000 in business anyway?

Yes.

Would we have done all that "extra" $50,000 in business without the Frequent Buyer plan? Absolutely, positively, unconditionally *No.*

But the greatest reaction was . . . surprise! The letter, received months earlier with the promise of bonus points and gift certificates, was forgotten. All the Customers knew was they opened up their mail one day and out came *free* gift certificates for merchandise.

What good feelings about our business!

What a story to tell their friends!

What a reason to come and shop with us when other businesses were complaining about . . . tough times!

Perhaps the ultimate Frequent Flier plan was recently announced by USAir to persuade funeral directors to use their airline when shipping bodies across the country. They established a TLC card (for Tender Loving Care) and promoted it heavily with the headline INTRODUCING: A HIGHER LEVEL OF CARE. After thirty shipments, the funeral director receives one free trip within the United States or Canada.

When the story was written in the trade publication *Advertising Age,* some of the comments were, well, let's listen in:

"We wanted to be first out of the box."—May Strite, USAir cargo sales.

"Northwest tried the idea, but it died. . . ."

"It almost makes dying worthwhile. . . ."

And this comment from James O'Donnell, the chairman of Seabrook Marketing: "It's really a Frequent Dier program."

How to Double
Your Business

———————■———————

Now you've seen how you can make Prospects climb to the top of the
Loyalty Ladder and become Advocates.

It's time to put these principles into action.

So here's a challenge for you. Can you **double** your business next
year?

Your first inclination is to answer "No!"

But your first inclination is wrong.

You can use your imagination and the information contained in this
book to dramatically increase your business next year.

Here are five ways of increasing your business, which correspond to
the five rungs of the Loyalty Ladder:

1. **Attract new Prospects.** You can make a major effort to
increase your business by expanding your Customer base. Here
are some ideas for you to consider:

Send mailings with special offers to Prospects who live or work
within two miles of your business. Visit the post office to determine the nine-digit zip codes and carrier routes that comprise
your primary market. Test other markets as well to see if there
are other areas where you can draw customers.

After doing some mailings with good offers to bring Prospects to your business, you'll be able to pinpoint where most of your Prospects live. Then you can mail to potential new Prospects with more precision.

Try sweepstakes or contests or games of skill that you can tie in with your business. Side benefit: A sweepstakes or contest is a great way to develop a Customer list. Sweepstakes have a history of boosting response rates 25 percent to 50 percent.

Have a local or area celebrity for a special in-person appearance. If you have a bookstore, invite an author to sign books. Publishers will work with you to line up someone who will attract a crowd. If you own a sporting goods store, hire a celebrity athlete for a day (or a hometown hero whose price will be a lot less).

Get some free publicity. Work with a public relations professional (the expensive option), or you can do it yourself.

Put yourself in the position of a newspaper editor. What is it about your business or you that merits a news article? Be creative. Send a press release with something newsworthy about your business. (The world being the way it is, your cause will be helped if you also happen to advertise in the newspaper where you're trying to get free publicity.)

Reward current Customers and other businesspersons for bringing new business to your establishment. Book and record clubs give their Customers free books and compact discs for signing up new members.

All your effort in bringing in new Prospects can increase your business by 20 percent next year.

2. Think of a new way of attracting Shoppers. If you're a restaurant, open early for breakfast. Or start a delivery service. Or try this year to obtain a liquor license. How about adding fancy coffees to the dessert menu? What about takeout?

Or you're a beauty salon operator. Add facials and pedicures to your basic service. Open your back room and have a special place for children to get their hair cut.

Or you're a dry cleaner. Increase your share of the drapery business in town. Send a reminder home with every Customer that you specialize in cleaning drapes. Include information on why they should clean their drapes every eighteen months (the average customer cleans drapes only once every forty months). Give each Customer a coupon for $10 off if they come to your dry cleaner with their drapes. Don't worry about making money the first time they come in. You're working on a lifetime relationship.

If you're an attorney or accountant, offer the local newspaper a free monthly column on your specialty. Be available to speak at the monthly luncheon meeting of the Rotary. And also volunteer to be a guest on the local radio station. The idea is to let Prospects know you are an expert.

Finding a new service to market to Shoppers under your present business umbrella can increase your business 20 percent.

3. Keep track of and reward your current Customers. Most businesses spend five times as much money finding new Prospects as they do on their current Customers. But it's easier to sell more to the Customer you already have than to sell to a new Prospect.

Here's why:

Your current Customers are satisfied with you and the product or service you offer. (That's why they are your Customers.)

Your current Customers are a great source of new business. Word of mouth is the strongest form of advertising.

Reward your current Customers . . . just for being your Customers! Give them a $5 gift certificate (no minimum purchase. The $5 is *free!*) for the next time they shop with you. Send them a gift on their birthday. Give them an extra, unexpected present when they shop in your store. Set up a frequent buyer program . . . the more your Customers shop with you, the more bonuses they earn.

You can increase your business 20 percent just from your current Customer base.

4. Involve your staff in satisfying Clients. One method many business owners neglect in trying to increase their business is the amount of ideas and energy they can generate from their employees. Properly motivated, employees can help all your Customers become Clients.

First of all and above all else, your employees want to know what is happening in your business. You can erase a lot of needless insecurity in your employees by telling them your plans for next year and what they can do to make those plans work.

Reward your employees for their contributions to your business success. Make sure they know that at least part of their compensation is based on the bottom line of your business. When the whole organization is working for the same objectives, the friction level at work is significantly reduced.

Think about instituting a commission structure in your business if you don't already have one. A commission structure makes your salespeople more like free agents. They are working for themselves as well as working for you. They have more *personal* interest in making the sale.

Make your employees understand they are responsible for your business's success or failure. And they are right! They are on the firing line every day. They are the faces your Customers associate with your business. If you have a philosophy of Customer service permeating your business, you will have more satisfied customers coming back time and again.

Remind your employees of the "lifetime value of a customer." If someone is dissatisfied and decides not to come back to your store, you haven't just lost a $50 sale. That same person may be spending $100 a week; $5,000 a year; $50,000 in ten years. Remind your employees that if they lose one single Customer, it's like losing $50,000 in business over the next decade.

Dissatisfied Customers also tell their friends about their mistreatment and discourage some of them from shopping with you. Make your employees aware of the significance of every Customer transaction, and they will begin to treat your Customers with the respect your Customers expect and deserve.

When your employees try every day to improve your Customer relations, your business is bound to grow. More and more of your Customers will become Clients.

If you motivate your employees so they are constantly working to grow your business by increasing the number of Clients, your business can increase 20 percent next year.

5. Expand your number of Advocates by expanding your horizons. Knock out a wall. Rent some more space. Buy that new computer. Expand your selling territory.

There is room for you to grow. You can start a small catalog to sell your products by mail. You can hire sales representatives who work totally on a commission basis. You can sell your product wholesale in quantity to a distributor.

Expanding your business dramatically may not increase your costs very much. You can advertise your product in a trade magazine for a percentage of sales.

You can give some of your product to a distributor on consignment.

Increase the hours of your business. If you close at 5:00 P.M., why not close at 7:00 P.M.? Try it, advertise it. Or open an extra day a week. What about Saturday hours? Or Sunday hours if you're already open Saturday?

Investigate the pros and cons of opening in another community. If you have a store or business operating efficiently and you can spare your time to help another location grow, it is worth considering. Ideally, the locations will not be too far apart, so you can share marketing and supply costs.

All these expansion ideas will give your Customers and Clients another reason for doing business with you. As your business grows, so will your number of Advocates.

If all goes well, expanding your horizons can increase your business 20 percent next year.

What have you done? You've expanded your product line, sold more to your current Customers, found new Customers, motivated your employees to increase their sales and expanded your horizons . . . and doubled your business.

But wait, what if . . . after reading this far and having followed these ideas you have not DOUBLED your business?

What if, by following some of the ideas in this chapter, you only increased your business 60 percent? Or 40 percent? Or even 20 percent?

That's 20 percent more than you thought you would do!

Now is the time for you to think of new ways to get Customers Up the Loyalty Ladder!

EPILOGUE
Checking Up

———■———

I was working in our clothing shop one afternoon in June. A fourteen-year-old boy, Tommy, came back to the counter where I was working and said, "Hello."

I've known Tommy since the day he was born. I delivered his baby clothes to his mother in the hospital.

"Mr. Raphel, may I use the phone?" he asked.

"Sure, Tommy, go ahead."

He picked up the phone, dialed, and I heard him say:

"Hi. Just went past your house. Saw you had a big lawn. I cut lawns to make some extra money. I also trim hedges. And I was wondering if . . . "

He paused, listened, and continued.

"I see. And are you satisfied with the work they are doing?"

Another pause.

"I see. Well, would it be all right if I called you back again in a month or so? I can. Thank you."

And he hung up.

I walked over to him and said, "Tommy, forgive me, but I was standing here and I heard everything you said. I want you to know that everything you said to that person on the phone was great. Promise me you won't be disappointed because you didn't get the sale."

And he answered, "Oh, Mr. Raphel, I got the sale. That was just one of my Customers. I was just checking up to see how I'm doing."

Index